If you've always dreamed of running your own business, or want to supplement your full-time income, this informative, idea-packed guide shows you how to mak~~~~

COMPUTER ~~~~

Start a remote computer ba~~~~ ~~~~ring service, or open u~~~~

♦

EYE FOR DETAIL

Become a wedding coordinator or party planner for every occasion.

♦

BEAUTIFUL HOME OR PRIME LOCATION

Put your house in the movies, rent your residence to vacationers, or host garage sales or craft shows.

♦

SPECIAL TOUCH WITH ANIMALS

Do you love cats, dogs, horses, birds, or exotics? Become a professional pet-sitter, dog trainer, or even a beekeeper.

♦

TALENT AT BEING A MOM

You've got know-how that's in demand. Offer your skills as a house childproofer, a lactation consultant, a baby-sitter for local inns and hotels, or a COMPUTERTOTS instructor.

♦

NOW YOU CAN

TURN YOUR TALENTS INTO PROFITS

WITH THESE AND DOZENS OF OTHER MONEY-MAKING IDEAS!

Also by Darcie Sanders and Martha M. Bullen

Staying Home
Never Throw Out a Banana Again

Turn Your Talents Into Profits

100+
TERRIFIC IDEAS FOR STARTING YOUR OWN HOME-BASED MICROBUSINESS

Darcie Sanders

AND

Martha M. Bullen

POCKET BOOKS

New York   London   Toronto   Sydney   Tokyo   Singapore

Some of the ideas in this book are unusual or creative. While to our knowledge, none of them are illegal or unsafe, the information contained herein is not intended to replace medical, financial, legal or other professional advice. We expect our readers to exercise normal good judgment when using the ideas in this book, to take reasonable precautions and to solicit professional advice as necessary when launching or running a business.

An *Original* Publication of POCKET BOOKS

POCKET BOOKS, a division of Simon & Schuster Inc.
1230 Avenue of the Americas, New York, NY 10020

Library of Congress Cataloging-in-Publication Data

Sanders, Darcie, 1953–
    Turn your talents into profits : 100 + terrific ideas for starting
your own home-based microbusiness / Darcie Sanders and Martha M.
Bullen.
      p. cm.
   ISBN: 0-671-01529-X
   1. Home-based businesses.   2. Small business.   I. Bullen,
Martha M.   II. Title.
HD2333.S257   1998
658'.041—dc21
                                     97-43196
                                        CIP

First Pocket Books trade paperback printing April 1998

10 9 8 7 6 5 4 3 2 1

POCKET and colophon are registered trademarks of
Simon & Schuster Inc.

Text design by Stanley S. Drate/Folio Graphics Co. Inc.
Cover design by Rod Hernandez, illustration by Hal Just

Printed in the U.S. A.

ACKNOWLEDGMENTS

A book of this scope is the work of many hands. The arduous task of research was made more enjoyable by the able assistance of Trish Ambrosio, Wendy Burbank Martin Karpel, Lenny Karpel, Margot Myers, Audrey Michaels, Patricia Minore, and Herb Sanders. The early support of Paul Mahon was extremely helpful, as was the good advice in time of need from Joe Esposito. Our agents Elise Proulx and Barbara Lowenstein furthered the work and found it a wonderful home at Pocket Books, where our editor, Greer Kessel, graciously brought the project to fruition.

And finally, we would like to express our deepest gratitude to all the microentrepreneurs who so generously shared their time, expertise, and experiences with us—and with you, the reader.

CONTENTS

◆───────────────◆

SECTION 1
ARTS AND CRAFTS BUSINESSES

◆───────────────◆

◆

SECTION 2
BUSINESS SERVICES

◆

◆

SECTION 3
PERSONAL SERVICES

◆

◆

SECTION 4

EDUCATIONAL AND ENTERTAINMENT SERVICES

◆

◆

SECTION 5
HOUSE AND GARDEN

◆

◆

SECTION 6
BUYING AND SELLING

◆

◆

APPENDICES

◆

TURN YOUR TALENTS INTO PROFITS

INTRODUCTION

For growing numbers of people, working from home is becoming the new American Dream. Forty million Americans work at home today—either running their own business, operating a side business, or telecommuting.

Work patterns have changed dramatically during the last decade. Over twenty-two million Americans are now working part-time—that's 19 percent of our nation's labor force! And over eight million of us work multiple jobs, reports the Bureau of Labor Statistics.

In *Turn Your Talents into Profits*, we introduce a new term to describe the fastest-growing type of small business. Microbusinesses have low start-up costs, are home-based, can be run by one person, offer flexible hours, and tend to be personally fulfilling as well as profitable. And best of all, almost anyone can start a microbusiness. All you need is a good idea for earning money, a useful talent or skill, and the desire to work for yourself.

Turn Your Talents into Profits features more than a hundred high-tech, low-tech, and no-tech moneymaking opportunities. We are focusing exclusively on part-time home-based small businesses because most people don't have the time, funding, or driving desire to be full-time entrepreneurs. (Of course, many of these businesses can be expanded into full-time ventures if you have the energy and opportunity to do so.)

Whether you're a full-time worker interested in moonlighting, an at-home parent, a part-time worker, a student, single parent, or retiree, you'll find dozens of microbusiness ideas to try. We'll show you how to use the skills and knowledge you already possess and how to expend your entrepreneurial energies for a profit.

We interviewed over a hunded microbusiness entrepreneurs and learned what they enjoy most about running their own small businesses. These are the reasons they mentioned most often: working part-time from home allows them to spend more time with their families; they enjoy being their own boss; they're able to do work that they enjoy, and that takes advantage of their talents; they receive a sense of personal achievement—as well as tax breaks; and they spend less money on child care, commuting, and business clothing.

Yvonne Barnes, the owner of a technical communications company, is one of the successful microbusiness owners we interviewed. We'd like to pass along her inspiring words on how she developed her own business:

> What a difference a work-at-home job makes! I have more time, more money, more freedom, and more happiness than I did when I worked full-time. I arrange my work commitments when it is convenient for me. I determine my vacations, raises, projects, and schedule.
>
> My professional background was in technical communication and education development. I developed training for dozens of different topics and had extensive experience as an instructor. I decided to take my skills, interests, and knowledge and use them as an independent contractor.
>
> I started my business with three children under the age of two. Since that time we added yet another child. Yet, in less than two and one-half years, I had too much work. That is, I had more than enough to keep me busy, knew when my next paychecks were coming, and had the opportunity to select projects I truly enjoyed. Today I subcontract work to others because I have so many contacts and projects.

I've learned that your opportunities are unlimited if you want to succeed. There are plenty of jobs you can do that require very low start-up and operating costs. You can order hundreds of business cards for less money than it costs to go to a movie and buy popcorn and a drink.

If you want it, you can do it. I had concerns, fears, and insecurities early on. A few successful projects and the commitment to continue gave me the inspiration and motivation to keep going.

Yvonne points out the greatest benefit of part-time, at-home work: You are completely in control. The businesses in this book will enable you to work as often as you like, when you like. How much you produce, and how much money you make, is completely up to you. Have you ever had any other job with such freedom, convenience, and autonomy?

In researching this book, we were delighted to discover how many people are successfully running innovative home businesses. Everywhere we looked, we found dozens of new and intriguing ideas for making money at home.

The craft market, for example, is booming. There are currently over eight thousand craft fairs a year in this country, and the vast majority of these are markets for amateurs rather than for professional artisans. In addition, a growing number of boutiques and galleries are stocking crafts. This book will show artistic types how to turn a hobby they already enjoy into a moneymaking venture.

Crafts, however, aren't the whole story. Countless people own a home computer that spends 95 percent of its life attracting dust bunnies instead of becoming the moneymaker it could be. We provide numerous ideas for professional part-time work from home—from running an electronic bulletin board service to designing Internet Websites or becoming a medical transcriptionist.

But you don't need to be artistic or a technical type to make money at home. If you don't like to get your hands dirty, or are scared of computers, then you can even earn extra money with your telephone by providing a telephone referral service. Or better yet, you may be able to make money with your house itself by renting it out as a set for commercials, movies, or outdoor weddings. (It's easier than you think, and we'll tell you how to hook up with location scouts for film companies and advertising agencies.)

Each entry provides a wealth of information on how to get started, the skills, materials and equipment you'll need, potential markets and how to reach them (without spending big bucks), and the going rate for that particular product or service. We also include expert advice from people in a variety of fields on the pitfalls and pleasures of making money at home—and discuss low-budget, do-it-yourself advertising and marketing strategies.

We are not the only ones who think that microbusinesses are the most exciting new trend in the American entrepreneurial landscape. The Small Business Administration (SBA) is so convinced of the growing importance of the microbusiness segment that they publish a nationwide customized list of banks willing to make extremely small business loans to undercapitalized microbusiness entrepreneurs.

And the SBA's faith is well placed: Microbusinesses have a much higher survival rate than other new businesses. Link Resources market researchers report that over the same three-year period, 85 percent of small home-based businesses will still be in business, as opposed to only 20 percent for small businesses in general. On a year-to-year basis, home-based businesses average a very respectable 95 percent survival rate.

Why do microbusinesses have such an outstanding success rate? Because of this built-in advantage: Their owners don't have to pay the heavy rent, salary, and utilities costs that hamper other enterprises. How do their owners develop their business, structure it, and run it in order to make the most of this advantage? Let us show you in this book!

TAKING CARE OF BUSINESS

STARTING UP

You might not have a background in business, but if you've ever managed a home, applied for a driver's license, supervised children, planned a party, or balanced a checkbook you have the basics of the managerial, financial, strategic-planning, follow-up, and interpersonal skills necessary to run a small, home-based business. Of course, having the basics doesn't mean you have the knowledge—yet. But being a part-time entrepreneur means you will have the time to study, seek out expert advice, and attend seminars to build your skills as you're growing your business.

For entrepreneurs on a budget (and what microbusiness person is not?), the single best source for excellent advice and educational programs is the federal agency known as the SBA (Small Business Administration) and its affiliated agencies, SCORE (Service Corps of Retired Executives) and SBDCs (Small Business Development Centers). These agencies holds thousands of free or low-priced workshops each year in numerous locations throughout the country to help small business owners exactly like yourself. Popular topics include start-up procedures, taxation, and market research.

The SBDC and SBA primarily offer educational services, while SCORE focuses on providing expert advice to individual businesses. The SBA used to offer loans directly, too, but the direct loan program has been cut back drastically. Nowadays the vast majority of SBA loans are actually made by local private lending institutions and are just guaranteed by the agency. The SBA does, however, offer a fabulous variety of programs designed to help small businesses manage their cash flow and capital problems, from Seasonal Line of Credit Guarantees to Pollution Control Financing. Get connected by calling 1-800-827-5722 and requesting publication OPC-2, *Your Business and the SBA*, which will give you a complete list of programs available plus the application procedures.

On the local level, go to your library and request the publication *How to Start a Business in* (*the name of your state*). Every state has its own version of this publication, usually in loose-leaf binder format. Besides general business information, it includes all relevant license, permit, and registration requirements particular to your location.

FINDING FUNDING

How much money do you really need to start a microbusiness? Less than you think. Almost a third (31 percent) of all new businesses begin with less than $10,000, and a relatively large 17 percent hit the ground running on under $5,000. Over half of the entries in our book can be started on less than $2,500, and many of those can easily be launched out of an existing hobby for well under $1,000.

Of course, how much you need will depend on your type of business. In a typical business plan the ten items for which expense projections are usually made are:

- ◆ Remodeling
- ◆ Equipment
- ◆ Installation
- ◆ Supplies
- ◆ Inventory

- Legal and professional fees
- Licenses and permits
- Telephone and utility
- Additional insurance
- Signage, advertising, stationery

Where can you find the financing you need? *Income Opportunities* magazine's recent survey of 200 readers found that 57 percent used their personal savings to get started; only 10 percent got a traditional bank loan. Other funding sources were credit cards, loans from friends, home-equity loans and pension savings.

Some of the entrepreneurs we interviewed also recommended making friends and family your first clients for your goods or services, and ask them to pay in advance. Even a fifty percent advance payment can provide a small operator with that invaluable start-up cash.

STRUCTURING YOUR BUSINESS

Technically, you don't *have* to write a business plan (unless you are applying for a bank loan), but it would be wise to make one anyway because of its usefulness to you as a planning tool. It needn't be fancy or formal. Your local library has many model books you can follow—ask for the Small Business section or hunt for the key word "business plan" on a search index. The SBA also offers these extremely helpful publications, which will outline for you the key points that should be included in any plan:

MP11	*Business Plan for Small Service Firms*
MP4	*Business Plan for Small Manufacturers*
MP15	*Business Plan for Homebased Businesses*
MP21	*Developing a Strategic Business Plan*

After preparing a business plan, the next step is to decide if you want to incorporate or not. It's not a requirement to run a business. In fact, many small (and even large) businesses started out and remain sole proprietorships and simple partnerships.

There are pros—such as protection of your other assets—to incorporation, and cons—such as expense and increased paperwork. How do you decide which is right for you? Consult a lawyer, accountant, or request the free publication MP25, *Selecting the Legal Structure for Your Business*, from the Small Business Administration.

While incorporation is not a requirement, maintaining a separate bank account for your business is a sound business practice. It goes a long way to establishing your activities as a "business" instead of a "hobby" to the Internal Revenue Service (IRS). This is important, because filing a tax form for your business, no matter how small, *is* a requirement.

You are required by the IRS to report and pay taxes on any profit from your business in addition to your personal income tax, and most state laws follow the federal model. Of course, no one wants to hear about extra paperwork, but filing may be very beneficial to your business, since there are a wide variety of deductions for which you will become eligible when you file. Some of these deductions include:

- ◆ Educational expenses
- ◆ Travel
- ◆ Business use of your car
- ◆ Depreciation of equipment

These deductions, to which business owners are entitled, can help reduce the total amount of taxes you end up owing each year. Make sure you keep your business records separate from your personal finance records. Though it is not required, many microbusiness owners maintain a separate bank/checking account, too. Besides helping you with record-keeping, a separate account is good evidence for the IRS that your activity is in fact a business, and not a hobby.

Unless you are very knowledgeable about the tax code, you may want to have a professional structure and prepare your taxes the first year in order to get things off on the right foot. You should also call the IRS toll-free at 1-800-829-3676 and order the YBTK, *Your Business Tax Kit*. This packet includes publications and guidelines for small business tax returns, including information on additional small business tax education programs.

Structuring Your Work Environment

Your business isn't the only thing that needs to be structured and organized—your work space will need special attention, too. The electrical and phone wiring systems of most older homes were simply not designed to handle the current (no pun intended!) gamut of household gadgets (such as microwaves, multiple TVs, electric can openers and crock pots, and VCRs, to name a few) plus the basic home office setup of computer, printer, photocopier, fax, scanner, and answering machine. We heard of one home-based graphic designer who found that he couldn't use the microwave at the same time as the computer because they were on the same circuit!

It will be well worth it to you to pay for an hour of an electrician's time to determine whether your business equipment list will overload your present system. You may need a separate fuse box or circuit.

Virtually every home-based entrepreneur we spoke to mentioned the need for a separate, dedicated phone line just for business use. This line should have its own answering machine with a message appropriate to your enterprise; it should also be off limits to other types of calls (so that you can deduct it as a 100 percent business expense)—even if your teenagers are desperate for another line to socialize on.

The problem of working around the house with young children underfoot is one that many of our respondents had to address early on. Several told us they had to make radical changes in the number of hours they worked, or when they worked, because they had been way too sanguine about their ability to work while infants or toddlers napped.

"Invariably," one computer consultant told us, "my daughter would get an ear infection the day before a deadline. She'd be up all day *and* all night. Eventually, I learned to add a 25 percent 'what if?' factor to all my dates, and didn't ever schedule a client meeting until after 3 P.M., when a neighbor girl came home from school and was happy to baby-sit for me."

The good news is that older children's activities can often be incorporated into your business activities. Youngsters of four or five will happily sort, sticker, and stuff envelopes—as long as you're not too particular if everything is exactly straight. A computer whiz of eight or nine is fully capable of handling a mail merge program. Older children can help write, edit, and proof promotional materials, distribute flyers and posters, and learn the rudiments of bookkeeping. And the fairs, farmer's markets, and conventions that many entrepreneurs attend in order to keep up their skills and catch clients can be an outing for the whole family. The consensus among our respondents was that children are not an impediment to an entrepreneur, as long as you are realistic about their—and your—requirements.

A final tip about working at home—if clients will be visiting you at home, make sure you post your business hours or have an "OPEN/CLOSED" sign for your door. Otherwise, clients tend to drop in at all hours (and *always* if you're in your bathrobe).

GETTING EXPERT ADVICE

Once you've read all the books on start-ups and operating small businesses, you still may have very specific questions about problems unique to your own enterprise. Most microbusiness entrepreneurs can't afford expensive consultants. But, how would you like the equivalent of an experienced board of directors to help you solve current problems and plan for the future? That's what you get when you sign up with SCORE, the Service Corps of Retired Executives.

SCORE is staffed by volunteer executives who donate their

time and expertise free to small business owners. They will have expertise in finance, accounting, sales, and general management, and their advice will be impartial. SCORE counselors can help you with your start-up, business plan, expansion, and the problems of the day-to-day running of your business. To find the SCORE office closest to you, call the Small Business Administration toll-free at 1-800-827-5722 for a referral. You can also ask them to send you Form 641, which will start your application procedure.

If you have access to the Internet, a lot of information is available on a Home Business site created by the Cooperative State Research Education and Extension Service. This site provides information on programs, conferences, seminars, and other activities for home-based and small business owners. Besides a 300-page resource directory you can download, there are also direct links to the IRS so that you can download necessary publications and forms, and links to the U.S. Patent and Trademark Office for information on patents, trademarks, and copyright. The address is: **http://decit.if.uidaho.edu/hbb/homebus.html.**

Other small-business sites worth exploring are:

Inc.online: **http://www.inc.com**

Entrepreneur magazine:
http://www.entrepreneurmag.com

Your Small Office: **http://www.smalloffice.com**

Home Office Association of America:
http://www.hoaa.com/

The Business Resource Center:
http://www.kciLink.com/brc/

EntrepreNet: **http://www.enterprise.org/enet/index.html**

CCH Business Owners Toolkit:
http://www.toolkit.cch.com

Should you plan on quitting your other job as soon as your financing is in place? Research by the Home Business Association shows that about 50 precent of all home businesses are part-time and intend to stay that way. Many other people use their part-time business as a test run for a full-time enterprise, but it's a prudent idea to start any new home-based business on a part-time basis at first. Yes, this does mean you'll be working two jobs for a while, but once your new enterprise takes off you'll have the luxury of choosing to do it full-time or keep it part-time. And, you'll still have the security of your day job income (and hopefully, benefits) while you grow your own business.

KEEPING COSTS DOWN

As we've said before, microbusinesses usually have a built-in advantage in that you don't have to pay the heavy rent, salary, and utility costs that hamper other enterprises. Many successful home-based entrepreneurs operate on a shoestring budget, but cash flow *can* be a constant worry. Here are our top tips for keeping your expenses low:

- For a fast jump start make family and friends your first clients, and ask them to pre-pay in cash so that you have the funds to buy inventory and supplies.
- If you have young children at home, trade out baby-sitting days with another parent so that you get large blocks of free time in which to work on your business.
- Use free publicity and inexpensive local newspaper advertising to promote your business.
- Get free advice and low-cost educational services from the SBA and SCORE.
- Use a bank that gives you a second account discount for your business account; if they don't give a discount, try to qualify for reduced fees and service charges based upon the combined total of both your accounts.
- Keep receipts for every single business-related expense and improvement in order to declare them on your tax return.

- Try to buddy up orders with other small business entrepreneurs such as yourself to qualify for wholesale discounts on supplies.
- Trade out for services and products you need; for example, an artist might design a new logo for a printer in
  return for having her business cards printed.

PROMOTING YOUR
MICROBUSINESS

Whenever possible you should promote your product or service
with free publicity instead of expensive advertising. Think about
how can you generate publicity:

- Offer a one-time finder's fee or "Thank-You Discount"
  to customers whose referrals actually generate new business.
- Include a referral sheet with quotes from satisfied customers on every job you bid.
- Send press releases to local media whenever you open or
  expand a business, or on an anniversary.
- Write a column or article on your area of expertise for
  local and national publications.
- Speak before civic, social, and educational groups as
  often as you can.
- Donate your goods or services to a worthy cause (and
  don't forget to keep records for the tax deduction).
- Network by joining every applicable club and association
  you can afford.

There are many reasons why so many people want to work
part-time from home. Of course, earning more money is at the
top of the list—but many microbusiness owners are equally interested in developing a new career, keeping current with an old
career while nurturing children through their early years, or sim-

ply making a hobby pay for itself and have some fun while doing it. Most entrepreneurs soon find that besides the pleasure of pursuing their dream, independence, and creativity, they also derive deep satisfaction from running their businesses properly. We hope you do, too.

ARTS
AND
CRAFTS
BUSINESSES

◆

WHAT YOU NEED TO KNOW TO GET STARTED

When you work from home as an artist or crafter you are joining one of the oldest traditions in the creative world—that of the studio. Of course, you need not starve in a garret for the authentic artistic experience—artists and crafters throughout the ages have craved a well-equipped corner of the house to work in where their tools are safe and they can have immediate access should inspiration strike at, say, 2 A.M. But, whether you have an entire basement workshop or a simple desk in a corner of the family room, an arts or crafts studio has some requirements above and beyond a simple home office.

First in mind should be safety. Do you work with glues or adhesives that require extra ventilation? Do you use power tools that need GFI (Ground Fault Interruptor) outlets or even a power upgrade? Do your projects create dust, shavings, or filings that will necessitate extra filtration for your heating or cooling systems? Do you work with chemicals, such as acids or solvents, that require special cleanup procedures? Do you have a nearby bathroom for emergency cleanups? Of course, these are questions that even casual hobbiests should consider when setting up a home shop, but there is never a better time to get serious about safety than when you upgrade your operation to a business. Where is the best place to go for safety information on the materials and tools you use? The manufacturer first, and then the Environmental Protection Agency (EPA) and Occupational

Safety and Health Agency (OSHA). Your local telephone book or directory service will have the number of the office closest to you.

A safety upgrade for your home studio may cost anywhere from $300 for a separate room air conditioner to $1,000 for an emergency eyewash station, but the good news is that the potential for profit in this area certainly justifies any additional expense. Freelance artists, writers, and designers have always been well accepted in the business world, and nowadays the craft market is definitely booming, too. There are currently over eight thousand craft fairs a year in this country, and the vast majority of these are markets for amateurs rather than for professional artisans. In addition, a growing number of boutiques and galleries are stocking crafts.

Many artists or crafters have a talent or interest—be it in painting, sewing, or woodworking—that goes back to childhood. But the key to taking your talent and developing it into something with profit potential is to specialize. What do we mean by specialize? Well, take calligraphy, for instance. A skilled calligrapher can make money through calligraphy in two different ways: by creating original designs and selling them at craft fairs and through boutiques, or by providing customized wedding invitations, envelopes, posters, and other items for individual clients. You should focus on one way or the other so as not to spend too much of your precious advertising budget and time on both markets. We provide tips for each approach in the following pages.

Similarly, when a hobby painter becomes a professional painter, you must become a painter of *something*. Thus, we profile for you house painters, furniture painters, mural painters—even fabric painters—to give you an idea of the variety of specialties available. If your skills extend to other types of graphic arts—say photography or illustration—numerous commercial opportunities are open to you. But remember—specialization is still the key. Read the profiles of the pet photographer, stencil designer, and greeting card companies for ideas on how to find your niche and develop it.

A woodworker's projects can run the gamut from simple toddler toys to museum-quality fine furniture reproductions. Well-crafted toys are best sold through the usual craft-show circuit and boutique placements, but marketing large furniture pieces represents a unique challenge.

In this age of ever-increasing technology, the consensus seems to be that Americans' appetite for handmade items has never been higher—we even found a designer of handcrafted fishing lures who has incredible demand for his creations. Some traditionally handmade items, like jewelry, have now even upgraded themselves to "wearable art."

Fancy needlework has been around ever since the first cave-woman fashioned a needle out of a sliver of bone. The tapestries that kept the drafts out of castles and quilts that our great-grand-parents snuggled under on cold winter nights are now the highly prized possessions of galleries and museums. Today's market for handmade quilts and all sorts of custom cloth fabrications shows no sign of letting up; we profile a wide variety of fiber artists to give you an idea of how wide open this field still is. However, as you read the write-ups please note, once again, how specific and targeted these businesses are—one of the designers specializes in doll costumes, another in decorations for lawn ornaments!

What if you have more appreciation for crafts than the talent to make them yourself? Can you still have a crafts business? Absolutely. The last two businesses we profile in this section—compiling craft kits and hosting craft shows—are ideal for individuals with a talent for promotion and a taste for the artistic. Both would work well for people who want a crafts involvement without actually being a crafter themselves, or as an add-on business for established artists looking to expand their markets.

A WORD ON CRAFT SHOWS

The consensus among crafters is that attending shows is worth your time, but not if it takes *all* your time. Remember, where you really want to be is back home in your studio, creating. But shows are an invaluable resource for gathering information on pricing and materials, continuing education, and permanent boutique outlets for your creations. Besides information and outlets, craft-ers can also pick up a goodly number of individual clients at well-attended shows. What follows are our top tips for general marketing of crafts.

GENERAL CRAFT SHOW TIPS

 ◆ Never, ever go to a show without a large supply of busi-ness cards and an order book.
 ◆ Most shows have a jury that evaluates your work before you're accepted. You need to send pictures or slides with your application. If you have a unique kind of speciality, it helps you get into the shows. Try to send in your appli-cation forms early, along with good, clear pictures. Abid-ing by their rules will help your acceptance rate. Booth rental fees range from $20 to several hundred dollars, or $100 to $150 for a few days at a shopping mall.
 ◆ Learn about upcoming craft shows by talking to other crafters, reading regional craft publications (available at craft stores), and reading the listings in your local news-paper.
 ◆ Join the ACCI (Association of Crafts and Creative In-dustries). They offer a huge international show in Chi-cago every year in July for crafters and craft store owners. You can go there to get new ideas, see new products, and take workshops on different crafting techniques.
 ◆ Since they are not driven by Christmas/Hannukah gift-buying, spring shows are not as lucrative as fall ones, and may not be worth your while. You may have to pay $150 for a spot, then sit there for two days and not sell any-thing. In the fall, shows are well worth it.
 ◆ Investigate selling your crafts through consignment and craft stores. Most consignment stores take 30 percent of your sales. An alternative is going through a chain of craft stores like the Country Sample, which has numerous lo-cations in the Midwest. You rent the space, pay a monthly rent, and a percentage of your sales (around 5 percent). You don't have to be there to sell your items,

just deliver new crafts now and then. This is not a consignment arrangement. The advantage of selling through them is that you can sell your crafts year-round.

◆ People aren't spending as much money on crafts and other nonessentials as they used to in the 1980s. Since they're watching their money now, keeping your price reasonable is important. If you sell them something well made and different for $10 or less, they'll get excited about that.

◆ Turn to other crafters for support and encouragement. It helps to have someone who understands what you're going through, will give you advice, and encourages you.

◆ Display your crafts at flea markets, outdoor art fairs, art galleries, gift shows, shopping mall exhibits, home craft shows, and specialty shops. Bring samples and photographs of your other work.

◆ Make sure you get a state resale registration number so you don't have to pay taxes when you buy your supplies wholesale.

◆ Set prices by carefully studying what other crafters charge in your area. Another pricing strategy is to add up the cost of your supplies and multiply by three or four.

◆ Note that currently the most popular items are: jewelry, porcelain pottery, art glass, handwoven clothing, quilts, leather items, wood sculptures, silk flowers and dried flower arrangements, folk toys, and holiday ornaments.

Unlike some of the newer technologies, crafts have been around just about forever, and there are many organizations and publications, both hard copy and on-line, to help you develop your talent and run your business. Here are the references and resources you just shouldn't be without.

ON-LINE CRAFT INFORMATION
CraftNet Village: **http://www.craftnet.org**
  This includes *Crafts 'n Things* magazine on-line, new product ideas and information, on-line BBs and craft libraries. For more

information on accessing this, send an SASE to CraftNet Village, PO Box 25286, Milwaukee, WI 53201.

Creative Industries Connection On-line Service:
http://www.connect2.org/cc
Includes E-mail, The Creativity Connection Web site, newsgroups, BBs, craft industry news, networking.

Crafts special interest groups on-line:

- ◆ Use keyword "Crafts" on AOL for dozens of different craft message boards.
- ◆ Use "Crafts1 BB" and "Crafts2 BB" on Prodigy.
- ◆ Go to "Fibercrafts Forum" on CompuServe.

MAGAZINES AND ASSOCIATIONS

American Craft Magazine
American Craft Council
72 Spring Street
New York, NY 10012
212-274-0630

The American Craft Council is a national nonprofit educational organization that includes the American Craft Association and American Craft Information Center. It also publishes *Contemporary Crafts Marketplace*, which tells how and where to sell crafts.

Crafting Traditions
5400 S. 60th Street
Greendale, WI 53129

Crafts 'n Things
Clapper Publishing Co., Inc.
2400 Devon, Ste. 375
Des Plaines, IL 60018
800-CRAFTS-1, or 847-635-5800

Association of Crafts & Creative Industries (ACCI)
PO Box 2188
Zanesville, OH 43702-2188
614-452-4541

This association offers an enormous annual International Craft Exposition—it gives crafters the chance to see lots of new products and take educational workshops. It also has a Professional Craft Artisan Program that includes a comprehenisve business seminar designed to help you start a craft business or improve upon an existing operation.

BOOKS

- *How to Start Making Money with Your Crafts* by Kathryn Caputo (Betterway Books, 1995)
- *Careers for Crafty People and Other Dexterous Types* by Mark Rowh (VGM Career Books, 1994)
- *Creative Cash: How to Sell Your Crafts, Needlework, Designs & Know-How, 5th Edition,* by Barbara Brabec (B. Brabec Products, 1993)
- *Craft Supply Sourcebook: A Comprehensive Shop-by-Mail Guide, 3rd Edition,* edited by Margaret Boyd (Betterway Books, 1994)
- *How to Be a Weekend Entrepreneur: Making Money at Craft Fairs, Trade Shows and Swap Meets* by Susan Ratliff (Marketing Methods Press, 1991)
- *How to Open and Operate a Home-Based Crafts Business* by Kenn Oberrecht (Globe Pequot Press, 1994)

See the Appendix for more information on craft associations, books and magazines.

MURAL PAINTER

Custom wall painting has become the latest style in home decorating, and you can make good money at this if you're artistically inclined. If this work appeals to you, you'll need strong artistic, design, and draftsmanship skills, as well as a variety of brushes, acrylic decorative craft paints, a large dropcloth, and a six-foot stepladder for those hard-to-reach places. When meeting new clients, you'll set up an initial consultation at their home, brainstorm a design together, choose colors, and estimate the time the job will take. Bring along photographs of other wall paintings you have done to show a variety of design possibilities.

The most popular patterns include ivy leaves, grapevines, sunflowers, and other flowers, although some people may request such elaborate murals as a fly fisherman in a stream or a trompe l'oeil (fool the eye) painting of a window on a windowless wall. Drawings of animals, trains, sports figures, and scenes reminiscent of E. E. Milne and Beatrix Potter illustrations are also frequently requested for children's rooms. It's a good idea to make a quick sketch in colored pencil after the first consultation so your clients can more easily visualize what the design will look like.

Janice Skivington, an illustrator, spotted this fashion trend when she went on a tour of an expensive new housing estate and noticed that most of the homes had a mural in the bathroom or a hand-painted decorative vine around the kitchen window. She thought, "I can do this," and took samples of her artwork to a local interior decorator's office. She asked, "Do you have clients who would like custom murals or wall painting?", was told "yes," and was hired on the spot. Janice Skivington offered this advice: "Learn to work neatly and quickly. Unlike illustration work, you can't be too detailed and meticulous, or you'll never finish. Anyone who can stencil nicely can probably do this. And approach the job confidently, since it can be a little scary at first drawing something permanent on someone else's wall."

This work can be physically tiring, since you may spend long hours on a ladder, but it pays well, and each job is enjoyably different from the one before. It's also very flexible—you can arrange the times you can work, whether you'd prefer to paint on evenings, weekends, or when your children are in school.

TOP TIP: "Since anyone can buy a wallpaper border at a store, you need to create a highly individual approach to each room," says Jennifer Holman of Holman Designs. "Find a niche by capturing clients' memories and incorporating their favorite scenes or pets into the painting. And be willing to make changes until they like what you've done—you'll need to put aside your artistic thin skin and make sure that your final painting is exactly what they wanted."

GETTING STARTED: Visiting local decorators and showing your work to them in person is usually more effective than sending out mass mailings. Printing up business cards and leaving a few cards once you've finished working in a home is a wise investment, since the best leads come from satisfied clients. You can develop new designs by painting murals for your children and for family and friends, or volunteer to paint a mural at your local school or library. Take a good-quality photograph of each job you complete so you can add it to your portfolio—the more examples of your work you can show, the more you have to offer potential customers. And pick up copies of *House Beautiful* (1700 Broadway, New York, NY 10019) and *Country Living* (224 W. 57th

Street, New York, NY 10019) magazines, since they often show-case decorative painting. You can clip these pages and add them to your idea file to show customers.

THE GOING RATE: $30 to $50 an hour; an average job lasts ten to twelve hours, although detailed trompe l'oeil paintings can take as long as twenty hours. Many custom painters charge $30 to $40 for their initial consultation as well, so they are compensated for their time if the customer decides not to hire them. Others offer free consultations, but charge an additional $12.50 a day if they have to drive a long way to get to a client's home.

FURNITURE PAINTER

Unlike house painting, you can set up shop as a furniture painter without so much as a ladder or even the ability to draw a straight line. How? By using ready-made stencil designs (available through craft stores and magazines). The term "furniture paint-ing" is actually a little misleading, since what the job really entails is furniture decorating. Designs can be realistic—such as the eter-nally popular pig and cow and ivy themes—or more abstract. The types of furnishings that are typically decorated are chairs, tables, room dividers, picture frames, and stools.

You don't need a background in fine art, but you need a good eye for color and design. You'll also need the patience and con-centration to be meticulous about preparing the surface, painting the decorations, and applying whatever sort of varnish or finish the client desires.

Though most of the work can easily be done in a basement, garage, or kitchen craft corner, plan on making one visit to the client's house to coordinate colors. It is usually the painter's re-sponsibility to transport the pieces back and forth, so owning a van or truck (or having access to one) makes good sense.

Kathleen McCann, home-based owner of Savoir Faire De-signs, started out as a mural painter. Today she is making a name

for herself as a specialist of realistic, tromp l'oeil cabinetry painting, though she has also painted fabric and even swimming pools.
McCann recommends using only acrylic paints because any mistakes can be sanded off. You can consult a variety of references
that discuss application and finishing of painted surfaces. Two
respected volumes are *Paint Magic* by Jocasta Innes (Pantheon
Books, 1987) and *Decorative Style* by Kevin McCloud (Simon &
Schuster, 1990).

TOP TIP: Build your clientele by donating a decorated piece
to a local charity event or designer showcase. One painter was
able to place a decorated headboard in the showroom of a
friend's fabric store. This was a good placement, since people
shopping for fabric are often looking for those personal finishing
touches that can pull a room together.

GETTING STARTED: Contact the American Academy of
Decorative Finishes (14255 N. 79th Street, Scottsdale, AZ
85260, 602-991-8560) for educational materials. Then hit the garage sales and junk stores to pick up a few small inexpensive
chairs and stools to practice on. If these pieces turn out well, sell
them to friends or relatives or place them in businesses around
town to develop visibility for your decorating services. One of the
best sources for stencil designs are the clip art books that Dover
Publications has been putting out for many years. Call 800-223-
3130 to receive their catalog.

THE GOING RATE: Your fee should vary with the complexity of the design. Some designers charge by the hour ($25), while
others charge by the number of colors ($40 for one color, $60 for
two, $80 for three, and so on). If you charge by the hour, remem-
ber to include the time it takes you to prep and finish the piece.
If you decide to sell ready-made pieces, the rule of thumb is to
double the amount the raw furniture cost you, and then add on
whatever your regular decorating fee would be.

HOUSE PORTRAIT PAINTER

This job beats getting up on a ladder with a bucket of paint. Instead, there's money to be made in painting or drawing detailed pictures of people's houses. Most homeowners feel a strong attachment to their homes, and many would be interested in buying an attractive drawing of their home to display on their wall. Some would like to capture memories of a favorite childhood home. Others would like to order these paintings as gifts for friends or family members who are moving, either to commemorate their previous house or to celebrate the purchase of a new house. These paintings also make popular Christmas and Hanukkah presents. You may find yourself busy painting before the holidays, so let customers know that they should expect four to eight weeks for delivery.

You'll need artistic training and skills, of course, before you can consider starting this business. You'll also need a good eye for details and the ability to make architectural drawings. An impressionistic style will not fit the bill—customers prefer a realistic rendering of their home and grounds. Once you receive a commission, you'll want to meet the homeowners on site and take a look at the house together. Ask which architectural features they'd like emphasized in your painting, and which season they'd prefer. Find out about the plants they'll have in summer if they're not in bloom when you visit.

Take several photographs or make sketches while you're there so you won't have to reproduce them from memory later on in your studio. Don't forget to capture such small details as curtains and bushes. James Walsh considers his art a relaxing hobby and sideline business. "I am very detailed down to the last brick when it comes to my architectural illustration work," he told a local newspaper reporter. "Of course, I use a little artistic license to clean up the grounds and enhance the plantings." You can also recreate happy childhood memories for customers when you create drawings of their previous homes by working from old photographs.

TOP TIP: You might want to join your town's historical society and volunteer to create paintings for a local housewalk or chamber of commerce brochure so your work will be widely seen.

GETTING STARTED: The first step is to develop a portfolio you can show to prospective customers. Paint your own home, your neighbors', and a sampling of other kinds of buildings around town to demonstrate your style and range. Watercolors, acrylics, and pen-and-ink drawings are all popular, so you can concentrate on the medium you most enjoy. After you put your portfolio together, you can find customers by displaying your work at local craft and art fairs, putting up posters and business cards on community bulletin boards, and taking out a small ad in your newspaper's "home" section. Visit local real estate agents and interior designers to let them know about your business. They may be willing to pass on your name to their clients, display a stack of your fliers in their offices, or even give your drawings as housewarming gifts to their clients. You could also place small classified ads in national home and garden publications, and work from photos that people send you.

THE GOING RATE: These paintings sell for between $90 and $350 for unframed, matted paintings, depending on their size. You may want to branch out by offering to create related artwork for your customers. You could promote your ability to paint garden scenes, landscapes, or pet portraits for similar prices. Or, you could produce printed notecards or stationery featuring your painting of customers' homes; a set of 100 engraved cards and envelopes sells for around $75 to $200. Other artists sell wooden boxes featuring customized home paintings for $245 and small three-dimensional sculptures of people's homes for $200.

CUSTOM TILE PAINTER

Here is a wonderful commercial outlet for artists who love to paint and work in clay, too.

Former art teacher Carolyn Payne, of Payne Creations Tile in Kansas City, MO, uses blank, commercially produced tiles as a canvas for her custom-designed murals, commemoratives awards, and historical house portraits.

Payne works out of her home studio, which is outfitted with several large kilns and one small test kiln. Many of her clients supply a photo, fabric, or wallpaper sample for her to match. Others may suggest a general theme, such as floral, historical, undersea (popular in bathrooms), animals, or fruits and vegetables. Payne likes to meet with them in person at least once to get to know their likes and dislikes.

After the first meeting, Payne prepares a first sketch done as a small watercolor. Clients review the sketch, make any changes they would like, and Payne incorporates the changes into another sketch. Only after final approval does work on the tiles themselves begin.

The sketch is enlarged and transferred to the tiles, which may need many firings as Payne builds up layers of color to a beautiful luminescence. She also takes care to mark each piece on the back so that the tile setters will be able to assemble the final mural in the correct order.

Besides murals, Payne also creates single tiles, crafting custom commemorative tiles for events such as golf tournaments, and gift-packaged tile portraits of famous historical buildings.

TOP TIP: Custom tiles pretty much appeal to a luxury market, and after you have your technical skills down, your main concern will be your marketing. To reach the luxury market you have to spend on advertising. Payne advertises locally and nationally, including *Giftware News* (Box 5398, Deptford, NJ 08096) and *The Guild Sourcebook*. Referrals from satisfied customers and luxury home builders also help build her business. If you have single tiles that can be sold nationally, you should attend one of the big trade gift shows in either Dallas, San Francisco, Chicago, or New York.

GETTING STARTED: Many community colleges offer classes in ceramics where you can learn to transfer your drawing and painting skills to tilework, in addition to learning how to fire and stack a kiln. Once you've mastered the necessary skills, a good kiln and nice supply of glazes can be purchased for under $1,500.

THE BOTTOM LINE: Single tiles are priced by the piece, while murals can run anywhere from $50 to $250 a square foot, depending on the amount of research needed. When pricing quantity orders for retail outlets such as gift stores and museum shops, you will be expected to offer the usual 50 percent discount off the final selling price to the store owner.

FABRIC ARTIST

If you enjoy painting but think that art doesn't sell, think again. Wearable art can be very salable. Artists and crafters who transfer fabric paint designs onto cotton clothing can quickly find an appreciative audience for their designs. Hand-painted children's clothes (usually sweatshirts and dresses) are particularly popular, especially during the holidays. Many customers like to buy coordinating clothing for infants and their older children, which they're unable to find in most department stores. By offering custom designs and personalized clothing, you can provide a service that shoppers couldn't find at the mall.

You'll need to buy a wide range of fabric paints, brushes, waxed cardboard to place the clothing on while painting it (available at craft stores), an industrial-size clothes steamer, and cotton clothes in a variety of sizes and colors. Glitter, rhinestones, lace, pearls and metallic trim are also used in many designs. *Craft and Needlework Age* (225 Gordons Corner Plaza, Box 420, Manalapan, NJ 07726) lists suppliers who sell ready-made clothing in small quantities. To succeed at this business, you'll need strong artistic and design skills, organizational skills (in order to keep track of orders and manage your inventory), and the ability to predict which colors and designs will be the best sellers.

Some of the most popular designs we've seen include angels, Santas, Christmas trees and reindeer, Easter bunnies, sunflowers, fall leaves, teddy bears, dinosaurs, and a wide range of animals, from pandas to tigers. Jeannette Esposito, who's built up a successful fabric-painting business over the past ten years, relies on her idea file to help her develop new designs. She told us, "Before I throw a magazine away, I clip color combinations I like and appealing designs. I pull out the idea files and flip through them to help trigger my imagination and creativity."

TOP TIP: The colors you choose can make or break an item. Jeannette Esposito commented, "I try to stay away from trendy colors. I've found that offering a few color choices is less confusing for customers than offering too many choices. I use mostly red and white garments around Christmas, along with a few navy blues, and stick to white and pink for spring. I cut costs by offering fewer colors and also have a better-looking display if I simplify."

GETTING STARTED: Join the Association of Crafts & Creative Industries (ACCI, PO Box 2188, Zanesville, OH 43702-2188; 614-452-4541), which offers an annual convention usually held near Chicago in Rosemont, IL in July. At the convention you can learn about new painting and crafts products and attend a variety of crafting classes. Once you've developed some designs, it's time to start exhibiting your wares at craft shows. You can network with other crafters to find out which shows are well attended and which are not worth your while. Developing a brochure is not such a good idea, since brochures can be expensive to print, and other people could use the brochure to copy your designs. Do set up a mailing list of all your customers, though, and send out regular flyers announcing your new designs and listing the upcoming craft shows where you'll be exhibiting. And visit local children's boutique owners, who may be interested in selling your clothes on consignment.

THE GOING RATE: Painted T-shirts sell for around $18, adult sweatshirts for $23 to $30, and children's clothes sell for between $20 and $35, depending on the complexity of the design and the cost of the garment. These are average prices; you may find yourself charging $2.50 for a pair of children's socks at the low end, and $75 or more for an ornate denim jacket at the high end.

CALLIGRAPHER

Is your handwriting beautiful and elegant? Are you artistically inclined? If so, you can fulfill the demand for unusual invitations for weddings, parties, and all sorts of events. You can also create elegant scrolls, certificates, and awards, or original notecards to mark and commemorate special occasions. Properly personalized, these graphics are highly prized.

Most calligraphers structure their business in one of two different ways: either by creating original designs and selling them at craft fairs and through boutiques or by providing customized wedding and party invitations, envelopes, posters, and other items for individual clients. This business's low start-up expenses are appealing to students and others who would like to set up a business on the cheap. All you'll need to buy is a fine set of pens, nibs and ink, high-quality paper, colored pencils and other art supplies, and a drafting table or light table. You'll also need a quiet room or corner where you can work and concentrate. Humidity can make paper curl, so make sure your work area isn't right next to the laundry room or the dishwasher.

Calligraphers receive training in their craft by taking classes at a local community college, art school, or community center and by reading *How to Become a Professional Calligrapher* by Stuart David (Taplinger, 1985). If you'd like to meet and learn from other practicing calligraphers, join the Society of Scribes (PO Box 933, New York, NY 10150; 212-475-1653) or Society for Calligraphy (PO Box 64174, Los Angeles, CA 90064; 310-306-2326). You may also want to subscribe to *Calligraphy Review* magazine (2421 Wilcox Drive, Norman, OK 73069). Then practice, practice, practice, until you are confident of your skills and can create polished-looking, standardized letters.

Karen Kramer, who has had her own calligraphy business for nineteen years, always brings her supplies and light table along to craft shows in order to personalize customers' orders. She's learned that it draws people to her booth to see an artist at work. Karen honed her skills by taking a job as a sign painter at a local store and as a hand letterer for a map company.

She advised, "Don't be afraid to try it. Take a calligraphy class, find out if you like it and if your teacher encourages you. It helps to have a good eye, be able to see details, and work with color well. Listen to your customers carefully to find out what they want. I use scripture and old sayings that encourage and comfort in my calligraphy. I clip verses and sayings that make you think, and save them for future designs. I like to take words and make them come alive on paper, and I love to see people get excited about what I do." Karen is also delighted that she's able to completely pay for her children's private school tuition through her calligraphy earnings.

Those with expertise in calligraphy are many times sought out to address envelopes in which invitations are mailed. But don't limit yourself to routine wedding and birth announcements. One woman, who works as a calligrapher in a retirement community, wasn't getting much business until she added dinner and anniversary invitations to her list of services. She also suggests adding creative touches along with the beauty of your handwriting. For example, for an invitation to a second marriage ceremony she used a copy of the sheet music for the song "The Second Time Around" as a border. This invitation made her reputation as someone who could bring a bit of creative humor to her work, and her orders increased.

TOP TIP FOR ORIGINAL WORK: Your work will be in more demand if you can draw a floral border or other original design to illustrate the sayings you've chosen. Creating an eye-catching business card or flyer is also a good way to promote your services. Mailing out a brochure to past customers before

Christmas is well worth doing, especially if you showcase new holiday designs or create unique Christmas and Hanukkah cards.

GETTING STARTED FOR ORIGINAL WORK: Volunteer your skills by creating posters and signs for local organizations, and experiment with taking a variety of sayings and turning them into framable artworks. Once you've developed a range of original designs, you can put samples or photographs in a large portfolio to show to customers. The next step is to display your pieces at art and craft fairs. Visit local craft fairs, talk to the crafters there, and get their recommendations on their favorite craft shows, as well as the ones to avoid. After that, you'll need to create as many different note cards and thank-you cards, prints, and framed quotations or poems as you can to bring along to the shows you've chosen to attend. Other promotional possibilities including sending fliers to past and current customers, posting your brochure at printing shops, bridal shops, and community bulletin boards, and taking out a yellow pages ad.

THE GOING RATE: You can charge a range of prices, from inexpensive individual greeting cards ($1 and up) to personalized, framed calligraphy sayings with decorated borders (larger sizes can sell for $75 to $125). Works on handmade paper and with detailed, colorful illustrations command higher prices than simpler black-and-white pieces. The average price for a framed eight-by-ten-inch saying is $5 to $10 for a print and $25 to $35 for an original. You can sell the frames separately for $10 to $15. Some calligraphers charge an hourly rate of $25 to $40 when they create posters, signs, certificates, greeting cards, menus, and letterheads.

GETTING STARTED WITH PERSONALIZED CUSTOM WORK: Contact the local print shops, bridal shops, and banquet halls and prepare business cards that can be left with them to attract clients. Prepare a scrapbook with some samples and ideas that you can show to prospective clients. Consider donating your services for a church, temple, or school event in order to get your work and name known around town.

THE GOING RATE: Your fees should vary with the time and effort spent. Figure on $25 per hour plus the cost of materials. Clients who wish to provide their own paper should be allowed to do so. Simple addressing of envelopes should cost about $1 to $3 per envelope, depending on the type of ink and complexity of the typestyle.

GREETING CARD ARTIST

If you have a talent for photography, painting, or calligraphy, there are opportunities for you to make money from your home art studio by freelancing to the greeting card industry. In fact, over half of all types of graphic artists are freelancers, and the greeting card industry is one of the largest markets for their work. You don't need to be a writer or even have a writing partner to submit material—if the company likes your work they'll buy it outright, or possibly assign you a writer.

It doesn't matter what medium or style you work in—pastel or oil, abstract or impressionist, illustrator or photographer, sentimental or serious—somewhere out there is a company producing cards, calendars, or wrapping papers in need of new designs. The best source for finding these companies is in the annual publication *Artists' Market,* which is carried by most public libraries. It contains listings of companies along with a brief description of their requirements and submission procedures. Most require samples (never, ever send originals—just prints or high-quality Xerox color copies) and an SASE to consider your work. A sample portfolio of four to six pieces is usual.

The amount of work these companies buy and the fees they pay varies widely. For example, Argus Communications of Allen, TX, publishes humorous cards, postcards, calendars and even posters. They usually pay from $50 to $125 per assignment.

Abbey Press, of Meinrad, IN, which is operated by the Benedictine monks and specializes in cards and gift wrap with a religious theme, pays in the $200 to $400 range and assigns several hundred designs each year.

TOP TIP: To be a success at greeting card design you need to be prolific and able to take rejection. As soon as a rejection comes back from one company, write a new cover letter and send your samples out to the next one.

GETTING STARTED: Increase your chances of success by doing the right research. Visit local card shops to find the names of companies whose product line is compatible with the kind of work you do. Then take your list to the library and look these companies up in the current issue of *Artist's Market* to find out their submission procedures. Don't waste your time and energy sending humorous photos to religious publishers, or photographic work to fine art reproduction houses.

THE GOING RATE: Varies by company. Check *Artist's Market* and *The Graphic Artist's Guild Handbook* for fair pricing practices.

PET PHOTOGRAPHER

Americans are crazy about their pets. More than 60 percent of all United States households have pets, and they spend $20 billion a year on pet food and supplies. Many people consider their pets as part of the family, and would like to include them in family portraits. If you enjoy photography and feel comfortable working with animals, this could be a rewarding niche business for you. You'll need a room set up as a studio, top-quality cameras and lighting equipment, tripods and film, and the ability to take clear, expressive portraits. A darkroom would be helpful if you plan to take a lot of black-and-white photos, but is not a necessity if you specialize in color prints. In that case, you'll need to find a good color processing lab you can trust.

You may want to take artistic black-and-white photos of pets and their owners, which could be sold at art fairs. You would need a signed release from the owner before you could resell their photograph. Or, you could compete with photo studio chains and take straightforward, color photographs at a reasonable price. Whatever approach you choose, you'll get the best pictures by getting down to the pet's level and using a variety of toys and props to get its attention. In order to photograph pets looking their best, you'll need to use squeaky toys, make funny noises and funny faces, flash a flashlight beam, or shake a can of pet treats so the pets will put their ears up and look right at the camera.

Cats can be particularly adverse to sitting still and doing what you want them to do, so make sure you schedule enough time for your photo sessions to get to know the pet. A soothing manner, understanding of animal psychology, and a lot of patience are definite assets in this profession. You should also enjoy working with people, since most of the pet owners will want to be in the photograph as well. It would help if you're a dog lover—one photographer has said that about 80 percent of his subjects are dogs. The other pets he's photographed are cats and more unusual animals, including a python and pet alligator. Unless you're squeamish about reptiles, you could help your business grow by publicizing your services at local herpetological associations.

If your photography skills are a little rusty, take some classes at a local community college before you set up shop. You may want to join the Professional Photographers of America Association (57 Forsyth Street NW, Ste. 1600, Atlanta, GA 30303; 404-522-8600) to learn about photography schools and workshops, and to subscribe to *Professional Photography* magazine. Or, join local photographers' clubs to network with others, learn new techniques, and get some tips on setting prices. Other useful resources are *Photographer's Market* (Writer's Digest Books), *Studio Photography* magazine (445 Broad Hollow Road, Suite 21, Melville, NY 11747), *Photographer's Guide to Marketing and Self-*

Promotion, 2nd Edition, by Maria Piscopo (Allworth Press, 1995) and *How You Can Make $25,000 a Year with Your Camera* by Larry Cribb (Writer's Digest Books, 1991).

TOP TIP: Make enlargements of a few of your favorite photos and offer to display them at your local library, veterinary office, coffee shops, and other places with good traffic, along with your business card.

GETTING STARTED: Establish a portfolio by taking portraits of your friends', neighbors', and your own pets. Select the best ones to put in a photo album to demonstrate your work. Create fliers and distribute them at pet supply stores, animal lovers' groups, and community bulletin boards. You may want to take a listing in the yellow pages and place an advertisement in your metropolitan newspaper and in pet magazines. If you're comfortable with public speaking, you could attract new business by speaking to local organizations and giving them your tips on taking memorable pet photographs. You'll attract more customers if you offer evening and weekend hours.

THE GOING RATE: Many photographers charge a basic sitting fee of $5 to $10 for each person or animal in the photograph, and then sell packages priced between $39.95 and $175, depending on the number of poses and portrait sheets the customer selects. Other photographers who have developed a name for themselves as experts in pet photography may charge as much as $300 to $1,500 per session. If you choose to sell pet photos at art fairs, you can charge from $20 to $200 per print, according to its size and whether it's matted or framed. You can also sell notecards and greeting cards featuring your photographs, and look into selling your best shots to stock photo agencies.

WOODWORKING SKILLS

CUSTOM FURNITURE MAKER

Whether it's a set of bookshelves for the fireplace alcove, a mission-style table to tuck into the entryway, or a headboard that's just the right height, more and more people are commissioning custom furniture. If you have always loved cabinetmaking and have a well-equipped shop space in your basement or garage, you can turn your hobby into a lucrative business.

Many of the most successful cabinetmakers specialize—either in pieces (such as rockers or hand-carved blanket chests) or a particular style (such as mission or Shaker or Early American). Start-up costs can be high if you are outfitting your shop from scratch, but if have been building up your tools slowly over the years, all you may need to go professional is an advertising campaign to get the word out about your work.

Word of mouth from happy clients is always the best advertising, but it can take several years to build up that big of a client base. The first few pieces you make will probably be for family and friends. Make sure you take a picture for your sample book and tell your satisfied clients to please brag about you to their other friends. Many of the cabinetmakers we spoke to all also took out paid advertising in local newspapers—usually in the arts or home furnishings sections. And don't forget free publicity—local weekly community papers are always eager to interview craftspeople about their work.

Woodworkers making expensive heirloom-quality reproduction pieces also advertised nationally in design and home-furnishings magazines—it was the only way, they said, they could find enough clients willing to pay $5,000 or more for a Sheraton-style desk. You can also try to place pieces in local upscale furniture stores, and make friends with local interior designers by offering them discounts.

Though most of your time will be spent in your own workshop, expect to visit the client's house, especially if the piece you are crafting needs to be custom-fitted or blend with the style of decorating already in the house. Be sure to bring along a sample book of color photos or color Xeroxes of your previous work. If you are just starting out, these samples may be freebies you made for your mother or friends—but the new client doesn't have to know that! A small sample case of fine furniture woods such as walnut, teak, and birch will also be useful.

TOP TIP: Sev Kemper, a Chicago custom cabinetmaker, uses a two-step approach to keep his customers happy and make sure he's not too out of pocket. He charges an initial fee of $100 for a home consultation and draftsman's drawings for the proposed piece of furniture. If the clients decide to sign a contract and have him build the piece, this $100 is applicable to the final price. If they decide not to go ahead, Kemper is still compensated for his consultation and drafting time.

GETTING STARTED: Solicit work from friends and family in order to get some of your pieces into circulation and provide samples for your sample book. You can also enter your pieces in juried fine furniture shows. To find shows, events, and classes, see the bimonthly magazine *Woodwork*, available through your local library or from Ross Periodicals, 42 Digital Drive, Novato, CA 94949 (415-382-0580).

THE GOING RATE: Will vary according to each piece, since they are custom-made. However, you should charge a flat fee of $50 to $100 for working drawings.

Porch Furniture Maker

Even if you have only low-to-average woodworking skills, you can turn a high profit making Adirondack-style lawn and porch furniture. This popular style of furniture is easy to put together—all the equipment you'll need is a table saw, jigsaw, electric drill, countersink, bar clamp, and your basic hammer and nail set. And since it goes together quickly you don't need a big separate shop. Just pull the car out of the garage for the weekend and set up a temporary shop there. It should take two days for someone of average skills to make a chair and footrest. Then figure on an additional day and night if you are going to paint the pieces with polyurethane gloss enamel for outdoor—as opposed to porch—use. By Monday morning you'll have finished furniture for sale and your car can move back into the garage.

TOP TIP: How do you sell your pieces? According to one teacher who makes his furniture as a summer business, the best place to display lawn furniture is on your own front lawn with a big Hand-Crafted Furniture For Sale sign. An attractive arrangement of pieces, perhaps with a bowl of flowers, will catch people's attention. If you don't live on a well-traveled street, ask a friend or relative to display your wares for you and take orders for a percentage of the profit.

GETTING STARTED: Check your equipment list and procure a set of plans. Many hardware and home improvement centers sell furniture plans, but you can also get a good set for free in the July 1995 issue of *The Family Handyman* (7900 International Drive, Suite 950, Minneapolis, MN 55425—check your local library for a copy).

GOING RATE: Individual enameled poplar chairs sell for $100—twice that if they're made out of cedar.

Porch Furniture Maker, Part 2

If you're interested in making outdoor furniture but live in a neighborhood of town homes and apartments where people don't have much need of big lawn pieces, consider making folding furniture for decks, patios, and balconies. Not only will these pieces be attractive to your neighbors, but they'll be easy for you to store, too.

Lightweight, foldable, attractive chairs and tables can be made in about eight hours each by someone of average skills with the following equipment: table saw, jigsaw, belt sander, electric drill, hand files, combination square, carpenter's square, screwdriver, power screwdriver, and sandpaper. You can use western red cedar or pine, but if you use the latter plan on an extra six hours to paint the furniture with waterproof enamel.

Display your pieces on your own front lawn or patio, and if your community has a common room ask permission to display a piece—or picture of your pieces—there, too. Make sure your sign includes prices and is large enough to be seen by passersby from the street.

TOP TIP: Don't overinvest in a big inventory—most furniture makers don't have the storage space or cash flow to tie up in a dozen or so pieces sitting around waiting to get sold. The most frugal operating plan would be to make one set for display and don't sell it—use it to get orders for other pieces, for which you collect a 50 percent deposit.

GETTING STARTED: Check your equipment list and procure a set of plans from your local hardware store or home improvement center. Or, better yet, get a set absolutely free from the April 1995 issue of *The Family Handyman* magazine (available at your local library).

THE GOING RATE: Chairs go for $90 and love seats $150 in top-grade western red cedar. Painted pine sells for about 20 percent less.

WILLOW-WOOD FURNITURE MAKER

Do you like making furniture? Do you have access to willow trees? Then making bent willow-wood furniture may be just the way for you to enjoy your hobby and make money too. You'll need carpentry experience and a variety of tools, including a camp saw, sureform rasp, hammer, galvanized nails (which hold particularly well), and some knives. Many carpenters find this a great way to make money between jobs and during the slow winter season.

Getting the willow branches may be the easiest part of this business. Since willows grow like weeds and are often considered a nuisance, most people will happily give you permission to trim their trees and remove some of the branches. One furniture maker told us, "I have never paid for any of the wood I use. I'm amazed because I'm always coming across a new stand of willows in my area. They're everywhere, and they regenerate quickly once you cut them." He has found that it's most efficient to build twenty to thirty frames at a time, and then "do all the bendy-bendy part." You can offer a variety of designs, including oval-back chairs, fan-back and heart-back love seats, porch swings, end tables, and rocking chairs.

TOP TIP: Demonstrating your work at craft and county fairs can attract customers and lead to additional sales. But flea markets are not a good place to sell, because everyone is looking for a bargain and may balk at your prices.

GETTING STARTED: Look at other people's designs in catalogs and brochures to get ideas for your own furniture. Buy some books on rustic furniture and practice a variety of designs. You can sell your furniture at local craft fairs and in antique shops. And let your previous carpentry customers know about your new trade, because they're likely to buy from you if they're already pleased with your work. Let customers know that your furniture will last almost indefinitely if kept inside out of the weather. People who insist on using the chairs and love seats as lawn furniture may get only five to seven years use of a set, since the exposure to rain and snow will eventually destroy it.

THE GOING RATE: You can charge between $160 and $190 for a straight chair or rocking chair, and between $280 and $325 for a love seat. Once you're experienced at this, it'll take about a day to make two chairs or one love seat. You could also sell tall plant stands for $45 and woven willow baskets for between $25 and $45 apiece.

WOODWORKING WORKSHOP INSTRUCTOR

Are you successful in your craft and looking to expand your business without having to carry more inventory? Do you enjoy woodworking and turn out beautiful pieces, but hate the selling part of the business? Or perhaps your schedule or location prevents you from getting out to the craft fairs and furniture marts where you could command top dollar for your creations. Never fear— you can still turn woodworking into a profitable home business by concentrating on teaching instead of selling. If you are patient—and what good woodworker isn't?—and not too paranoid about letting other people use your tools, you might make an excellent mentor and tutor to other aspiring woodworkers.

After twelve years as a woodworker, Jeff Miller of Chicago had made a name for himself as a superb craftsman of collector-quality handmade furniture of his own design. In Miller's case, the decision to start a school was made for two reasons: first, as a complementary extension of his existing business, and second, as a way to test his teaching skills for a book he intends to write on his craft.

Miller offers a variety of courses through his company, J. Miller Handcrafted Furniture, running from a day to a week at $100 to $925. Students get to keep the pieces they work on, of course, and to simplify his instruction Miller initially limits the number of selections to a box, end table, or chair. Miller provides equipment, excellent quality wood, the design, and personal instruction. He says that there is a tremendous demand for woodworking instruction in general and fine furniture making in particular.

To provide a good educational environment your shop needs to be well lit and well equipped, with plenty of room around each piece of equipment to accommodate a student and instructor. Miller uses two each of table saws, band saws, joiners, and lathes, but points out that his emphasis is on a lot of bench work. He has half a dozen workstations so that he can start each student off on a different station, then move from bench to bench helping each person individually.

There are a couple of things a woodworking instructor needs to keep in mind that other types of instructors—say, piano teachers—might not worry about. Remember that whenever you let someone into your home to work with equipment there is some risk of injury, so always observe standard shop safety rules, and make sure your students do, too. Post the safety rules in the shop, and repeat them in the lesson contract that the students sign. Check with your insurance agent to see if your liability coverage should be increased, and don't let one student cross your threshold until you are adequately covered.

There should also be a clean-up station and a good emergency medical kit nearby. If you are going to provide the niceties of a cooler for soft-drink refreshment, make sure students will also have access to a washroom. If you would like to run classes with several students at a time, make sure there is enough parking so that the neighbors won't be put out and complain. A one-on-

one tutoring setup may be better for you if parking or zoning requirements would make a large group difficult to handle.

TOP TIP: The best place to post flyers advertising your school would be specialty lumber yards, craft stores, and fine furniture galleries. The most effective flyers will include a photo of one or two of your pieces. Craft fairs are also a great source for students—even if you don't sell a single piece, you could pick up a year's worth of students. Come well equipped with plenty of flyers and business cards.

GETTING STARTED: Inventory your equipment and evaluate your shop space to see if it will accommodate students. Volunteer to make a presentation at the local high school or technical college shop class to make sure you like teaching.

THE GOING RATE: If you structure your instruction as full-day workshops and provide instruction and materials, you can charge $100 a day or more, depending on the complexity of the piece and the value of the wood. If you are merely renting out time in your shop and providing minimal supervision and no materials, figure on an hourly fee of $5 to $10 an hour.

SEWING SKILLS

CUSTOM CURTAIN MAKER

Savvy sewers who have an interest in interior design can special-ize in designing, sewing, and installing window treatments. By providing all of these services, you can charge a great deal more than if you just stitch together basic curtains for customers. As a drapery designer, you'll set up an initial meeting at a prospective customer's house, take into account the colors of walls and furni-ture in the rooms, then suggest curtain fabrics and styles that would pull the room together. Once you and your customer agree on a window treatment plan, you'll need to track down the right fabric, sew the curtains, and arrange for their installation.

This business requires little up-front capital investment, and can be run comfortably out of your home. Many people start with one basic sewing machine, then buy additional commercial sewing machines, sergers, ruffling machines, and blind-stitch hemmers as the business takes off. People skills are important, since you'll need to sell your services, and a computer can be useful for keeping track of proposals and billing. You'll also need access to a wide variety of fabrics and materials. Shopping at a merchandise mart is ideal if there's one in your metropolitan area, since you can see five thousand different fabrics there in-stead of the five hundred choices at a typical fabric store. Or, you can set up an account with several different fabric companies and carry their sample books—many offer sample books for free.

Once you've gained experience in sewing curtains, valances, and swags, you may want to branch out into making coordinating bedding, or ordering wooden or vinyl blinds for customers. You'll want to develop a good relationship with an installer if you'd rather not do the installation yourself. Offering a quick turn-around time will be a good selling point for your business, since many designers take up to two months to finish and install custom window treatments. It's wise to charge a deposit once you receive an order so you won't be out of pocket on the cost of the fabric.

TOP TIP: Molly Burkart, who runs a thriving home-based business called Curtain Call Ltd., offered the following tip on finding new clients. She reads real estate listings in the newspaper, finds out who's new to the area, then drops off a plant and letter of introduction with references. Since most people who have just moved into a new house are thinking about doing some redecorating, this approach has really paid off. Referrals by other clients account for the rest of her new business leads. She commented, "This is an excellent business to supplement a family's income."

GETTING STARTED: Keep your eyes open for ideas on the latest curtain fabrics and styles by visiting showcase homes and reading *Window Fashions* (4225 White Bear Pkwy, Ste. 400, St. Paul, MN 55110; 612-293-1544) and *Draperies and Window Coverings* (450 Skokie Blvd., Suite 507, Northbrook, IL 60062) trade magazines. Consider attending the conferences sponsored by *Window Fashions* magazine to learn from others in this field. Or join The Window Coverings Association of America (825 S. Waukegan Road, Ste. A8-111, Lake Forest, IL 60045; 847-480-7955).

THE GOING RATE: The rates vary dramatically, depending on the fabric, design, and amount of work you need to do for each project. Most curtain makers charge a fee for labor and materials on the curtains they sew, add a markup on blinds or any outside products they market to their customers, and charge an installation fee on top of that. An average markup is 20 percent to 30 percent on each order. Shop around in your community to learn more about the going rate.

QUILT DESIGNER

If you enjoy embroidery and hand sewing, you can turn this talent into a thriving quilt business. Monogrammed baby quilts are particularly popular, since they make wonderful new baby gifts.

You'll need a variety of sewing materials, such as cotton broadcloth and soft flannel for the backing, and high-quality threads and lace trimming. Carol Valde, who has recently started her own quilt business called Carol's Creations from her home, even uses gold-leaf thread and bridal lace on her top-of-the-line baptismal quilts. Carol told us, "You really need to love to sew—this is not a business for everyone." Her goal is to start a new American tradition of sending newborns home from the hospital in an heirloom quilt. She cautioned, "Make sure you charge a 50 percent deposit when you take an order to cover the cost of materials, since people can change their minds."

TOP TIP: If you have a home computer, you can also learn by exploring the quilting forums on America Online, CompuServe, Prodigy, and Microsoft Network. To get a free copy of *Computer Quilter's Newsletter*, send a large SASE to BON Creations, 4072 E. 22nd Street, #329, Tucson, AZ 85711.

GETTING STARTED: You can find embroidery kits at most fabric and craft stores, or you can create your own designs. If you plan to use another company's design and resell it, you'll need to write that company and get permission to use and modify their designs. Reading *Quilting Today* (2 Public Avenue, Montrose, PA 18801) and *Quilter's Newsletter Magazine* (Box 4101, Golden, CO 80401; 303-278-1010) can give you good ideas for new quilting designs and techniques. When it comes to selling your quilts, word of mouth usually results in the most business. Distributing flyers at local fabric stores and placing small classified ads in parenting newspapers and magazines are inexpensive and effective ways to publicize your business, as is exhibiting at craft shows.

THE GOING RATE: If your quilts are one-of-a-kind and completely hand embroidered, you can charge between $200 and $750 for each quilt (since each quilt can take six weeks to create). Less complex quilts are usually priced between $75 and $300. You can also sell quilted Christmas tree skirts for between $30 and $60, or quilted place mats for $3.50 to $5 apiece.

DECORATIVE PHOTO ALBUM DESIGNER

Decorative photo albums are perennially popular for gift giving, especially for wedding and new baby presents. If you're someone who enjoys crafts and would like to earn some money from your hobby, specialty albums are a nice niche.

A popular and fairly easy-to-make album is an upholstered cloth-covered album decorated with lace, flowers, teddy bears, or any other trim that suits your fancy. Your start-up costs are surprisingly low—all you need is a selection of colorful fabrics, a glue gun and some gluesticks, scissors, and sewing materials. You can buy the fabrics during sales at fabric stores, and find generic photo albums in a variety of sizes by shopping your local office supply or craft store. If you're adept at hand sewing, a sewing machine isn't necessary. A visual imagination is also helpful in developing your own range of designs.

We spoke to Betsy Caruso, who has built up a large clientele through word of mouth. Since she sells several popular albums for brides, her busy season is primarily May and June—though Christmas can be hectic as well. Fortunately, babies are born year-round, so she can work on baby books throughout the year.

According to Betsy, "The best part about making these albums is that it can be done in your home at your leisure, and you can enjoy yourself while you're doing them. They're popular enough that you can make as much money as you want to."

TOP TIP: Betsy Caruso advised us, "Keep an eye on color trends. When I first started twenty years ago, everybody wanted pastels. Now people prefer bright, vibrant colors."

GETTING STARTED: Make up one type of album for a sample book and fill it with fabric swatches and photos of your other styles. Take this around to flower shops, film developing stores, and bridal shops to get orders.

THE GOING RATE: You can charge $20 for smaller, five-by-seven-inch quilted photo albums, $25 to $30 for larger baby photo albums, and $35 for large wedding albums.

MONOGRAM SERVICE

Clothing and linens personalized with an embroidered design of the owner's initials have been a prestige item for hundreds of years, and show no sign of going out of fashion now. Once the laborious work of specialized seamstresses, modern monogram machines make it possible for anyone to start a small, personalized monogramming business out of their sewing room.

The most popular items brought in to be monogrammed are sweaters, shirts, towels, and bed linens. The business is somewhat seasonal, with a rush of orders for newly married couples in the spring. Some monogram services try to get as much of this wedding business as possible by offering a discount for doing a complete set of bed linens and towels.

Since the machine does most of the embroidery work, sharp sewing skills are not a prerequisite for this business. You must, however, have an artistic flair for color and material combinations, and have good people skills for dealing with customers on a one-to-one basis. A background or interest in fashion or graphic design would be a big plus, too.

You can expand your business by also offering for sale the items to be monogrammed, such as sweatshirts or towels. By buying these items in bulk through a wholesaler (check the business pages) and reselling them along with the monogram to your customers, you can increase your profits. For example, you can buy a dozen top-quality heavyweight all-cotton T-shirts for $3 a piece, which, when monogrammed, will sell for $18 a piece. This gives you a profit of $15, whereas if you sold only the monogram alone you would probably only be able to charge $10.

TOP TIP: Get clients by leaving your card and a sample book at bridal and gifware shops. Of course, the best advertising is always word of mouth. One woman turned her daughter's entire softball team into her sales force when she monogrammed their jerseys for free. If you don't have an entire team available, consider making a few pieces as gifts for close friends and family and ask them to spread the word.

GETTING STARTED: Find a new or used monogram machine through the business pages of your phone book or call a national distributor such as Meistergram Machines (910-854-6200).

THE GOING RATE: You can charge from $5 to $12 dollars per monogram, depending on size, complexity, and number of colors.

HALLOWEEN COSTUME DESIGNER

If you're a whiz with a sewing machine, you can start a seasonal business creating original Halloween costumes. Many parents panic at the thought of whipping together a costume for their kids, and are more than willing to pay someone else to produce a costume instead of struggling with it themselves. You'll need a variety of fabrics and fabric paint; you can purchase patterns from your local sewing store or come up with your own designs.

Do some market research in your community to find out which costumes are most in demand each year. Besides such TV-inspired costumes as Power Rangers and Barney, dinosaurs, fairies, brides, princesses, cowboys, monsters, and pirates are always popular. You can publicize your costumes through parents' groups, bulletin boards at local schools, day-care centers, libraries, and grocery stores, selling on consignment to costume rental shops, and advertising in community newspapers or parenting papers.

TOP TIP: Once Halloween is over, set up a meeting with the head of the drama department at local high schools and colleges to show sample costumes you've made. If he or she likes your work, you can make costumes all year-round for student productions.

GETTING STARTED: If you've already designed some costumes for your own children or grandchildren and like to sew, you've had all the training you need. If not, you can take a sewing class at your local sewing store or community college and practice at home. Janice Wood, an illustrator, has made costumes that were the envy of the neighborhood for her own children, including a flying horse, a ten-foot dinosaur, a bald eagle, a monarch butterfly, a peacock, and an enormous fish, so she has already established the word of mouth she needs if she decides to sell her creations.

THE GOING RATE: You can charge between $20 (for simple costumes) and $50 or $60 (for more elaborate or more elegant costumes).

Custom Bridal Veil Designer

This home business is for anyone who enjoys sewing and designing elaborate creations but doesn't want to spend weeks working on one outfit. It's also a good way to enter the lucrative bridal market. Since most veils are mass produced and available in one-size-fits-all from large manufacturers, you can provide a distinctive service by crafting one-of-a-kind veils and headpieces. Unlike bridal stores, you can create veils that will properly fit the bride's head, create any design that she has her heart set on, and even find lace and beading that will precisely match her wedding dress.

A talent for design is crucial, as are top-notch sewing skills, good people skills, and the ability to choose a headpiece that is most flattering to a particular bride's facial structure. You'll need to own a sewing machine and serging machine, and hunt for places to buy a variety of pearls, beading, combs, glue, thread, specialty fabrics, ribbons, wire, appliqués, and illusion tools for veiling and lace. Headpieces are crafted out of buckram forms (buckram is a thick cotton fabric that is heavily sized with glue, also used in bookbinding). You can find buckram manufacturers through sewing stores or sewing magazines.

One custom veil maker stumbled into this business when she was working as a hairdresser in a salon. A bride came in late for her hair appointment a few days before her wedding in tears. She had just had a fitting of her wedding dress and veil and hated her headpiece. The hairdresser said, "Well, I'll see what I can do," and took the headpiece home to work on. She was shocked how badly it had been made—just glued together with a hot glue gun. So, she trimmed it, changed the style, and brought it to the bride, who loved it. After that, the bride showed the headpiece to everyone in the hair salon, and other customers began asking the hairdresser to perform the same service for them. She discovered that she loved the challenge of designing and sewing custom headpieces, and started her own business out of her home.

This successful veil maker advised us, "The headpiece should not wear the bride. It should blend in with her dress. People should say, 'What a beautiful bride,' not 'What a beautiful headdress.' If the headdress stands out too much, then I've done something wrong."

TOP TIP: You can branch out by making first communion veils, which sell for between $20 and $50.

GETTING STARTED: Take a sewing class or two if your sewing skills are rusty. Most veil makers have started by creating veils for friends and family, and then attracting new customers through referrals. Attending wedding expos and taking out a small display ad in local newspapers and bride's magazines are also good ways to get started.

When you are ready to market your business, let prospective customers know that your headpieces are made to order and have hand-sewn beading; the majority of headpieces made by large manufactuers have glued-on beading and tend to run large. Encourage brides to come in two months before their wedding so you have time to discuss the options, agree on a design, and track down the fabric and laces that would look best with her dress.

THE GOING RATE: A simple headband without a veil sells for $50. More elaborate headpieces can sell for between $150 and $600, depending on the complexity of the design and the materials that are used. Veils are an additional $40 (for short veils) and $90 (for long ones).

DOLL DRESS DESIGNER

Turn your favorite hobby into a moneymaking proposition. While doll clothes may be small, the demand for them is not—especially if you sew dresses for the American Girl dolls (which retail for $82 and have expensive wardrobes) or everyone's favorite fash-

ion doll, Barbie. Creating glamorous Barbie gowns and histori-
cally accurate reproductions for the American Girl collection fills
a real need, since millions of these dolls have found homes. Girls
(and their parents) are always eager to expand their special doll's
clothing choices without having to pay retail prices.

You should have strong sewing skills and a talent for dress
design, at least one sewing machine, and a wide variety of fabrics
and trimmings. Some dressmakers own three different sewing
machines for different purposes, since some machines make ruf-
fles and others specialize in zigzags. You may also want to invest
in a serger, which makes a professional seam that never frays.
You'll need a well-lit room with a comfortable corner for sewing
in and a place to store all of your dresses.

It's a good idea to call 1-800-845-0005 to request a free catalog subscription from Pleasant Company, which makes American
Girl dolls. You can buy doll dress patterns from this catalog, or
find patterns at sewing stores, which you can modify. Subscribing
to *Doll Reader* (6405 Flank Drive, Box 8200, Harrisburg, PA
17105) magazine can also give you inspiration for new dress designs.

Then, take the time to do some market research—ask as many
little girls as you can what kinds of doll clothes they like. If you're
not in touch with what the kids like, your clothes won't sell. One
woman who's been making doll dresses for ten years noticed that
her best-selling Barbie clothes are "bright, glitzy, and sparkly."
Red and purple ball gowns with full skirts are always the first
items to sell when she displays at craft shows. For American Girl
clothes, she found that it's just the opposite—country cottons in
more muted tones, like mauves and rust, are the most popular.
This dressmaker spends hours in fabric stores finding just the
right fabrics, since it's hard to find a match for clothes found in
the American Girl catalog. Her average $10 dress includes $2 of
materials and takes about an hour to make.

Offering such accessories as doll hair ribbons, hats, socks,
tights, and slippers can be good for your business. One woman
told us, "Anytime I put a hat with a dress, it sells." Designing a
wide range of doll dresses for holidays—such as Easter dresses,

swimsuits, Christmas party dresses, and even Halloween costumes—will give your customers a reason to keep coming back to check out your new inventory. We've noticed that more and more doll dressmakers are teaming up with furniture makers who sell handcrafted wooden beds, tables and chairs, wardrobes, and other items for the American Girl dolls. Some seamstresses are fortunate enough to have a crafty spouse or other family member who likes to make furniture; others get in touch with a local woodworker in their community and offer to display both of their wares at craft fairs.

TOP TIP: Contact local children's clothing shops, toy stores, gift shops, and resale shops—many retailers may be interested in selling your creations on consignment.

GETTING STARTED: Once you've accumulated a wide selection of dresses, it's time to publicize your services in local newspapers and bulletin boards, parenting publications, and by participating in craft shows. Visit several craft shows before you decide to exhibit there, since you can lose money if you choose a show that doesn't get good traffic. Keep in mind that you'll need to have fifty to a hundred dresses ready to take to the show in order to make exhibiting worthwhile. Offering such accessories as doll hair ribbons, hats, socks, tights, and slippers can also be good for your business.

THE GOING RATE: Barbie clothes are priced between $5 and $55, depending on their complexity and material. Dresses made of velvet, sequined fabrics, lace, or satin will naturally sell for higher prices than more basic cotton frocks. American Girl clothes sell for between $8 and $25.

GARDEN GOOSE-WEAR DESIGNER

Lawn ornaments lend that extra bit of enchantment to a well-tended home, and selections are available to match any house style, be it formal Victorian fountains or cheery country geese. (In fact, some goose owners like to dress their statues in a different outfit every day depending on the season and the weather— from bikinis and barbecue aprons in summer, to football and cheerleading outfits in autumn, to Santa costumes and miniature fur coats in the winter.)

Though statuary and sewing skills might not seem like your automatic ideal marketing mix, Debby Ryan noticed that concrete geese dressed in a variety of costumes have become popular. When a friend suggested she begin making clothes for geese, Ryan commented, "I thought she was nuts. I gave it a whirl—and the rest is history."

Ryan has been running her home-based garden ornament clothing business, called Goose Get-ups, for four years. She offers sixty-six different clothing choices, and has been so successful that she's hired three people to keep up with the demand.

When asked for her advice, Ryan cautions, "Plan on spending a lot of time on this. I average about twelve to sixteen hours sewing a day, and I spend an insane amount of time right before big holidays. So you really have to enjoy sewing." Debby displays at three to four different craft shows a month, and brings in as many outfits as she can create before each show. The average booth cost is $60 to $75, and she tells us that it's well worth it—so much so that she does no additional marketing or publicity. Oh, and plan on taking a lot of showers as well—Debby always gets her best ideas for new outfit designs while she's in the shower.

TOP TIP: Since you'll need to buy a few geese (available at lawn and garden stores) in order to size your patterns, you can create an eye-catching advertisement by having your geese model your clothes in front of your house.

GETTING STARTED: Good sewing skills are essential, as is a good-quality sewing machine. You'll need a wide variety of fabrics, trimmings, and notions—you can buy these on sale at fabric stores, and save more by giving the store your tax number so you don't have to pay sales tax. Then develop several different designs and start displaying them at craft shows in your area, or sell them by consignment through local craft stores.

THE GOING RATE: Prices vary according to the size of the geese. These are the approximate prices you can charge for each outfit: $10 to $14 for small geese (fourteen inches high from base to head), $13 to $16 for medium-sized geese (nineteen inches high) and $16 to $20 for large geese (twenty-two inches high).

CRAFTING AND ◆ ORGANIZATIONAL ◆ SKILLS

CRAFT KITS SELLER

There's more than one way to make money from crafts. Rather than making and selling your own handiwork, you may want to assemble craft kits for beginning crafters. A craft kit usually contains an illustration or photograph of the item to be made, all of the necessary supplies, and some written instructions. Craft kits run the gamut from needlework to sand art, Christmas ornaments, stained glass, dolls, beaded jewelry, and children's art projects. You're right for this business if you enjoy working on crafts, like using your creativity to develop new designs and projects, and are willing to hunt for suppliers of the craft materials you need. Your start-up expenses are extremely low. You just need a table to work on, storage space for completed kits and materials, and such basic supplies as scissors, Ziploc bags, paper, and a paper cutter. You can get good ideas for new kits by reading craft books, joining the American Craft Council (72 Spring Street, New York, NY 10012; 212-274-0630) and reading its publications, or joining a local crafters' association.

Elaine Rusling started a home business called Creative Kits for Kids eleven years ago, after she found that she never had the right supplies at hand whenever she sat down to make a craft project with her children. She thought, "I bet this happens to other people too. Wouldn't it be convenient if you could buy everything you needed for a craft project in one kit?" So Elaine set out to look for local manufacturers of craft materials (such as feathers, beads, "googly eyes," felt, and construction paper), and then started creating some original projects using simple materials. Some of her most popular kits include pom-pom critters, bracelets and necklaces, and such holiday kits as wooden spool reindeer and angels. Once she found that Brownie and Cub Scout troops were flocking to buy her kits for their meetings, she started packaging six identical kits in a bag and offering a small discount to make it easier for group leaders. These larger packages also sell very well as birthday party activities.

You'll probably sell most of your kits through word of mouth and direct mail, so the packaging does not have to be too glitzy. If you establish a niche, as Elaine has, by selling convenient and inexpensive craft kits, you can package them simply by putting the supplies in a resealable plastic bag, include easy-to-follow handwritten or typed directions, and provide a photo or drawing of the finished product. If you branch out by selling through local toy, gift, craft, and hobby stores (either through consignment or outright at a wholesale discount), you can add a brightly colored paper header to each bag and make up extra samples so the customers can see how the kits will turn out.

TOP TIP: Make sure you send a press release and samples to the family and home editors at your metropolitan newspaper. Getting a feature in the paper quickly increased Elaine's visibility in her community and led to lots of new customers.

GETTING STARTED: Visit local craft shows in order to learn which types of crafts are most in demand. Then look for manufacturers of craft supplies by getting in touch with suppliers to the school and hobby markets. Once you've set up accounts with several craft suppliers, begin developing and perfecting your own kits at home. If you sell kits for kids, you can do market research by testing them at friends' and family members' birthday parties. Adult craft kit makers can get feedback from local women's and crafters' organizations. After you've created a number of different designs, put together a brochure to show or mail to prospective customers, and sell the kits at community craft shows. If you have the space, offering craft classes or crafting parties would be a natural extension of your business and an additional money-maker. You could also bring all the supplies and demonstrate crafts at birthday parties.

THE GOING RATE: Kits range from $2 for a minikit or $5.95 to $9.95 for larger kits. Since $10 and under is the ideal price point for birthday gifts, try to keep your kits in that price range. Some kit makers set their price at four times the cost of their materials.

CRAFT SHOW HOST

Are you fascinated with crafts and can't get enough of going to craft shows? If so, consider hosting a craft show in your home. In-home craft shows have become increasingly popular in the last few years, since people enjoy buying handmade, distinctive crafts in a cozy home environment. You can start a tradition of hosting several artisans and crafters in your home at a once-a-year craft show. Staging your show in early or mid-October is a good idea, since you can provide an opportunity for shoppers to buy Christmas and Hanukkah gifts, and you can get in ahead of other holiday bazaars and craft shows held in November and December.

Before you begin, visit several established craft shows in your area to discover promising crafters. Look around carefully—what kinds of crafts tend to attract the most customers? You should know enough about crafts to be able to distinguish between outstanding and ordinary handcrafted items. Look for crafters who specialize in fabric painting, pottery and ceramics, calligraphy, jewelry, handmade children's toys, wood carvings, dolls, baskets, quilts, stained glass, gourmet food and baked goods, floral arrangements, vests, tie-died clothing, wall hangings, rag rugs, painted Santas and other holiday decorations, and more. Then recruit at least eight to ten people who will agree to display and sell their crafts at your show. Try not to invite two crafters who directly compete with each other. Choosing one person to represent each category will still give shoppers the variety of choices they're looking for. While you'll want to display a range of crafts that appeal to differing tastes and budgets, remember that customers are increasingly price sensitive. Many are looking for stocking stuffers, teacher gifts, and grab-bag gifts priced under $10.

Once you have selected a weekend for your craft show and booked several reputable crafters, you'll need to think about ways to publicize your show. Creating flyers and giving a supply to each of your crafters is a good way to get the word out. Then put up signs in your neighborhood, at local schools and community bulletin boards, put posters in nearby stores, and take out a newspaper ad. You can advertise your show as offering convenient "one-stop holiday shopping." Make sure you take down the names and addresses of everyone who attends, so you can create a mailing list and send out invitations to next year's event.

TOP TIP: If you have some well-known or unusual artisans displaying their work at your show, send out a press release to the community affairs or arts editor at your local newspaper. This may result in a feature article about your show.

GETTING STARTED: As the show date approaches, you'll need to clear out the furniture from as many rooms as you can to make room for tables and craft displays. You'll also need a variety of folding tables and chairs, as well as boxes to hold extra inventory and bags for customers. It's easier to keep track of sales if you give each crafter a code, which is put on all their price tags. You can use a small business software program on your home computer to keep track of sales for each crafter present. Joan Kramer has a business called Joan's Country Crafts, and has held craft shows at her home for the past six years. She told us she puts all her furniture into storage and makes room for crafters in all of her ground-floor rooms (including the kitchen), along with her back porch and garage. When asked what skills you would need to run a successful craft show, Joan replied, "A sense of adventure—this can be a lot of work. You'll also need a sense of what will sell. I've found that my customers will buy things that are reasonably priced and well made. It can take several years to build a good clientele. Still, this is a profitable venture for me. I only hold one show in the fall because more gift items are purchased at that time of year."

THE GOING RATE: Charge a modest booth fee of $20 to $30 for each crafter attending, as well as a percentage of their sales (between 10 and 20 percent).

JEWELRY DESIGNER

Jewelry making is one of the oldest crafts. It's a satisfying art form, because the creations are long-lasting and can be passed on through several generations of mothers and daughters. If you have some skill in manipulating materials, an interest in developing your own designs, and a desire to make and sell beautiful objects, this may be a fulfilling home business for you to consider. Read *Beginning Jewelry* by Roger Armstrong (Star Publications, 1992), *The Book of Jewelry* by Jo Moody (Simon & Schuster, 1994), or other jewelry books at your local library to learn more about the variety of jewelry techniques that are worth exploring.

Those who have little experience in jewelry making may want

to try some simple designs made of copper, brass, or sterling silver wire. These require no soldering and are relatively easy to manipulate with pliers. You can buy several coils of wire for a small expense and experiment with them to make necklaces, earrings, bracelets, or pins. Sterling silver is most often used by serious jewelry makers, since it's extremely strong and malleable. After you try working with a number of different materials, from metal to beads, polymer clay, household objects, fabrics, or gemstones, you should discover which medium is most appealing to you.

You can exercise your creativity by combining different materials together or incorporating found objects into your designs (such as shells, driftwood, polished stones, and pebbles). For inspiration, look to forms in nature. Others may be inspired by paintings, sculptures, and graphics they glimpse in museums or magazines. Practice your design skills by carrying a sketchbook with you to capture ideas as they occur. You'll gain a feeling for your materials and improve your technique as you experiment.

TOP TIP: Craft shows, art fairs, and holiday bazaars are the best places to sell your work. Make sure you take down your customers' names and addresses so you can send them flyers about your new creations and upcoming shows. Offering to design custom jewelry can be a good way to set yourself apart from mass producers of look-alike jewelry. Visit local jewelry shops, art galleries, and gift stores as well to show the owners your wares. Finally, wearing some of your most striking pieces daily may be your best form of free publicity.

GETTING STARTED: Take classes at local art schools or community colleges, and visit craft fairs to talk to other artisans. Becoming an apprentice to another jeweler would be an ideal way to learn the finer points of your craft. If you discover that you do have a talent for and interest in jewelry making, it's time to set up your home workshop. Your workshop should include a workbench and jewelry pliers (both diagonal cutting, chain-nose, half-round nose, and round-nose pliers), files, a ball peen hammer, a rawhide mallet, tweezers, an anvil or stake, a six-inch file, a jeweler's saw and saw frame, a jeweler's vise, a hand drill, a buffing machine, chemicals for oxidizing, a propane torch or soldering iron, and steel wool. Buy the raw materials and findings (wires for earrings, backs for cufflinks, necklace clasps) from jewelry supply houses, craft stores, and hobby shops. Consult *Jewelry Crafts* (4880 Market Street, Ventura, CA 93003) magazine and *Lapidary Journal* (60 Chestnut Avenue, Suite 201, Devon, PA 19333) for dealers of jewelry supplies and cut and uncut precious stones throughout the country. Alpha Supply (PO Box 2133, Bremerton, WA 98310; 800-257-4211) is one of the biggest mail order suppliers.

THE GOING RATE: Varies from as little as $5 for a barrette or ring to hundreds of dollars for a dramatic silver or gold necklace.

PERSONALIZED FISHING LURE MAKER

This is a relaxing hobby anyone who is fond of fishing will enjoy. You can make your own colorful fishing lures, then personalize them by stringing small letter beads onto the lure. That way, no one else will walk off with your customers' prized possession.

You'll need a variety of fishing supplies, including molds, hooks, wire, paint, and spray guns for painting, which can be found at most sporting good stores. Many of these stores also sell flytying kits with directions, which is a good place to start if you're a beginner. You can get small "baby blocks" with letters painted on them for personalizing your lures at most craft stores.

Joe Divis started a business called Put Your Name on a Lure after he had been doing some hard thinking about new products he could develop. He wanted to create a different kind of lure as a moneymaker, and the idea for personalized lures just hit him on the head one day. He said, "I've been making lures most of my life—I got interested in this hobby when I was ten—and my mother used to work craft shows. So I sent these lures along with her one day and they sold like hotcakes." Joe takes a booth at a dozen craft shows a year, and does no other form of advertising or publicity. As far as he knows, he is the first person to have created this kind of lure.

TOP TIP: This business tends to be seasonal, since spring and summer are the prime buying times. Joe Divis's advice to others is: "Try to be creative, and come up with a different hook. I now make lures out of everything I can get my hands on."

GETTING STARTED: People who enjoy fishing and know what kinds of lures work best for different kinds of fish would be most suited for this business. Although all ages can enjoy this hobby, it helps to be good with your hands. Start off small by experimenting with different lures until you're comfortable with your skills. You can find books about flytying and lure making at many libraries and bookstores, including a helpful series of books and kits by Worth Tackle.

THE GOING RATE: $3.50 to $5 for each handmade lure, which measures about 3½ inches in length.

SECTION 2

BUSINESS SERVICES

◆

WHAT YOU NEED TO KNOW TO GET STARTED

Unless you've been living on another planet for the past decade, the news that home computers have revolutionized the business world should come as no surprise. But if you are a small, home-based business owner looking to provide services to other businesses, the change is much more profound than simply changing the way you work. The computer revolution also changes the quality and quantity of the types of jobs you can bid on. In short, home computers and all their attendant home office paraphernalia (such as fax machines, scanners, voice mail, E-mail, and laser printers) put you on an equal footing with any large company. You are, as self-employment gurus Paul and Sarah Edwards put it, an "equal competitor" with the big boys. A great deal of the explosion in home-based businesses can, in fact, be attributed to this new level playing field created by the computer. And home-based entrepreneurs have been quick to catch on—according to *Home Office Computing* over 60 percent of home-based businesses are in the business-computer-desktop publishing category of services.

You may, for instance, provide services to the burgeoning computer industry itself, such as training or remote backup. Or, you may use your home computer and specialty software packages to provide financial services such as bookkeeping and auditing to other businesses—an enterprise that formerly required office support staff. E-mail, faxes, and a home database permit individuals to do editorial or consulting work for a large variety of corporate clients—clients for whom your up-to-date technical capabilities will go further to establishing credibility than any downtown address.

The first concern of anyone contemplating a home-based business that provides services to the business world is to establish credibility. Of course, you may be working at your desk dressed in your usual working attire of jelly-smeared bathrobe, but your clients won't know it. Don't stint on well-designed stationery, billing forms, fax cover sheets, and business cards. Trade out services with a local designer or print shop to keep costs down if possible, but don't compromise on quality here. If your billing and communications forms are all your clients ever see of you, they will derive their impression of the quality of your work from these materials.

When you do meet with clients in person, take an extra minute to review your dress, briefcase, and any proposal materials you'll be bringing along. People who work at home tend to trend toward the casual, but when you travel corporate corridors dress up to their level.

Your minimum equipment requirements are a computer-fax-modem, photocopier, printer, and at least one dedicated telephone line. An ergonomic chair and correct-height desk should bring your basic setup charges to around $5,000—depending on your software requirements you might need an additional $1,000. Operations providing more complex services—such as a bulletin board site or color separations—have additional equipment requirements.

Where is the best place to look for clients? The absolute best first place to look for business service clients is with a previous employer. Many secretarial services, desktop publishers, editorial services, and bookkeeping services are actually the fruit of the current fashion for large companies to downsize and outplace services formerly provided by employees. The logical first place to look for these services is among former employees who already know the job—again, that credibility factor.

Once you have a credible operation, attract more clients with visibility for your company. Hometown newspapers are usually happy to send a reporter out to cover a new or expanding local enterprise. Join every community organization you can think of: chamber of commerce, Lions, PTA fund-raisers; and join the appropriate professional association for your business, too. Professional associations may not give you visibility with your clients, but they are the best source for the continuing education you need to keep your technical skills up and thereby maintain that all-important credibility.

Donate, when applicable, your services to a worthy municipal or charitable event. And get a business listing in the phone book, even if your name and your business name are exactly the same.

◆ COMPUTER SKILLS ◆

INTERNET WEB PAGE DESIGNER

This is probably the fastest-growing profession we've profiled in this book. According to the Business Research Group, a Massachusetts-based market research firm, the Internet's rather modest $20 million in transactions in 1993 should grow to $30 billion annually by the year 2000. Home page designers—and the Webmasters who maintain their pages—are key players in the exploding field of electronic commerce.

If you are a proficient computer user, familiar with the Internet, and willing to teach yourself how to program in HTML (the Internet programming language), you could develop a business as a home page creator for businesses. What is a home page? Home pages (also known as Websites) are locations on the Internet's World Wide Web. Like a page in a magazine, a home page displays information, advertisements, photographs, and other graphics. Due to the vast amount of hype about the Internet in the media these days, most companies are convinced that their competition will leave them in the dust if they don't develop a home page of their own. That's where you come in. These companies need someone who knows how to design a visually compelling, informative Website that will attract thousands of prospective customers.

To create top-rate Web pages with integrated graphics, you'll need to own a powerful computer with at least 16 megs of RAM, a color monitor, a 500-meg hard drive, along with a high-speed modem and a scanner. You'll also need access to the Internet through a local access provider and Web browser software. You can download the Web browser from the Internet. Two highly recommended books used by many Web authors are *Teach Yourself Web Publishing with HTML in 14 Days* by Laura Lemay (Sam's Publishing, 1995) and *HTML Publishing on the Internet* by Brent Heslop and Larry Budnick (Ventana Communications, 1995). Both books come with a CD that includes plenty of shareware programs and design tools to help you get started.

You don't need a computer degree; many successful Web designers are self-taught librarians, marketers, graphic designers, or engineers. Reading a variety of magazines like *The Net* (150 North Hill Drive, Brisbane, CA 94005), *Internet World* (20 Ketchum Street, Westport, CT 06880) and *Online* (462 Danbury Road, Wilton, CT 06897) will also help you keep up with the rapidly changing developments in the field. Attending a conference or class on home page design would also be helpful, if you can find one at a computer society or college in your area.

As you might expect, several Internet sites are available to help you design, target, and market your services. Check out these three top Websites for on-line business:

Business Sites: **http://www.rpi.edu/~okeefe/business.html**
Miniprofiles of Net success stories maintained by a professor at Rensselaer Polytechnic Institute's School of Management.

Yahoo Business Directories: **http://www.yahoo.com/business**
A huge and frequently updated catalog of business life on the Web; consortiums, sites with information on specific subjects in commerce; business directories; plus valuable info on taxes, intellectual property rights, and legal issues of doing business on the Web.

CommerceNet: **http://www.commerce.net**
Information and guidance on dozens of ways businesses can use the Internet; good background info to convince prospective clients to use your services.

After you've done your homework, you can start by creating a home page to advertise your own or a friend's business. The process of designing and programming a Web page is best learned by doing. We spoke with Vykie Whipple, who designed her first home page for her family's manufacturing business making performance driving accessories for Porsches. Vykie commented, "Creating my first Website was like giving birth—it was a similar experience. I had a burst of creativity, and felt really good after the page was done." The response was so overwhelming that she sensed a need for more Websites for Porsche owners browsing the Internet. So, she went on to found Computer Wizardry, Inc., and create the *Platz Mall, a one-stop on-line "shopping center" featuring listings from manufacturers, distributors, restorers, and service people. These advertisers pay a monthly fee to her company for their space in the mall.

While the mall is a commercial enterprise, Vykie provides services to her customers by linking her site to all Porsche clubs with on-line pages and by listing racetrack schedules and local Porsche service centers. Providing a service is key to offering a successful Website. Vykie said, "You need a feel for the Internet as a medium. I see home pages from large advertising houses and they stand out like a sore thumb because of their blatant commercialism. It's important to give people helpful information as well as product information. If you have a home page selling products for new mothers, for example, you would also want to include links to pages on day-care centers and health services for women."

TOP TIP: "There's such an incredible market for this stuff," Vykie said, "that you could probably get enough work to start immediately if you mention your service to all your contacts in the business world." Other publicity approaches for your business include developing a home page advertising your business, linking that home page to other pages of interest to your prospec-tive customers, and taking out ads in trade publications for the industries you've targeted.

GETTING STARTED: Once you've gained some experience, you can go after new business by targeting a market that would work well in a mall concept. A mall made up of dozens of compa-nies offering a similar product or service draws people in because it has more to offer than a single company's site. Once you set your target, send out some letters to area businesses and make follow-up phone calls to present your service. A big selling point is that a home page is a way to sell products internationally. Even a small mom-and-pop business can develop a glorious-looking home page and garner new customers all over the world. Don't forget to contact associations and clubs in your area as well. Non-profit associations are increasingly interested in serving their members through a customized Website.

After creating a home page, you can become a Webmaster and charge a prorated $50-an-hour fee to maintain the page by updating the information on a monthly or weekly basis, handling correspondence, and troubleshooting. You can also provide con-sulting services to businesses wanting to know more about going on-line, or help them acquire new computer systems and learn to use them, and charge the same hourly rate.

THE GOING RATE: Many home page designers charge a flat fee for creating home pages, housing them on their servers, and registering them with the major Internet search engines. This fee ranges from $500 for a very simple page to thousands of dollars for more complex Websites. The rate also varies depending on whether you need to start from scratch and write all the text and design the graphics, or whether you simply need to take existing advertising copy and insert HTML commands, which takes a lot less time. Average projects usually fall within the $1,000 to $2,000 range; a flat monthly maintenance fee (not including order fulfillment) of $200 is standard. All the above nonwith-standing, a first-time designer out to build up a portfolio of Web pages should be willing to take on a first-time client for $250 to $300 in order to build a business.

COMPUTER BULLETIN BOARD SERVICE PROVIDER

There are currently 150,000 computer bulletin board services (BBS for short) running in America today, and many people are surprised to learn that over three-quarters of them are private enterprises that can easily be run from a home or small office. BBS provide users with an electronic means to share data, news, or just express views.

The trick to running a successful BBS is to develop such a special-interest group. A natural choice would be something that you are already interested in so that you can start the conversational pot boiling. It could be, for instance, science fiction, organic gardening, or software development. After a BBS is up and running, your main input should be billing, keeping the equipment in good shape, and searching out new subscribers. All that can be done in small snatches of time or even at night after your regular workday.

Your minimal equipment requirements are a personal computer with a hard drive and five modems and phone lines so people can call into your board. You'll also need the software to let your callers talk to each other. Several such BBS software programs are available—try your local software store or any of the computer magazines. Two popular ones are called *TBBS* and *PCBoard*.

Depending on the special-interest group you decide to service, you can find subscribers (as customers of BBS are commonly called) through flyers, posters, and press releases sent to any magazines or newsletters that currently service the same market. You can also send an announcement to *Boardwatch Magazine* (5970 South Vivian Street, Littleton, CO 80127; 800-933-6038), which features articles and announcements about bulletin board services.

TOP TIP: Choose a subject you're interested in, because in the start-up phase you'll be the one providing most of the information.

GETTING STARTED: Order several back issues of *Boardwatch* to familiarize yourself with the special-interest bulletin boards already operating.

THE GOING RATE: You can charge for your services in one of two ways: either a flat monthly subscription fee (the current range is $20 to $50), or use your BBS software to bill time at a rate of one to ten cents a minute.

COMPUTER BACKUP
SERVICE PROVIDER

More and more small businesses are coming to rely on computers for their daily operations, yet that reliance also puts them at risk of losing all their data through power failure or simple human error. In addition, few small business have the resources to hire a full-time data administrator to make sure disks are backed up on a daily basis. With phone lines, a modem, a backup zip drive, and your own computer you can offer other businesses and self-employed professionals with crucial files (such as lawyers and architects) a valuable remote backup data service, also known as an RBS.

While most offices know they should be backing up their computers every night, many don't. Your remote backup service is a form of business insurance in the information age.

This is an ideal business for someone with reduced mobility or a hermit-type personality who doesn't want the kind of home business that will bring a lot of clients actually knocking on his door. Since most of your clients will already be on-line, you can even advertise your business via computer. Rob Cosgrove, who literally wrote the book on RBS services, claims that "you don't have to leave the house to sell it, run it, or restore it." One Detroit RBS provider comfortably services over two hundred clients, even though he is partially disabled by a stroke. An RBS is also a good add-on candidate for any other type of business that has you interacting with your client's computers, such as bookkeeping, tax preparation, or secretarial services.

An RBS is simple to install and doesn't require you to be a skilled programmer or computer jock. You'll need a PC 486 with 100 to 200 megabytes of free memory, high-speed telephone lines, a modem, and a zip drive memory cache to back yourself up. The computer backs up your clients automatically, and should they suffer a data loss and need restoration you can mail them replacement disks or, with new remote restoration software, modem the necessary files back to them without ever leaving your desk chair. The hardware and software are generally available through computer stores and catalogs, or you can purchase everything but the hardware as a business kit from Precision Data Corp. (901-682-0732).

While setting up and running the system is relatively simple, you'll need marketing smarts to develop your client base. Your target clients will be doctors, lawyers, CPAs, and bookkeepers who need data insurance. Since your service is, by definition, remote, you don't have to limit yourself to local advertising. You can advertise on-line or through direct mail with a professional-looking brochure followed up by a personal phone call. Write an article for professionals' association newsletters. Closer to home, send the local paper a press release about your unique form of "Information Age Data Insurance." Join the local chamber of commerce and offer to talk for free to professional organizations. Offer a community discount to the local library, hospital, or village hall as a gesture of goodwill to create visibility.

TOP TIP: Rob Cosgrove recommends offering a finder's fee to accountants and computer stores for recommending their clients to you.

GETTING STARTED: Contact QT Inc., 720 Harbor Ave., Memphis, TN 38113, 800-552-7814 or **www.Alice.net** for an information packet on their RBS Business Kit.

THE GOING RATE: Clients pay $300 to $500 monthly for the service. You can also offer to charge them $300 or the amount they would lose if they lost one day's worth of billing data due to computer malfunction—whichever is less!

INTERNET SEMINARS INSTRUCTOR

Can you surf the net without breaking into a sweat? Do you know people who are curious about going on-line but are baffled by all the computer jargon being tossed around in the media? If so, starting a home business to help others get up to speed can be a smart and timely move. *Entrepreneur* magazine has called Internet consulting and computer-training classes some of the hottest businesses. Before you begin, you'll need to own the best computer you can afford and a fast modem. Make sure you have plenty of technical knowledge and computer experience before you start teaching others. You can teach a few students at a time in your home office, or offer seminars at corporate offices. If you want to offer larger seminars, you'll need access to a meeting room (try your local library or community college) and will need to hook your computer up to an overhead for demonstrations.

During your seminars, you can introduce students to such commercial on-line services as CompuServe and America Online, discuss these services' strengths and weaknesses, and give advice on navigating and finding specific types of information. Your students will also want to learn about E-mail, Usenet Groups, the World Wide Web, and how to understand technospeak. You might want to offer separate workshops on the Internet, since it's a complex subject that requires a lot of time to explore.

Jodie Slothower offers a series of "Travellers' Guides to the Information Highway" through her home-based business The Text Kitchen. She helps participants learn everything from accessing on-line connections to saving time and money once they're plugged in. "Many people are nervous about this subject to begin with, so I start by helping them get over their anxiety," Jodie said. She advises, "Realize that you can't answer everyone's questions about every aspect of the Web or Internet, but you can point them in the right direction."

TOP TIP: Since technology is changing rapidly and it's hard to keep up with all the latest developments, it's good idea to specialize—for example, by concentrating on women, teachers, or small businesses.

GETTING STARTED: Once you've educated yourself in these subjects, advertise in your newspaper and try direct mail. Jodie sponsored some spots on her local public radio station, which ended up interviewing her about her workshops. Word of mouth brings in a lot of students, so work on developing your reputation as someone who can cut through all the hype to let people know exactly what on-line services can do for them.

THE GOING RATE: $50 per student for a two- to two-and-a-half-hour workshop. You can also charge around $25 per hour or more for individual consultations at your home.

COMPUTER CONSULTANT AND TRAINER

This home-based business is ideal for anyone who knows computers inside and out. Former programmers, self-taught computer experts, and adept computer users are in great demand to guide and teach the technologically challenged. It doesn't matter whether you've earned a master's in computer science or just spent hundreds of hours as a teenage hacker—as long as you can solve people's computer problems, you'll be in business. Although computers have been around for quite a while, many people still feel intimidated and frightened when confronted by a flashing cursor or incomprehensible error message. If you are well-versed in a variety of software programs and computer systems, you could offer computer training, troubleshooting, and consulting services. There is also ample opportunity for gurus with expertise in a specific area such as JAVA, database connectivity, and HTML.

Before you begin, you'll need at least one recent-model computer at home—many consultants specialize in either Macintosh or IBM machines and clones, although some are generalists—and an up-to-date collection of the most popular software programs. You can develop expertise in new software packages by taking classes at a technical or community college, or you can train yourself by spending some time exploring the software (and even reading the manuals). In addition to a solid grounding in computer technology, you'll need strong interpersonal and teaching skills to do well in this business. A soothing manner and the ability to translate computer jargon into plain English are essential traits of a good trainer. You can travel to people's workplaces or homes to teach them, or have them come to your home office.

Offering individualized training programs can help your business take off. Lois Morton has been doing computer consulting for a few years, and told us, "My focus is on training and helping people to get their skill level up. By coming in and training people on exactly what they need to know at a particular time, I offer an alternative to their having to take a ten-week computer class at a community college. That's my niche, and my market strategy." Lois told us that her consulting has run the gamut from showing clients where their computer's hard drive is to teaching them how to program in Excel. "It's good money, but there's a lot of preparation work when I teach someone a class designed just for them," she commented. "Still, I'm enjoying this immensely. I really recommend it for people who want interesting part-time work."

TOP TIP: Read *How to Be a Successful Computer Consultant* by Alan R. Simon (McGraw-Hill, 1993). Reading *PC* (One Park Avenue, New York, NY 10016) or *Macworld* (501 Second Street, San Francisco, CA 94107) magazines and *Home Office Computing* (555 Broadway, New York, NY 10012) will also help you keep up with new products and changes in the industry.

GETTING STARTED: Businesses are looking for people who can quickly bring their employees up to speed on such popular programs as Microsoft Word, Excel, and the Windows '95 operating system. Schoolteachers and principals are looking for consultants who can help them understand the intricacies of their new educational computer systems. And parents are looking for help in selecting appropriate hardware and software for their families. You can reach these markets by leaving your brochure at computer and software retail stores, putting up business cards on local bulletin boards, and sending a letter and brochure to local businesses. To reach parents, place flyers at schools, preschools, and day-care centers, and take out an ad in a local parenting newspaper. After you gain some satisfied clients, word of mouth generally leads to more consulting assignments. Also, consider joining the Independent Computer Consultants Association (933 Gardenview Office Parkway, St. Louis, MO 63141; 314-997-4633) to network with others in this growing field and to subscribe to their magazine, *The Independent.*

THE GOING RATE: You can charge between $60 and $150 an hour for consulting and troubleshooting, and around $40 an hour for individualized computer training.

FINANCIAL SKILLS

BOOKKEEPING SERVICE

Small businesses are the fastest-growing segment of the U.S. economy, and very few companies with fifty or fewer employees have the wherewithall to hire a full-time bookkeeper. Many of them turn to freelance bookkeepers to handle their financial record keeping.

Bookkeepers may offer their clients a wide variety of services, such as payroll, billing, accounts receivable and payable, making bank deposits and reviewing statements, and preparing financial statements. Since the services cover such a wide range, most bookkeepers charge by the hour. Certain services, such as complex preparation of corporate tax returns, may carry an additional hourly charge.

A background in bookkeeping or accounting is ideal, but if you are good with numbers, enjoy detail work, and are familiar with—or willing to learn—the computer, many reputable programs are available to provide you with the additional knowledge you'll need to run a good service. Your previous work may not have been in bookkeeping at all, but lead you to specialize in a specific industry that you have intimate knowledge of, such as bookkeeping for restaurants, contractors, or commercial artists.

One bookkeeper who has been in the business for twenty-five years cautions prospective bookkeepers to not even think about getting into the business without a computer. "The days of long

green ledger books with meticulous hand entries are long gone,"
she stresses. This bookkeeper went to a local community college
for her basic computer education at a cost of around $250—an
investment in herself that has paid her back many times over.
With the costs of home computers continuing to drop every day,
you should be able to set up a home office with computer,
printer, calculator, fax, modem, and accounting software for
under $3,000. "If you develop a lot of business and your phone
lines are often busy you should also consider voice mail," she
adds, "since clients have a habit of calling up in an extreme state
of urgency needing an answer to a question *right now*. A busy
signal only increases their anxiety."

While most of your work will be done at home, you should
plan on going to your clients' offices once or twice a month to
pick up and return paperwork. And if you plan on having small
children at home when you are working, take the advice of one
bookkeeper mother of two toddlers and pay for a baby-sitter in
your home or plan on working on the books at night—this type
of work requires extreme care and concentration since one error
can cost your clients thousands of dollars—and lose you their
business and your good reputation.

TOP TIP: A listing in your local yellow pages and community
paper are essential advertising for small business bookkeepers.
After personal recommendations, these publications are often the
first place small business owners look when they are trying to find
a service. In order to get those personal recommendations make
sure you join the chamber of commerce. In addition, contact
local tax preparers, accountants, financial planners, and business
loan officers of local banks in order to get referral business.

GETTING STARTED: Contact the American Institute of
Professional Bookkeepers (6001 Montrose Rd, Rockville, MD
20852; 800-622-0121) for information on their well-respected
home-schooling courses on all aspects of bookkeeping. This
membership organization also offers newsletters, keeps its members up to date on tax laws, runs a telephone question-and-

answer hotline, provides free federal and state tax forms, and publishes the *Journal of Accounting, Taxation, and Finance for Business.* Community colleges are often good sources for classes in bookkeeping and computers. In addition, the IRS periodically offers in-depth seminars on federal taxation.

THE GOING RATE: Typically $20 to $40 an hour.

REFUND AUDITOR

Are you a demon for details? Do you go over your phone bill with a microscope to make sure you were billed at the correct rate and for the right amount of time? Is your checkbook balanced every month? Do you run your electric dryer at 2 A.M. in order to take advantage of cheaper off-peak rates? Congratulations—you have the instincts of a natural-born refund auditor.

A refund auditor specializes in locating and collecting hidden business overcharges. Refund auditors review the electric, gas, water, waste disposal, freight, and telephone bills for their corporate clients. They check to make sure that the charges are figured correctly and look for errors in computation, keypunching, or misapplication of rates.

Utility companies *do not* guarantee that you will always be charged the most favorable rate, so auditors also check that their clients have been given any and all discounts that might apply. Some companies may be eligible for reduced rates based on special circumstances, which vary nationwide. For example, if the company is located in a specially designated "enterprise zone" it may qualify for a discount. Refund auditors may also make recommendations to their clients about switching services or service plans (for example, a long-distance phone carrier) in order to get better rates, or request a peak demand monitoring device from the utility company in order to help the client stagger their demand and reduce their expenses.

Finding the overcharge is only the first part of an auditor's job.

The second part is to negotiate the refund with the utility company. Your fee as an auditor will come out of this refund for past overcharges. A typical fee structure is 50 percent of past savings, with an additional smaller percentage on the upcoming savings for the next year. If no refund is available, your contract should call for a percentage of the upcoming savings for the next year or sometimes even two years.

Of course, large industrial or corporate clients who use a lot of energy or make a lot of phone calls offer the greatest potential for large profits; however, these types of companies may already have internal auditors. Local hospitals, small municipal governments, township school systems, and churches may be better bets for someone just starting to build a clientele.

What sort of background do you need in order to break into bill auditing? While the ideal previous job would be in the billing department of a phone company or electric utility, a background in bookkeeping or purchasing will also be useful. Luckily, several instructional programs exist to train bill auditors. See below for the particulars. Besides the technical aspects, you'll also need to be a whiz with the adding machine, love detail work, and feel profound satisfaction in your ability to track your elusive prey— big savings!—through a jungle of paperwork every month.

TOP TIP: Experienced auditors recommend soliciting clients through direct mail pieces followed up with a personal phone call. If you don't have good design or copywriting skills, pay for a professional to create your brochure—you want it to look sharp and credible. Emphasize the economy of your service—you only get paid out of refund money you are getting them, so the company is actually making money as it pays you your fee. Another good idea is to join your local business or merchant association and make other members aware of your service.

GETTING STARTED: Contact these companies regarding their training programs:

Institute of Consulting Careers
222 SE 16th Street
Portland, OR 97214
800-696-4594

Public Utility Consultants
25800 Ward Ave.
Fort Bragg, CA 95437
800-833-2998

Utility & Tax Reduction Consultants
1240 Iroquois Dr.
Naperville, IL 60563
800-321-7872

THE GOING RATE: The profit potential will be greatest if
your clients have utility billings of at least $2,500 a month, but
no matter how large your clientele your income will vary widely
from month to month. It could be $0, $200, $1,000, or $5,000,
depending on how much overcharging you find.

INSURANCE POLICIES
AUDITOR

If you have financial skills or used to work in the insurance industry—and your eyes don't glaze over when you encounter a
densely written insurance policy—you've just found a good niche
for a home business. (Some people offer this service as part of a
bookkeeping or tax preparation business.)

An insurance auditor will ask his clients to bring in copies of
their home, business, and automotive insurance, and will show
them how to save money by cutting down on duplicate insurance
coverage. Most people are bewildered by the numbing language
and endless small print in their insurance policies, and often end

up with more insurance—and higher premiums—than they really need.

You can audit your clients' insurance policies for coverage that is not cost-effective, and decide when they could save money in the long run by raising their deductibles or getting rid of unnecessary provisions. For example, people who add car rental coverage to their car insurance rarely need to use it. It would be far cheaper to pay for a car rental yourself if your car breaks down once instead of paying extra for your auto insurance for five or six years without benefiting from it.

TOP TIP: Some auditors offer a guarantee that they can save their clients more than their $50 fee over the course of a year.

GETTING STARTED: Build a clientele by putting ads in your local paper and mentioning your service to parents at your kids' preschool, neighbors, members of your Rotary Club or church, or any other organization you belong to. People who already know you and people in your community are your best bets for potential customers.

THE GOING RATE: $50 per consultation.

INSURANCE CLAIMS ASSISTANCE CONSULTANT

Filling out medical insurance claims forms is right up there with filling out tax returns for most people. It can be tedious, time-consuming, and frustrating for people who are not used to dealing with Medicare and insurance companies. Others may be battling serious illnesses and don't have the energy to battle their insurers as well to make sure that they're receiving fair reimbursements. If you have a background in the insurance business, you could set up a home-based business as a medical claims adjuster, otherwise known as an insurance claims assistance consultant.

In this business, you would act as patients' advocate, check on the accuracy of every medical bill they receive, help them file medical claims, get the largest insurance payments possible, and mediate disputes with insurers and with Medicare over whether your clients are entitled to reimbursements. You'll need strong organizational skills to sort out all the medical bills the patient receives, and good follow-up abilities and negotiating skills when questioning insurance company denials of claims. You'll also need to be concerned with details and accuracy, since many times claims are denied when a minor mistake is made on an insurance form.

TOP TIP: If you're computer savvy, you can expand your business by becoming an Electronic Claims Professional and helping doctors reduce administrative costs by filing medical claims electronically.

GETTING STARTED: You can become qualified for this profession by joining the National Association of Claims Assistance Professionals (5329 S. Main Street, Ste. 102, Downers Grove, IL 60515; 800-660-0665). Membership is open to anyone with an interest in health insurance. The NACAP runs The Claims Academy, a series of courses that will help you understand claims-processing techniques, develop skills in marketing your business, and learn how to process claims electronically. They publish an informative monthly newsletter, *The Claims Advisor,* hold a national conference, and offer discounts on buying professional liability insurance. The NACAP also offers referrals to customers in your area seeking help with their claims.

THE GOING RATE: You can charge between $30 and $60 an hour for your services, depending on your experience.

TYPING AND OFFICE SKILLS

MEDICAL TRANSCRIPTIONIST

Home business experts Paul and Sarah Edwards call this one of the ten fastest-growing fields for home-based workers today. This flexible job is for anyone who's interested in health care but does *not* want to spend years in medical school. A medical transcriptionist listens to and types doctors' dictated notes, making a permanent printed record for patients' files. (So relax, you won't have to interpret doctors' handwritten scrawls.) An in-depth knowledge of medical terminology is essential. Beginners will need to take one to two years of medical transcription classes before they can start their at-home business. Many community colleges offer certificate programs in medical transcription, and are more economical than the $995 correspondence course offered by *MT Monthly* newsletter (1633 NE Rosewood Dr., Gladstone, MO 64118; 800-951-5559).

You'll need a computer with word-processing software, a fax and modem, a printer, and a transcribing machine. You can find base models that play microcassettes at office supply stores for around $150 to $200. These include a foot pedal to control the tape's speed and a set of headphones. Or, you can rent a transribing machine that plays full-size cassettes for around $30 a month—or buy one for $300 to $400. You can buy or lease more sophisticated recording equipment with new digital recording abilities, but it's unlikely that you'll need to do that until you've built up your business.

Strong typing, editing, and proofreading skills are required, since the records you type become legal documents. "Accuracy is crucial," says Michele Miller. "You are taking a certain responsiblity for what you type. Errors and omissions insurance is theoretically a good thing to get, for that reason." Acquiring several reference books—such as Stedman's series of *Medical Word Books, Stedman's Medical Speller, Current Medical Terminology* by Vera Pyle (Health Prof. Institute, 1994), and a pharmaceutical reference book—is also a must, so you can look up unfamiliar medications and procedures and their spellings. You can now get software versions of some of these resources, including Stedman's Plus.4.0 Medical/Pharmaceutical Spellchecker and Stedman's Electronic Medical Dictionary. (You can order Stedman books and software by calling 1-800-527-5597.)

TOP TIP: To find customers, introduce yourself to doctors (including psychiatrists and veterinarians) and small health clinics in your area and hand out your business card, or send a brochure to local medical practices. It's worth targeting hospitals as well, since many are laying off their in-house medical transcriptionists and switching to services or freelancers. You can also contact large transcription services to see if they're hiring: The MRC Group is a large national firm with 60 branches throughout the country.

GETTING STARTED: Read *Health Service Businesses on Your Home-Based PC* by Rick Benzel (TAB Books, 1993) for start-up tips. After you've completed your training, join the American Association for Medical Transcription (PO Box 576187, Modesto, CA 95357; 800-982-2182). The AAMT offers local chapters, which are good places for networking with others in the field, and publishes a bimonthly journal, *Journal of the AAMT.*

THE GOING RATE: Rates vary, depending on whether you bill by the line, the page, or the hour, and whether you're asked to provide a fast turnaround time. Some transcriptionists charge between eight to ten cents a line or $3 to $5 per page; others receive $9 to $12 per hour and up.

ANSWERING SERVICE

In this era of high-tech voice mail systems you'd think that something as simple as a good old-fashioned operator-run answering system would be hopelessly out of fashion, but there is in fact a growing population of business and professional customers who insist upon a personal answering service—because their customers do.

Who needs the judgment, warmth, and problem-solving capabilities of a personal answering service? Doctors, plumbers, electricians, psychologists, dentists, and any other repair person or professional whose customers may call up with an emergency situation that needs an immediate answer. Personal answering services can also screen calls and make callbacks to customers—something no voice mail system can do—yet.

An answering service is a 100 percent at-home business. People running answering services need to be extremely reliable. You can't leave your post to run a few errands or deal with the four-year-old twins fighting over a toy in the backyard unless you refer calls to your personal cellular phone. If you go out for dinner or away on vacation you'll have to hire someone to cover for you. House-bound entrepreneurs or couples who can split shifts without having to pay for someone else to cover their time off will have an easier time living with the mobility restrictions running an answering service puts on you.

A pleasant speaking voice is a plus, as well as a reassuring manner with people. If you take message slips by hand you'll need a good handwriting that isn't hard for your clients to decipher, or you can run your whole system by computer and fax message records back and forth.

Advertise your service with flyers or brochures to local businesses of the type mentioned above. Offer a referral fee to accountants and office-building managers who steer new clients your way.

TOP TIP: To sign up new business, offer a trial discounted three-month contract.

GETTING STARTED: Contact your local phone company to determine equipment needs, or contact The Complete Answering Machine (800-229-1753) for information on a PC voice-mail board for your computer.

THE GOING RATE: Charge clients $150 to $300 a month, depending on whether you answer their phones full-time or only after regular business hours, and whether or not you'll be making callbacks to your clients' customers for them.

TRANSCRIBER OF TESTIMONY FOR COURT REPORTERS

Ever wonder what happens to those miles of testimony type we all see court reporters producing on *Perry Mason* and *The People's Court?* They get turned into readable transcriptions by special typists called "scopists" (or sometimes "notereaders").

According to our local court reporter, scopists are most often used by court reporting agencies in large metropolitan areas. Scopists commonly work from home, though you usually will have to stop by the courthouse once a week to pick up and drop off work. Still, 95 percent of your work time is spent at home in front of the word processor or computer.

To be a scopist you'll need good typing skills and familiarity with legal terminology. Knowledge of some other area, such as medical, tax, or police procedurals can be a big plus, as can the ability to transcribe directly from audiotapes. Present your flyer or résumé directly to reporters at the courthouse or contact one of the agencies listed in your local yellow pages.

TOP TIP: No matter how good your skills are, you won't get your first assignment sitting home waiting for the phone to ring. Develop a friendly, colleagial relationship with the other scopists and the court reporters. Hang out at trials. Take your coffee break or lunch in the municipal building. Sometimes others will have overflow work and pass it on to you, and that's how you'll get your break. Once you've developed your clientele, you'll only have to leave the house once a week.

GETTING STARTED: If you have the typing skills but no legal background, contact At-Home Professions (12383 Lewis Street, Garden Grove, CA 92640; 800-359-3455) and ask about their home study course in court reporter notereading.

THE GOING RATE: Varies with municipality and region.

RESEARCH AND ORGANIZATIONAL SKILLS

INFORMATION BROKER

An information broker has been described as "a reference librarian for hire" or a "private librarian." Brokers are asked to sift through the mountains of information available through reference books, newspapers and magazines, and on-line services to find out exactly what their clients need to know. You're right for this job if you have strong research skills and experience in library reference work. A master's degree in library and information sciences would be a definite plus. Alternatively, you could take your expertise in a certain profession, like law or engineering, and offer specialized searches for one industry. You'll need to be a proficient computer user, since most search requests can be fulfilled by going through on-line services and the Internet. For that reason, you can't start setting up your business until you have a computer with a high-speed modem, a dedicated phone line for your modem, and a few subscriptions to major on-line databases.

Most clients can be found at local businesses who need specific types of information, and need it in a hurry. The first step with new clients is to set up a reference interview. By asking the right questions, you can clarify what information they are seeking, set parameters, help them narrow their focus, and make suggestions about sources to use. You may be asked to find out about upcoming engineering conferences, look up patent information and federal regulations, find a list of banks in Missouri for an employee relocation firm, or compile a family history for an amateur genealogist.

You'll need to keep your eyes open for new reference sources, both in written and electronic form, because you never know what you'll be asked to look up next. Since Internet resources change daily, be willing to experiment, and look up lists of new Websites regularly. One information broker told us, "No guidebooks are up to date, so it's up to you to discover new on-line information sources. I'm a big believer in going into Yahoo (one of the Internet's major search engines) once a day and looking at the lists of new sites." It's also important to train yourself to be a speedy and efficient on-line searcher—you'll be working under deadline, and clients won't be willing to pay for wasted time.

Terry Beck has had a part-time information brokerage business for a few years, in addition to working as a reference librarian. She advised, "Remember that you're offering the same service a public library can do for free. Set yourself apart by knowing your sources, being speedy and very service-oriented. Let clients know that you'll give them personal attention and will take as much time as they need to fulfill their request." She's found that the volume of work can vary dramatically from month to month, so you can't count on a steady stream of income.

TOP TIP: The best leads for new clients come from referrals from friends, businesses you've worked for, and librarians, who may find a particular search request too time-consuming for them to handle. For that reason, make sure you let all the libraries in the area know about your business. In addition, you should contact local financial companies, public relations firms, and attorneys, since they are likely to use (and pay for) your services. Present seminars to local organizations and publicize your business in relevant trade journals.

GETTING STARTED: It's a good idea to join the American Library Association (50 E. Huron Street, Chicago, IL 60611; 312-944-6780) to stay up to date with the information services field and to network with other librarians and researchers. Once you're a member, you can attend ALA conferences and receive useful publications from the Reference and Adult Services division of ALA.

If you're not a librarian, you can join the Association of Independent Information Professionals (245 5th Avenue, Suite 2103, New York, NY 10016; 212-779-1855), which offers special member rates to on-line services. Read *The Information Broker's Handbook* by Sue Rugge and Alfred Glossbrenner (TAB Books, 1992) before you set up your business. Then buy some key reference books like the *Encyclopedia of Business Info Sources* by James B. Woy (Gale Research, Inc., 1994), *Basic Business Library: Core Resources* by Bernard Schlesinger (Oryx Press, 1994), and *Finding Facts Fast* by Alden Todd (Ten Speed Press, 1992). You can also subscribe to such professional journals as *Information Today* (143 Old Marlton Pike, Medord, NJ 08055) and *Database* (462 Danbury Road, Wilton, CT 06897).

THE GOING RATE: You can charge anywhere between $15 and $20 an hour up to $50 to $100 an hour. The rate will vary depending on your background (a library or other professional degree will allow you to charge more for your services), the region you live in, and whether you have an individual or corporation for a client. You should also pass on-line charges along to clients, and charge an additional fee for photocopies of documents.

GRANT WRITER AND FUND-RAISER

Fund-raising and grant writing skills have never been more in demand. Since the government has made a balanced budget one of its top priorities and cut back on social spending, nonprofits, social service agencies, and private companies are feverishly searching for new sources of funds. This would be an ideal business to start if you have some experience as a grant writer, enjoy researching grant opportunities, and have strong factual writing abilities and good interpersonal skills when dealing with clients. You should also have an interest in public service if you plan to focus on working with nonprofits or the government. Many people specialize in working with school systems, since so many schools are in need of additional money to buy basic supplies and class computers.

A computer and a modem have become the most essential tools for this business, as in so many other fields. While grant writers used to have to travel to several different government and public libraries to learn about new grants, now they can discover the same information at home by logging onto the Internet. You can find a wealth of information on the latest grants by going through thousands of on-line sources, such as Grantsweb, Grantsnet, and Handsnet.

You can access portions of the *Federal Register* on-line, and most departments of the federal government have home pages as well. This makes it easy for you to go directly to the source, learn what you need to know, and download the applications in a few minutes, instead of waiting a couple of weeks for the information to arrive in the mail. These improvements in technology make it much easier to do your job more efficiently, and to stay up to date on the latest grant opportunities as soon as they are posted. Then, you can communicate with hard-to-reach or busy clients through E-mail. With the right computer setup, you may never have to leave your home office again!

It's a good idea to subscribe to the *Chronicle of Philanthropy* (1255 23rd Street NW, Suite 700, Washington, DC 20037) because it offers informative articles and regularly lists organizations and people who are looking for freelance grant writers. Once you're on this mailing list, you'll receive lots of information from other fund-raising organizations and publications. Visit your state branch of the Foundation Center (79 5th Avenue, New York, NY 10003; 212-620-4230; 800-424-9836) to learn about private funding and to explore their extensive libraries of books on fund-raising. You can also access the Foundation Center database through the Internet at **http://www.fdncenter.org/.**

TOP TIP: Join every local networking organization you possibly can, from the chamber of commerce to the Elks or Women's Business Owners, and then talk about what you do. If you enjoy grant writing work and can convey your enthusiasm and commitment to others, you will attract new clients wherever you go. You could also publicize your business through on-line services.

GETTING STARTED: While taking classes and seminars in grant writing is a good idea, you may find that experience is truly the best teacher. Kim Smoyer became interested in grant writing while searching for funds to send herself to graduate school. She discovered that she enjoyed doing the research and found that grant writing was a good way to apply her technical writing skills. She gained more experience in looking for funding possibilities and in filling out state aid applications when she worked for a township manager and a state government agency before forming her own business, Smoyer & Associates, Inc., five years ago. Kim has learned that her services are particularly in demand by arts organizations, such as local theaters, opera companies, and historical societies, by such nonprofits as YWCAs and AIDS organizations, and by local corporations.

Kim told us, "I've always wanted to work in social service and public service. Now I combine public- and private-sector work, which is the best of both worlds for me. I make private-sector wages, but do the kind of work I want to do with public-sector people. I really like and believe in what I'm doing, and that comes across when I meet people. I've never advertised anywhere—all my business is from word of mouth."

THE GOING RATE: Whatever the market will bear in your area. You can earn an average of $30 an hour in this business. Some grant writers offer a sliding scale. They may charge $20 an hour for their work for small nonprofit organizations that are low on funds, and $40 an hour when they work for large corporations.

MEETING AND CONFERENCE PLANNER

It seems that every week there are thousands of conventions going on across the country, from pizza makers to plastics industry shows. These conventions may be local, regional, national, or international, and can contain as few as eighty booths, or as many as three thousand. Organized, detail-oriented people are in demand to help corporations and associations plan their trade shows, meetings, conferences, and expos. You'll need to have a background in planning meetings or expositions within a company, hotel, or trade association, and be skilled in negotiating contracts, getting the best prices for the best services, finding suppliers, and troubleshooting.

Independent meeting planners offer the following services:

budgeting, exhibit booth sales, planning, and on-site management. Some clients may want only one of these services. They may ask you to get bids from suppliers, create a budget for a show, and make your recommendations before any of the planning begins. They may want you to handle registration, badges, and generate a list of show rules and other printed materials. They may hand you a list of corporate leads and ask you to fill the booth spaces by making sales calls. (If you're hired to sell exhibit space, you will probably work on a commission arrangement.) Or, they may request a comprehensive meeting plan, including the show's location, food and beverages required, equipment needed, and all other details. Finally, you may be asked to fulfill the role of floor manager, and be on-site during the show to make sure that everything is running smoothly and that union workers and contractors are performing their jobs properly, and to solve problems as they occur.

Most importantly, you must be able to prepare and stick to a budget. "To succeed at this business," Laura Kruchko Rich, president of Exposition Resources, told us, "you need to determine if the conference or exposition is financially feasible, and have a plan to achieve the bottom line. You also need to be able to communicate effectively. There is no substitute for real-world experience on the job." Laura has found that the essential equipment for this job are a computer, fax machine, telephone, printer, a business phone line and another line dedicated to the fax, and an answering service, so it doesn't sound as though clients are calling her home. She usually meets clients at their workplace or at the conference site, but spends most of her time working out of her home office. Another meeting planner, Jennifer Hodge Jerzyk, commented, "What I always liked about this job is that it is project-oriented. The challenging part of the job is that things can easily go astray at the time of the event, and keeping a cool head and being prepared with contingency plans is essential."

TOP TIP: Join as many local organizations as you can, from the chamber of commerce to service and professional organizations. Then, volunteer your services to plan a civic or charitable event. Read the local newspapers to keep track of community events and people on the move and network with managers at convention centers and visitors' bureaus in your region.

GETTING STARTED: Joining the International Association for Exhibition Management (PO Box 802425, Dallas, TX 75380; 214-458-8002) or Meeting Professionals International (1950 Stemmons Fwy, Ste. 5018, Dallas, TX 75207; 214-712-7700) is a must. By reading these associations' monthly publications, attending conferences and continuing education programs, going to local chapter meetings, and talking to other planners, you'll learn an enormous amount about the field. You can also tap into MPINet on-line, which offers access to hundreds of documents and forms used by the meeting industry, along with conference rooms, message boards, and E-mail.

THE GOING RATE: You can charge a flat per project fee or an hourly rate between $45 and $65 an hour, plus phone and travel expenses. Make sure you develop a contract that spells out exactly which tasks you've agreed to take on, or you can lose money by ending up doing much more work than you had bargained for initially. Also, make sure your contract includes a liability clause, stating that you're covered under the show management's liability insurance.

WRITING AND PUBLISHING SKILLS

COPYWRITER

If you know how to write clearly, concisely, and persuasively, you could be sought after as a freelance copywriter. Copywriters write brochures, catalogs, book jackets, press releases, annual reports, and other materials for companies, both small and large. A computer is an essential tool, although you can get by with a basic word-processing system. A fax machine or fax modem has become just as important in giving you a professional image and enabling you to meet your deadlines.

If you have worked in a specific field, you can continue to specialize while you work at home. For example, a former copywriter for a publishing company can focus on writing catalog and back-cover copy for local publishers. Engineers are in great demand as technical writers. Liberal arts majors make good copywriters as well, since they need to be quick learners who can absorb and synthesize new material. As a copywriter, you may find yourself writing about computer software one day and pig farming the next day. Copywriters enjoy the flexibility of their work and the fact that projects are self-contained. You can get a sense of completion and satisfaction in a short period of time.

TOP TIP: Beware of taking on too much work at once, since you don't want to develop a reputation for missing deadlines. You can find work by contacting former employers and by talking to small businesses within your community.

GETTING STARTED: Do volunteer work for a community organization to help you develop a portfolio and spread the word about your business.

THE GOING RATE: This varies, according to the size of your client. You can charge about $25 an hour for writing copy for publishers, but can get as much as $50 an hour when writing for large businesses. Some copywriters charge a flat rate, such as $500 for a standard 8 1/2-by-11-inch folded brochure, but are willing to offer lower rates for struggling new businesses.

BUSINESS COMMUNICATIONS WRITER

The great thing about freelancing in corporate communications is that it's much more lucrative than most forms of freelance writing. Writing articles for local newspapers can pay only $25 to $50 per article, and magazine journalism is extremely hard to break into. By contrast, business writing is a good way to make money from your writing skills. You can succeed in business communications if you're a good writer and interviewer and have an interest in the business world. Your job would be to write articles for corporate publications, such as company newsletters and magazines, and to write news releases, brochures, and catalogs.

A background in writing is essential, and some experience in journalism would be helpful, since you'll usually need to do some research and conduct telephone interviews before you can write your articles. You're expected to present the company's point of view in your writing—you will use the skills and techniques of a journalist, along with a public relations perspective. You'll need to be able to make business news seem lively and interesting. You'll also need to have a computer, fax machine, and a separate business phone line.

"All it takes is one big assignment, which can lead to others," said a freelancer in this field. "When I started I had a public relations and communications background, but did not have experience writing for corporations. I lucked out when a company saw my samples, called me, and asked me to write a major feature for their magazine. I've used that piece as an example of what I can do, and built on it to get freelance jobs from other corporations."

TOP TIP: You may want to specialize in a particular field and gain expertise in that area. One communications consultant we spoke to has focused on health-care writing, which has led to numerous writing assignments from a number of health-care companies, ranging from magazine cover stories to booklets on knee surgery for patients.

GETTING STARTED: To get started as a freelancer, start contacting former employers, local businesses, and associations. You'll need to be comfortable with marketing yourself, and be willing to make cold calls to local organizations. Following up with a letter, your bio, and several samples of your work attractively presented in a folder can drum up interest in your services. Becoming active in local organizations such as the chamber of commerce or Rotary will bring you into contact with businesspeople who may need help with business writing. Joining the International Association of Business Communicators (1 Hallidie Plaza, Suite 600, San Francisco, CA 94102; 415-433-3400) and getting listed in their directory can also lead to new clients—and you can attend local chapter meetings to meet other business communicators and hone your skills. Once you've been freelancing for a while, you'll find that you get most of your clients through referrals.

THE GOING RATE: You can charge between $30 to $100 an hour, depending on your track record and experience in this field. Many writers prefer to bid on a per project basis, but will work on an hourly basis if they don't know the scope of the project.

TECHNICAL WRITER

Did you have trouble choosing between the arts and the sciences in high school? Do you enjoy a good algebraic proof as much as a good novel? And have you ever been frustrated by a poorly written operating manual, confusing instructions, or needlessly complicated diagrams? Then congratulations, you have the right interests and attitude to be a technical writer.

Technical writers work for industrial, technological, and manufacturing companies. They write operating manuals, document software, and provide specifications, and as business becomes increasingly high-tech, their services will be more and more in demand.

You need to have good basic editorial skills plus some background in your specialty field—be it software, geology, medicine, or electronics. You may be expected to write a manual from scratch or "revise" (read "turn into English") a technical report from a scientist. Sometimes you'll be called upon to create an index, too.

Good technical writers also need to be good interviewers. Andrew K. McCarter, whose company, Sculpted Technologies, specializes in computer manuals and documentation, insists on as much "upfront" interview time as possible—usually two full days—because, he says, "You have to ask a million and one questions before you start writing. In essence, you yourself define the parameters of the project."

TOP TIP: Currently the highest demand for technological writers is in the software industry.

GETTING STARTED: It is unlikely that you will be equally skilled in both areas. Be honest with yourself and evaluate your skills to see if you need more education in a technical area or editing skills. Many state universities and junior colleges offer reasonably priced programs in technical communication; there is also an association that provides education, pricing guidelines, and a state-by-state jobs listing. For the name and number of your local chapter, contact:

The Society for Technical Information
901 N. Stuart Street
Arlington, VA 22201
703-522-4114

THE GOING RATE: Varies with the job; full-time technical documentation writers make about $30,000 a year; freelancers bid jobs on either an hourly or per-page basis.

COMMUNITY SPEECHWRITER

Do you have that special talent for expressing yourself? Are you always ready with the right combination of words to express thoughts and feelings in a meaningful fashion? You can cash in on the instinctive fear and distaste that most people have for speaking in public. You can help them gain confidence and assurance by providing a meaningful script that is certain to get positive response from an audience. Become the Village Wordsmith and turn your words into dollars.

You don't have to be a politician to need a speechwriter. Regular folks are routinely called upon to make speeches and presentations at retirement, birthday, and anniversary parties, in addition to other special occasions. Of course, local politicians are always a possibility. If you are familiar with the issues you can be of service in organizing and presenting them properly.

Plan on spending at least half an hour interviewing your client in order to gather material about the subject, since you will need to include anecdotes and details to personalize the speech. Professional interviewers recommend you use a simple tape recorder instead of taking notes, since the tape will help you preserve the style and character of the person involved. Have a list of questions you intend to ask prepared ahead of time, making sure you get anecdotes that tie in to the special event.

Besides a tape recorder, you will also need a word processor or computer and printer. Prepare the final text double or triple spaced so that it is easy to read. Review it with your client and suggest proper delivery and emphasis to instill confidence.

TOP TIP: Be prepared to offer your services free to your first client or two in order to gain experience.

GETTING STARTED: Create a flyer outlining your service. Post it on bulletin boards in local houses of worship, schools, village halls, civic organizations, banquet halls, and the library.

THE GOING RATE: Charge $15 per double-spaced page and $25 per hour for research (if necessary).

DESKTOP PUBLISHER

Desktop publishing actually covers a wide range of editorial and graphic services, such as copywriting, design, proofreading, layout, and logo design. Ten years ago you could set up shop and count on being the only publisher on the block, but today's dropping prices on computers and printers has resulted in a proliferation of publishers trying to sell their services to the same number of clients—and by now those clients may own the equipment themselves.

The only way to set your service apart from the pack is, according to Maryanne Ingratta, whose Ingraphics Desktop Design of Palatine, IL, has been a successful business for over ten years, is to provide creative services along with production services. "You have to run the gamut," she notes, "from technical expertise on the computer to creative artiste at the drawing board." Ingrata's own background is in graphic design, which is something her clients consider when choosing her service. She does many flyers and brochures, but her favorite category of job is newsletters, because they are repeat business.

A desktop publishing business is easy to set up in a home office. Busy designers recommend that you buy the largest monitor you can find—your eyes will appreciate it. You'll also need a hard drive, scanner, laser printer, and two phone lines, one for "live" calls and the other to hook up to your modem/fax/answering machine. If you need a brush-up on your computer skills, contact your local community college. At a bare minimum you'll need to know Pagemaker or Quark Express, Freehand, Illustrator, and Photoshop software packages.

TOP TIP: The best place to find clients is among businesses or people you worked with previously. Send out self-designed "birth announcement" cards to publicize your new business. Take out an ad in the local yellow pages under "Desktop Publishing" and be sure to add specific mentions of the type of work you specialize in, whether it be logos or newsletters or annual reports. Consider donating a freebie flyer to a public venue—such as a special program at the library or annual chamber of commerce banquet—to increase your visibility.

GETTING STARTED: Evaluate your own skills to see if you need additional education, and survey local businesses to make sure there is demand for desktop publishing services in your area. Read the manual *Desktop Publishing Success: How to Start and Run a Desktop Publishing Business* by Felix Kramer and Maggie Lovass (Irwin Professional Publishing, 1991) and consider subscribing to *Publish Magazine* (501 Second Street, Suite 310, San Francisco, CA 94107).

THE GOING RATE: Work is usually quoted on a combination of hours plus materials. Hourly fees usually fall in the $15–$25-a-hour range, depending on complexity. Materials fees of $1 to $2 a page are common for black-and-white master pages, double that for two-color, and $10 a page for full four-color master pages. Even if you figure your fees on a time and materials basis, be prepared to have prospective clients request you to bid on the job as a whole so that they can compare costs.

COLOR SEPARATOR

This can be a wonderful sideline business if you own a computer and such popular desktop publishing and graphics software as Quark Express, Pagemaker, Adobe Illustrator, or Photoshop. You'll also need a color scanner, a color printer, and a fax machine, along with some design experience and technical expertise. You can master these programs by taking a class at a community college, learning through trial and error, or taking a course at Elektek or CompUSA on specific software packages. After you've honed your skills, you can start providing color separation and other graphics services.

In addition to local printers, other possible customers include nearby companies with in-house publications, nonprofit associations, churches, community groups, and anyone who produces color brochures, catalogs, or newsletters. Many of these places will not want to invest in expensive color-processing equipment, so they'll consider farming out their color work. Once you receive a customer's artwork on disk, you can do the separations (usually by using Adobe Photoshop), then send it to a graphics arts service to create the negatives.

TOP TIP: If you have desktop publishing skills and experience, you can also design publications for your customers.

GETTING STARTED: Local print shops are your best bet for customers, since many use outside service bureaus to do their color separations for them. Visit printers in your area, show them some samples of your work, and let them know that you can provide competitive prices and fast turnaround time.

THE GOING RATE: You can charge an hourly rate (around $20 to $25 an hour) or by the job.

INDEXING SERVICE

While there is no stereotypical "indexer personality," David Billick, past president of the American Society of Indexers, notes that most people drawn to indexing have a "passion for detail and a persistent need for coherent structure." Your personal interest and reading tastes might range from romance to military history, but to succeed as a freelancer you'll need the intellectual capacity to grasp a wide range of subjects and properly organize a book's contents into a coherent, detailed index. Most indexers read a lot, and are familiar with and have degrees in an academic discipline; many stray into the profession from related fields such as editing, research, or education. Indexing is probably as close as you can get to being a professional grad student who actually gets paid.

Indexing is truly a solitary, anytime kind of work. It is deadline driven, but within that time frame it doesn't matter if you work at your craft at 2 P.M. or 2 A.M. Clients are usually not put off if the answering machine picks up instead of a person. You don't even need any special equipment to do it, though the overwhelming majority of indexers working today are using computers and a printer because it makes their work easier and produces a better-looking, more professional final product.

What skills make an indexer more marketable? Knowledge of a foreign language and familiarity with the specialized terminology of any of the sciences or professional disciplines are especially valuable assets. (Here's where your hated high school Latin or the summer you spent shuffling papers in a law office can really pay off.) Besides specialized knowledge, good proofreading skills that produce clean final copy and an absolute adherence to deadlines will keep your clients coming back with more work for you.

There are many books available to help you learn how to prepare an index—you'll probably need more than one.

- *Indexing Concepts and Methods* by Harold Borko and Charles L. Bernier (Academic Press, 1978).
- *Indexing Books* by Nancy C. Mulvany (University of Chicago Press, 1994).
- *Indexing from A to Z,* by Hans Wellisch (Bronx, NY: H. W. Wilson Company, 1991).

While indexing is not a licensed profession and formal training is not a requirement, numerous opportunities for professional training exist locally and nationally. Many colleges offer indexing in their extension programs; library science or information science courses are also valuable. For example, the University of Chicago Publishing Program (312-702-1682) offers semester-long and short courses; indexers looking to develop a specialty may also want to take their medical editing course. The Graduate School of the U.S. Department of Agriculture offers two courses through its Correspondence Study Program: Basic Indexing and Applied Indexing (202-720-7123). In addition, off-the-shelf indexing software programs contain their own tutorials.

TOP TIP: Prepare a one-page résumé of your background, areas of knowledge, and specialized indexing education, and include a sample index that you have prepared. Send this to the editorial directors of general, academic, and scientific presses nationwide—indexing is *not* a localized business. Your best sources for lists of publishing houses are *Literary Market Place* (LMP) and *Writer's Market,* both available in public libraries. Magazines, newsletters and journals also hire freelancers to do annual indexes.

GETTING STARTED: "No matter how skilled or experienced you may be, or how impressive your educational background and previous work experience, it's generally hard to get started," warns David Billick. As a novice, be prepared to do your first project for a reduced rate or flat fee: Billick's first indexing project was done for just $100 in order to get some book-indexing experience on his résumé. Join The American Society of

Indexers, Inc. (Box 48267, Seattle, WA 98148; 206-241-9196). Review their publications, and request their book *Starting an Indexing Business*. The national office can provide Recommended Indexing Agreements and put you in touch with your local chapter. They will be the best source for information on local educational resources and prospective clients. Check out their Website at **http://www.well.com/user/asi/.** You can also find work through temporary agencies that staff technical writing and editing positions.

THE GOING RATE: Hourly rates for indexers range from $15 to $40. Some charge by the entry (50 to 70 cents per) or by the page ($2–$4). David Billick uses a combined approach: $25 an hour for the intellectual work of indexing, and then $15 an hour for the mechanical work, such as the inevitable proofreading and corrections. When do you charge at the high end of the scale? According to Billick, when the text demands additional expertise, such as a foreign language or complex technical knowledge. Experienced indexers caution neophytes not to negotiate too hard with publishers regarding fee structure—save the hardball haggling for later in your career, when your reputation is established. In any case, after you have a job from a client set down the rate, deadline, final form, and level of index in a letter of confirmation.

ABSTRACTING SERVICE

If you love to read and have the ability to condense lengthy material into a few concise paragraphs, an abstracting service may be your dream business. But heed this warning—romance readers need not apply, since most of the market for abstracts is in journals, magazines, and newspapers, and nonfiction books.

And make no mistake—that market is growing. By some estimates information is doubling every year, with journals on everything from *Apartment Life* to *Zoology News*. Companies, researchers, and writers do not have the time to wade through this proliferation of magazines, journals, and on-line databases in order to keep current. That's where the abstractor comes in. You read the articles for them and write a short one- or two-paragraph synopsis.

Users generally access abstracts through subscriptions to one of the numerous database publishers. These database publishers are almost as numerous as the magazines they abstract, and often hire freelancers to provide the huge volume of material they need for their subscribers. There is a great variety among the publishers. Some will hire only locally, others specialize in academic or technical databases. The publishers will usually provide you with the journals or magazines to be read and condensed, but you should have your own computer and printer. Payment is made on a per-article basis, not hourly.

TOP TIP: While the need for good abstractors is high, publishers tend to rely on a small group of freelancers they already know, many of whom have worked for them previously. Your best bets for breaking in are persistence, contacting someone already doing abstracting and begging for their overflow work in order to get experience, and having the technical background to handle engineering or chemical or biomedical literature. You can also join the National Federation of Abstracting & Information Services, 1429 Walnut Street, Philadelphia, PA 19102; 215-563-2406. Make sure to request their publication *Abstracting and Indexing Career Guide*.

GETTING STARTED: Your search for database publishers to sell your abstracts to should start in the library. If your local branch doesn't carry *The Index and Abstract Directory* (EBSCO Publishing, Box 1431, Birmingham, AL 35210-1431; 800-825-3024) or some other abstracts service publication, try the closest college library or hunt on-line using the *BiblioData Fulltext Sources Online* (617-444-1154) to find the on-line service address and phone. The research librarian is usually more than willing to help you. Use these industrywide references to familiarize yourself with a target publisher's style and special areas covered, and then write up a few samples yourself. Send these, along with a cover letter explaining your background and any areas of special interest or expertise, to the personnel officer in charge of freelancers. Follow up in a week with a phone call, and don't get discouraged—freelancers have to be able to take rejection.

THE GOING RATE: The range for abstracting an article is usually $5 to $15, depending on length and complexity. Obviously, the more articles you can abstract for more databases, the more money you can make.

MAGAZINE CONTRIBUTOR

Can a reader make money as a writer—even if you don't have much writing talent? You bet. Many magazines have columns made up of reader hints and tips, for which the editors pay good money even though the contributor is not a professional writer. You don't need to have a slick style or new invention to get published—just a good idea. One editor told us that tips that save time or money or show a safer way of doing something are always in demand. For example, recent issues of various home improvement publications included reader-supplied tips on better ways to drill ceramic tile, how to retrofit a garden hose reel as an extension cord winder, and how to square up kitchen cabinets.

If you're handy or creative—or live with someone who is who'll let you pick their brains—you can share your tips and make money.

TOP TIP: Don't even think about sending in previously published material. Nonoriginal ideas are not acceptable to any editor, and if you try to sneak one by you'll ruin your credibility for any future submissions.

GETTING STARTED: Go to your local library and browse through their magazine collection to see which magazines publish reader contributions. Each publication will have its own set of guidelines, so remember to bring a notepad or change for the photocopy machine. You can also look for *Writer's Market* in the reference section for information on magazines your local library doesn't carry.

THE GOING RATE: Payment for reader contributions can range from $25 to $500, depending on the publication. For example, *Better Homes and Gardens* pays $25 for a tip, while *Rodale's American Woodworker* (33 E. Minor Street, Emmaus, PA 18049) pays $50, plus a special $200 for the entry editors decide is the "Best Tip" of the issue.

PROOFREADER

Proofreading is an extremely flexible home-based business that requires no start-up capital or expensive equipment. All you really need is a comfortable chair and desk (even the kitchen table), a good desk lamp, a sharpened pencil, and a strong attention to detail. Owning a home computer would be useful, but is not essential. While some companies are beginning to do all their editing and proofreading on computers, many still proofread by using paper printouts and plenty of red pencils. This is a good job for people who enjoy reading—but don't expect to be proofing thrillers or quality fiction. You'll also need a passion for detail and a burning desire *to get things right*!

Most of the proofreading opportunities you'll find are for associations, technical journals, newspapers, and other publications concerned about accuracy. Your job is to compare an original or edited manuscript to the typeset version to catch any typographical, grammatical, or spelling errors. Proofreaders should own and be thoroughly familiar with the principles of grammar and usage and proofreader's marks as outlined in *The Chicago Manual of Style* as a starting point. Some clients may request that you follow the style book of their particular field or provide you with additional resources to follow a particular house style.

TOP TIP: You can sharpen your skills by volunteering to proofread articles for your local library, school, or nonprofit association's newsletter. Joining the Editorial Freelancers Association (71 W. 23rd Street, Suite 1504, New York, NY 10010) can also help you learn more about the industry.

GETTING STARTED: Once you've gained some experience, prospect for jobs by looking in your telephone book or chamber of commerce business directory for book and magazine publishers, associations, and other companies likely to put out publications. Then call some of those companies, find out the names of their top editors, and ask if they hire freelance proofreaders. You could offer to complete a sample assignment at no charge to demonstrate your skills.

THE GOING RATE: Beginning proofreaders earn about $6 an hour; experienced ones can earn $10 to $25 an hour.

MARKETING AND PUBLICITY SKILLS

Freelance Publicist

Keeping up with a national media list—and keeping your contacts fresh—can be a full-time job. If you want to work part-time in public relations, your best bet is to concentrate on your own community or metropolitan area. That way, you can develop a relationship with a smaller, more manageable group of local media.

Specializing in a particular type of business is a smart way to begin. Retail stores, real estate developers, universities, and hospital and health-care facilities are businesses that often hire outside PR experts to set up events and tell their story. Once you become a specialist, it'll be easier for you to sell stories to national trade magazines that cover that particular business.

You'll need a home office equipped with a telephone (call waiting or a second phone line is essential, as is an answering machine), a computer (for writing news releases and maintaining your mailing list), and a fax machine or fax modem. Access to a photocopier is also important. Previous job experience in public relations is important, as is a polite but persistent telephone manner and the creativity to develop newsworthy angles that will catch journalists' attention.

TOP TIP: Keep up with your media contacts even during periods when you don't have any clients. A birthday or holiday card can go a long way to maintaining goodwill—after all, producers and editors are people too, and appreciate the personal touch. Also, if they remember your name it's easier to get through to them when you *do* have a client to represent.

GETTING STARTED: A great way to get started as a freelancer is to make your former employer your first client. To attract new clients, consider making a special trial offer of your services at a lower salary structure for a limited time period—say three months. If you deliver results, employers are likely to continue to offer you work at a higher hourly rate.

THE GOING RATE: You can charge $25 an hour for this service, plus expenses, in most areas. But you'll need to be adaptable, since each business has its own fee structure and each in-house project has its own budget.

Market Researcher

Here's a great line of work for a sales-type personality who doesn't want to sell. If you are a good communicator, gregarious, and genuinely interested in people but nonjudgmental, market research firms and opinion pollsters may want to add you to their list of independent contractor researchers. Researchers work a specified neighborhood, known as the "sampling area," to gather answers to survey questions prepared by the firm. The surveys themselves and some additional tracking paperwork is then sent back to the company. Payment is usually by the piece rather than by the hour.

Some market research is done totally over the phone, while other firms may want you to go into a mall or even door-to-door in a specific neighborhood. If the project description calls for "field surveying," the work will probably be outside the home. Typical outside sites are malls, bowling alleys, movie theaters, and supermarkets. The work is almost always part-time and on a per-project basis.

To succeed as a market researcher you need to truly like people and have good verbal and written communication skills. According to the National Opinion Research Center of the University of Chicago, which is the oldest research center in the country (founded in 1941), a good interviewer needs to be "people-oriented, an independent worker, outgoing, somewhat aggressive, and able to follow instructions precisely." If you plan on doing fieldwork you'll also need to be able to present yourself in a pleasant, nonthreatening manner, since nowadays many people are wary at the approach of a complete stranger. Researchers who work malls told us that clothing cues are important to breaking down initial fear: wear conservative, casual clothing, display your clipboard, and get some sort of large badge or button that says "SURVEY" or "MARKET RESEARCH" on it.

TOP TIP: You should also consult your local business telephone directory and chamber of commerce to find research firms operating locally—many medium- and large-size cities have firms that do strictly local research for local businesses.

GETTING STARTED: Get your foot in the door with one firm, then use that experience on your résumé to list with several companies as a way of ensuring steady work. If you have absolutely no experience in market research, interviewing, or surveys but possess the interpersonal skills and want to break in, try volunteering your services to a local nonprofit group to get some experience. Then try the big national firms again.

THE GOING RATE: Varies by project, but $10 to $50 is the average range.

Below is a list of some of the better-known national market research and opinion poll firms. Most of them do sampling all over the country, but to work for them you may have to live in or close to one of their specified sampling areas. The usual procedure is to send them your résumé, which should note any previous market research, interviewing, or survey experience (paid or volunteer) that you have. Your résumé will usually be kept on file and you'll get a call when work is available in your area.

Certified Marketing Services
Route 9, Box 447
Kinderhook, NY 12106
(Primarily field surveys; pays by the hour.)

Dale System, Inc.
1101 Stewart Avenue
Garden City, NY 11530
(Field surveys; pays by the survey.)

Far West Research
438 25th Avenue
San Francisco, CA 94121
(Primarily phone interviews on the West Coast; pays by the survey.)

Gallup Poll
47 Hulfish Street, Box 310
Princeton, NJ 08542
(Pays by the hour; uses almost two thousand door-to-door interviewers around the U.S.)

Louis Harris and Associates
630 Fifth Avenue
New York, NY 10020
(Has several hundred sampling areas across the country; pays by the survey.)

Harvey Research Organization
600 Perinton Hills Office Park
Fairport, NY 14450
(Primarily field surveys in major American cities; pays by the survey.)

Information Resources, Inc.
150 N. Clinton
Chicago, IL 60606
(Phone surveys; pays by the project.)

National Opinion Research Center
Social Science Research Center of the University of Chicago
6030 South Ellis Avenue
Chicago, IL 60637
(Needs interviewers for long-term sociology research
projects, by phone and in the field. Provides training and
pays by the hour.)

Simmons Market Research Bureau
380 Madison Avenue
New York, NY 10017
(Primarily field surveys; pays by the survey.)

SECTION 3

PERSONAL
SERVICES

◆

WHAT YOU NEED TO KNOW TO GET STARTED

Health and consulting services currently make up 15 percent of the home-based businesses pie—and that slice is growing, fast! Two factors are contributing to the steadily increasing demand for all sorts of personal services, be it wardrobe consultant, party planner, or personal trainer. The first factor is the increased pace of life for the typical American family: Between work, school, commuting, and children's activities many people don't have the time (or the willpower) to get to the gym, pull together a business wardrobe, or spend weeks researching a new vehicle purchase or family history. And the second factor is the inevitable aging of the baby-boomer generation, whose members are entering their peak earning years and have the income to spend on exactly these types of services necessary to make their harried lives run a little smoother and healthier.

Coupled together, these two factors make a fabulous opportunity for people with specialized knowledge and skills in the area of personal services. But, unlike business service providers who can get a quick jump start in their own businesses by providing services to former employers and colleagues, personal service providers need to devote extra time and energy and to pay particular attention in their plan to who, where, and how they are going to find clients.

Every single person we spoke to with a personal services small business stressed the importance of word of mouth for building business and finding suitable clients. For the small businessperson, there is simply no better, cheaper, or more effective advertising. Word-of-mouth business building actually consists of two parts. The first part is to structure your operation to make sure you have satisfied customers, and the second part is put in place strategies that will encourage these satisfied clients to make referrals to you.

What are the top tips successful personal service providers have for you on keeping your customers satisfied? Of course, everyone tries to provide the highest-quality service possible, but what can you do beyond being a good planner or savvy stock selector? If we had to sum it up in one phrase, it would be to "make the relationship personal, not just the service." That personal touch is what builds trust and confidence. Some of the ways people do this is by keeping a database on all customers, on which they note items such as how many children they have, whether they travel a lot, if they are a film fan, or have a hobby or sport. Before each meeting refer briefly to this file to refresh your memory. After each meeting, update the file. Your clients will be impressed with the impression they made on you—"She remembers so much about me!"

Your database will also come in handy as a mailing list for a quarterly or monthly letter that you send to all your customers. It needn't be as slick as a professional newsletter—standard letter style on your regular stationery will be fine. Keep the length to one side of one 8½-by-11 sheet, so you can fold it in thirds, address the back, and send it as a self-mailer (thereby avoiding additional envelope costs). In a chatty tone update your clients on new equipment or products, upcoming sales, seasonal tips, and current trends in your service area. For example, in a springtime letter personal trainers, masseuses, and wardrobe consultants might remind clients to stock up on sunscreen and summer clothes, referral agencies and professional organizers might offer a spring-cleaning discount, and a genealogist might provide highlights of his spring-break visit to the Ellis Island Immigrant Museum. This letter will keep your name in the front of your clients' mind, and also let them a feel a personal connection to you and your business. This letter is also a great place to announce a pre-release discount price for a new product or service—something available only to current and valued customers.

Once your operation has these structures in place to ensure satisfied customers, what strategies can you employ to encourage referrals? The very first thing you should do is to make better use of something you already have on hand: your business card. Give your client another card every time you see them. If they protest that they already have one, suggest that they take it anyhow and "pass it on to a friend." You can make it worth their while to pass your card on by offering a one-time 5 or 10 percent discount on their next service to anyone who refers a bona fide new customer to you. This reward, or "finder's fee," gives your customers some incentive beyond goodwill to send referrals to you.

HEALTH AND BEAUTY

MASSAGE THERAPIST

This is a rewarding job if you like people and enjoy helping them feel better. Therapeutic massage is designed to relieve muscle tension, headaches, and chronic pain, ease stress, and alleviate such ailments as pulled muscles and tendinitis. Swedish massage is the most widely practiced technique, but you'll have more to offer your clients if you learn a variety of other techniques as well, from Esalen-style massage to Jin Shin Do. Good communication skills, a sense of empathy, and the ability to inspire trust are essential skills for this job. You'll also need to earn a certificate from a massage therapy institute and gain quite a lot of clinical experience before you can hang out your own shingle.

The most important piece of equipment you'll need is a massage table. You can find brochures and catalogs selling massage tables on display at the massage school you attend. Folding massage tables are most useful if you plan to make house calls. You should also buy a lot of sheets and blankets, massage oils and creams, and some relaxing music tapes. If you work out of your home, you must create a quiet, private environment for you clients. A guest bedroom or warm, furnished basement can work well; setting up your massage table in front of the picture window in the living room is not a good idea. If you have children, schedule clients when the kids are at school or hire a baby-sitter to make sure you won't be distracted.

Developing a specialty can be a good way to set yourself apart from your competition. Popular specialties include sports massage, acupressure, and reflexology. Jody Naples, a certified massage therapist, has built a successful practice centered around women's health, and attracts women by offering infant and pregnancy massage, help with stretching exercises, and tips on relaxation and deep breathing. She cautioned, "This is a very physical job. Be careful you don't overdo it by scheduling too many massages in a day. You need to take care of yourself too, since massage therapy takes a lot of physical and emotional energy." When asked how she's found clients, she answered, "Word of mouth is 90 percent of it, and the rest is networking with people. I offer seminars on what massage therapy is and what it can do for you. It's important to educate people when you're massaging them. Tell them what you're finding, what the problem is, and how they can help themselves."

TOP TIP: To gain some experience, practice on family and friends. Then, contact local chiropractors, sports medicine clinics, health clubs, and women's health clinics, since they often hire part-time massage therapists.

GETTING STARTED: Before you do anything else, take courses in fundamental massage techniques, basic anatomy and physiology, kinesiology, and wellness concepts. Look in your phone book for state-certified massage therapy schools, or contact the American Massage Therapy Association (820 Davis Street, Ste. 100, Evanston, IL 60201. Call 1-800-296-0664 for information on becoming certified, or 847-864-0123 to find out more about joining the organization, participating in a local chapter, and receiving its *Massage Therapy Journal*). You can also purchase group liability insurance through the AMTA. Completing your education can take one to two years. Most states do not regulate massage therapists, so certification is a way to set yourself apart from more dubious practitioners of massage in beauty parlors or storefronts.

THE GOING RATE: $25 to $30 for a half hour, $50 for an hour and $75 for ninety-minute massages. Some massage therapists charge more if they have to travel to clients' homes. You can also sell massage gift certificates to your clients.

PERSONAL TRAINER

Personal trainers aren't just for Hollywood stars. They're becoming increasingly popular with regular folks who want to get or stay in shape and need some help achieving their fitness goals. If you're athletically inclined, actually enjoy exercising, and like working with people, this may be just the job for you. Don't come to this cold, though—you'll need to educate yourself in sports medicine (including anatomy and applied kinesiology) and get plenty of hands-on experience working in health clubs or teaching aerobics before you can go into business for yourself. You may also find it useful to read *The Personal Trainer Manual* (Reebok University Press, 529 pages, $38.95) before you begin.

The National Academy of Sports Medicine (Chicago, 312-929-5101), the American College of Sports Medicine (Indianapolis, 317-637-9200), and the American Council on Exercise (San Diego, 800-825-3636 or 619-535-8227) each offer highly regarded training and certification programs. You can also become certified by attending classes held at many YMCAs, park districts, and health clubs, but these courses are usually not as comprehensive. Wherever you get your training, becoming certified shows that you are capable of conducting healthy, safe workouts. And, many insurance companies will only sell that all-important liability insurance to certified instructors.

You may find yourself "making house calls" for some clients and training others in your home. When you travel to others' homes, you'll need to bring along such equipment as dumbbells, exercise bands, tubing, ankle weights, and a step for step aerobics. Your exercise room at home should include a variety of fitness equipment, including an exercise bike, Nordic track, weight stack machine, and rowing machine, since clients will expect access to this equipment. When you see new clients, you'll need to provide an initial fitness assessment to find out their strengths, weaknesses, and medical history. Then, you develop an individualized program based on their needs and goals. You'll teach effective exercise techniques and monitor and record their progress. Some personal trainers also provide nutritional advice. The average client has two one-hour workout sessions a week.

TOP TIP: Deborah Majka, CPFT, came to personal training after twelve years of teaching aerobics in several health clubs. Deborah advised, "I would encourage you to have your clients sign contracts, so you know they'll be coming back. People have a tendency to cancel, which is not good for your business. You could offer them the option of a ten-session or three-month deal."

GETTING STARTED: Word of mouth is most effective, as is placing your business card on local bulletin boards. Many trainers never have to advertise, since they get quite a few referrals from the health clubs where they used to work. Deborah Majka commented, "You should know your stuff. If you're training someone for a triathalon, you should already have trained for a triathalon. You've got to be motivated yourself to motivate others. And try to incorporate as much variety as you can to combat mental and physical boredom."

THE GOING RATE: Between $35 to $70 an hour, depending on whether you have to travel to see your clients and what kind of workout they've requested. If you're asked to conduct a personal aerobics session, that's more physically demanding than monitoring a workout, so the price you charge can be higher. If a client balks at the price, you could offer them the chance to share sessions with a friend for a reduced rate.

LACTATION CONSULTANT

Learning to breast-feed is not an easy task for exhausted mothers of newborn babies. Women who are interested in helping mothers learn to breast-feed can consider becoming lactation consultants. People come to this field from two basic tracks: either as medical professionals (usually delivery room or postpartum nurses) or as La Leche League leaders or volunteers for the Philadelphia-based Nursing Mothers Council.

You'll need several years of experience and training in this field before you can start your own practice. This job requires terrific people skills and sensitivity to babies' cues as well as the ability to communicate well with adults. You'll also need to respond quickly to emergencies—you may be asked to make home visits in the middle of the night if a breast pump is needed, or if breast-feeding is not going well and a baby is at risk of dehydration. You can see clients in your home or come to them—it's most helpful to brand-new mothers if you can help them in their own homes. And, you'll need such equipment as a supply of breast pumps, a baby scale, nursing pillows, and cooler cases for breastmilk, for example.

The Breastfeeding Answer Book by Nancy Mohrbacher and Julie Stock (La Leche League, 1991) is a problem-solving guide used by many consultants. Nancy Mohrbacher gave us this advice: "The most common pitfall I've seen is women who don't take this seriously as a business. Since many women who go into this area are not materialists, they tend to view it as a service to humanity and undervalue their services."

TOP TIP: Nancy Mohrbacher recommends these marketing methods: "Build relationships with lactation consultants in hospitals, since many of your referrals will be through them. Introduce yourself to doctors and get to know La Leche League leaders in your area, since they also are good sources of referrals. Satisifed customers are another great source of new leads."

GETTING STARTED: Gaining accreditation through the International Board of Lactation Consultant Examiners (IBLCE, PO Box 2348, Falls Church, VA 22042; 703-560-7330) will give you a lot of credibility. They offer a certification exam, usually in late July and provide referrals for women seeking consultation and advice. You can take other courses through the UCLA Extension program and Georgetown University. La Leche League International publishes a helpful magazine called *New Beginnings* and offers breast-feeding groups throughout the world. You can call 1-800-LA-LECHE to find out more, or write them at 1400 N. Meacham Road, Schaumburg, IL 60173.

THE GOING RATE: You may provide several different services, from private consultations to renting and selling breast pumps and other nursing supplies. A consultation usually takes between one and two hours, and the fee is anywhere between $40 and $150 a consultation, depending on the location and credentials of the lactation consultant. The average rate for consultations is $50–75 per session. When renting such equipment as electric breast pumps, you can charge around $2.50 per day or $30–$45 a month, in addition to requiring a deposit.

CONSULTING SKILLS AND SPECIALIZED KNOWLEDGE

AU PAIR COMMUNITY COUNSELOR

If you want to experience the world without leaving your neighborhood, become a community-based counselor for an au pair organization. Most parents have heard of au pairs—those young European women who provide live-in child care to American host families. Au pair organizations consider themselves cultural exchange services as much as employment agencies and use local counselors to act as liasons between families, the au pairs, and the au pair organization.

Counselors help families through the selection process, then orient the au pair to the community. They organize monthly outings for au pairs in their area, and make quarterly home follow-up visits to families and their au pairs. They're also asked to market the program to companies and individuals in their area and make occasional on-site presentations.

Counselors' most challenging role is to step in and solve problems when they occur. Strong organizational, communication, and mediation skills are a must, since they need to listen to both sides and help them understand each other's concerns and come to an agreement. If an unresolvable problem arises, the counselor can remove families from the program or place au pairs in a different family.

Laurel Johnson, who worked as an au pair counselor for two years, told us, "It was very interesting meeting girls from different countries and learning more about their cultures. It was nice to be accepted as a professional and feel needed as a problem solver, and I liked that I could do the work at home in about ten hours per week. The only problem was that I was responsible for housing an au pair temporarily if I couldn't find another home for her!" Laurel found her job through an ad for AuPairCare in her metropolitan newspaper.

TOP TIP: Publicize your au pair services at local community fairs, business showcases, and to local newspapers.

GETTING STARTED: Contact AuPairCare at their international headquarters: One Post Street, 7th Floor, San Francisco, CA 94104 or call 1-800-4AU-PAIR. A similar organization, AuPair in America, can be reached at 1-800-928-7247.

THE GOING RATE: $45 per month per family in your region. (One counselor is usually assigned between seven and twelve local families.)

WARDROBE OR IMAGE CONSULTANT

Today's competitive job market has made professional image increasingly important for people who'd like to get ahead in their careers (or simply hang on to the jobs they already have). If you have a flair for fashion and a background in retail sales, you could become a wardrobe consultant. Wardrobe consultants help other people find clothes that fit well, look good on them, and help them present a positive image. Your best clients will be professionals who hate to shop, have no time to scour the stores for the right clothes, or are anxious about shopping and afraid of buying the wrong things. This latter group may have a closet full of out-moded fashions and impulse buys, and need guidance in choosing more flattering clothes. Some image consultants also branch out into advising clients on their best colors, makeup and hairstyles, while wardrobe consultants stick with clothes.

As a wardrobe consultant, you would help clients evaluate their needs and their current wardrobe, and then offer your services as a personal shopper. You'll put in the time shopping at a variety of stores looking for classic clothes in your client's size, and then assemble a collection of coordinating outfits and accessories in a dressing room. Your clients can show up only for the fitting stage. Kathryn Roth started her business, Chicago Wardrobe Consultants, after spending ten years selling women's designer clothes in an upscale department store. After she had her second child, she decided she wanted to work flexible hours by setting up her own consulting business. Kathryn always sets up a lunch meeting with prospective clients. The first question she asks is, "What is your lifestyle, and what kind of image do you want to project?" Most of her clients are midlevel executives (both men and women) who want to take the next step on the corporate ladder. She also has quite a few clients who are looking for attractive casual and evening clothes, or want to look good when it's their turn to drive the carpool.

Many people hire a wardrobe consultant to help them build a whole new wardrobe. Others plan to add clothes to their existing wardrobes. They would like the consultant to come to their homes, look through their closets, and help them decide which clothes and accessories are keepers and which are hopeless. Kathryn is surprised how many people tend to buy clothes that don't fit correctly. She usually sorts their wardrobe into three piles: to be donated to a charity, to be taken to the tailor for alterations, and to go back in the closet. Then she asks clients how much they're comfortable spending on shirts or blouses, suits, shoes, and so on. After that, she goes into her personal shopper mode and helps find clothes that are timeless, well made, and well suited to the person she's shopping for.

TOP TIP: Skip the expensive newspaper display ads and spend your money on bold listings in the yellow pages under "Clothing" or "Fashion." They're much more cost-effective in bringing in new customers.

GETTING STARTED: The best way to begin is to start slow. Taking a job selling clothes in a department store, men's clothing store, or women's boutique will give you invaluable experience in matching clothes to individuals and in putting complete outfits together. If you're talented at this, you'll find that you will attract repeat customers who trust your recommendations. You should wait to set up your own business until you have a track record of pleasing shoppers in a retail setting. Taking fashion classes and art classes focusing on colors can also help you prepare for setting up your business. You can join The Association of Image Consultants International (1000 Connecticut Avenue NW, Suite 9, Washington, DC 20036; 301-371-9021; 800-383-8831) to meet others in the field and to receive *Fashion News and Views* magazine. Most of your clients will come through word of mouth and a listing in the telephone book. You can promote your services by giving talks to women's groups, clubs, service organizations, and at public libraries.

Giving corporate seminars on image and employee presentations is another way to expand your business. A recent survey has found that 42 percent of office workers are now permitted to wear casual clothes once a week, up from 17 percent in 1992. The advent of "casual Fridays" in the workplace has been a godsend for the image business, since so many employees have no clue about what to wear. Personnel directors are interested in presentations that tactfully give employees and new hires directions on what's appropriate to wear to work.

THE GOING RATE: You can charge between $25 and $150 an hour, depending on your level of experience. You'll probably spend an average of ten hours with each client. This includes the initial consultation, time you spend shopping on your own, helping your client try on and fit the clothes you've selected, and a follow-up call to make sure your client is satisfied.

GENEALOGIST

Genealogy is an ideal home-based business if you enjoy doing research and would like to help others track down information about their ancestors. To succeed, you should be a careful, accurate researcher, and—most importantly—know your sources. You'll need an in-depth knowledge of the records at your county courthouse, local genealogical libraries, and nearby branches of the National Archives and LDS (Church of Latter Day Saints) archives. You'll find these reference books particularly helpful in pointing you toward the best sources: *The Source: A Guidebook of American Genealogy* by Arlene H. Eakle and Johni Cerni (Ancestry, 1984), and *Cite Your Sources*, edited by Richard S. Lackey (University Press of Mississippi, 1985). After you've developed a solid grounding in the basics, it's a good idea to expand your services by finding a specialty. It makes sense to specialize in your state or region if you don't want to travel too widely. Other genealogists focus on the Civil War, Native Americans, or European ancestors. Choose your specialty based on your interests and the resources available in your area.

A computer is a must for entering your research information and putting out polished-looking reports. Computers have also speeded up the process of genealogical searches enormously. You can now buy CDs containing thousands of government records and software programs that allow you to quickly construct a family tree—and you can learn about other genealogists' research by going on-line. You may find that a laptop computer is a good investment, since it'll enable you to enter your findings while you're researching instead of having to write them down, then type them up at home. A basic photocopier will also come in handy. You'll need a car to travel to local courthouses and libraries. Buying a microfilm reader is optional, since most of the libraries you'll be researching at will have microfilm readers you can use for free.

"Every time *Roots* comes on TV, I get swamped," said one Certified Genealogist we interviewed. He advised, "Hang in there. It can take several years to build up your business, so you'll need another income during that time. But it's hard to do this part-time on evenings or weekends because most courthouses are only open from nine to four Mondays through Fridays." This genealogist's most important billing tip: "It's best to ask clients to set the amount they want to spend before you begin, then get something in writing. This protects them and you."

Other genealogical services you can offer include these creative ways to expand your business: writing a family narrative in verse or prose; offering workshops in autobiographical writing and family history; finding missing relatives, lost loves, old friends, and birth children or birth parents; preparing family medical histories; translating European records from their original language; and taking photos on location of clients' ancestral villages in Europe.

TOP TIP: You'll find clients through referrals from libraries, genealogical societies, courthouses, and prior clients. If you're comfortable with public speaking, giving talks to local organizations is the best way to get your name out. You can also publicize your services on such on-line bulletin boards as America Online's Genealogical Forum and the Genealogy BBS in Atlanta (404-949-0643). Joining local genealogical and historical societies in your area is also smart, since they're more apt to refer people to you if you're a member.

GETTING STARTED: Take as many classes and workshops as you can at local community colleges and genealogical societies. Or take the correspondence course from Brigham Young University (contact Brigham Young University, Independent Study, 206 Harmon Bldg., PO Box 21415, Provo, UT 84602; 801-378-2868). Then, volunteer to research friends' and neighbors' family trees. Once you've gained some solid experience, work toward becoming a Certified Genealogical Records Specialist (write the Board for Certification of Genealogists, PO Box 5816, Falmouth, VA 22403). You could also join the Association of Professional Genealogists and the National Genealogical Society to stay connected with others in the field. The most popular magazines are *The Genealogical Helper* (Box 368, Logan, UT 84323), *Heritage Quest* (Box 329, Bountiful, UT 84011), and *Ancestry* (Box 486, Salt Lake City, UT 84110). In addition to offering helpful articles, these magazines are excellent publicity and advertising sources for you.

THE GOING RATE: $15 to 20 an hour for archival research plus expenses (including photocopying, microfilm rentals and parking), and thirty cents a mile for your travel costs. Do charge a deposit (of $50 to $200, depending on the size of the search you're undertaking) to cover your initial costs. If you do field research and travel to the county where a client's ancestors lived, you can charge around $150 a day plus $50 for expenses. Some genealogists also provide photographs or videotapes of local landmarks and birthplaces for an additional fee.

CAR BUYER'S CONSULTANT

Shopping for new cars is a dreaded ordeal for most people—they're afraid they'll be taken for a ride by smooth-talking salespeople. So, it should come as no surprise that, according to a J. D. Powers and Associates study, more than 1.7 million Americans go to "buying agents" to purchase new cars every year. If you're knowledgeable about cars and comfortable with negotiating with car dealers, you can take the pain and strain out of new-car buying for your clients. As a car buyer's consultant, you first sit down with the customer and find out what he or she really wants: two-door or four-door, American, Japanese, or European, sporty or sensible, pricey or economical. You also need to talk about whether a trade-in is involved, where to go for loans, the cost of insurance for specific models, and which dealer incentives and discounts are currently on offer.

After narrowing the choices down to a few models, you call up several dealerships to find out who is willing to give the best deal on those particular cars—and who will offer the most for a trade-in. You'll need to read the automotive section of your local newspaper every day and subscribe to the *National Auto Research Black Book* (PO Box 758, Gainesville, GA 30503-0758), the same book the dealers use, to know the current invoice prices of each car on the market.

Bruce Fisher, a former car salesman, meets potential customers for lunch to discuss their car needs and budget. "People are usually unrealistic—they want Cadillacs for the price of a Chevette. I have to wake them up to what cars cost today," he said. After he makes several phone calls and determines the best deal, he sets up an appointment at the dealership for the customer. He told us, "All the customer has to do is show up, sign the papers, and drive the car home. It takes about an hour." The hardest part of the process is selling used cars as trade-ins to a dealership—you'll need to shop the car around to two or three different dealers in order to get the best price.

TOP TIP: This is most important—get paid up front before you have your consultation. If you're not paid first, customers could take all of your advice and go off and make the deal on their own.

GETTING STARTED: You'll need an in-depth knowledge of cars, negotiating skills, and the ability to sell your service to others. It also helps to know the managers of several different dealerships. Printing up five hundred business cards and handing them out liberally to family and friends and displaying them on local bulletin boards is often enough to bring in some business. Word of mouth is most effective—one happy customer can bring in several more.

THE GOING RATE: Anywhere from $150 to $500 for the entire process, including the original consultation with the customer, closing the deal, and sitting in on the final signing of papers.

House Childproofer

There's nothing more important to parents than their children's health and safety. New parents are particularly anxious about protecting their babies. They're aware that the average home is full of potential dangers to young children: open outlet covers, unprotected stairways, cupboards filled with cleaning supplies, and other lurking hazards. You can provide a service to the community if you start your own childproofing business. Childproofing businesses help educate parents by showing them the potential dangers that exist within their homes and then installing safety products to correct those problems.

This is a fast-growing field. Ten years ago there were only 50 childproofing firms in America, and now there are closer to 350. Since there aren't any official training programs in childproofing, most of the knowledge in this field comes from personal experience. If you're a parent and remember how much trouble a curious baby or determined toddler can get into, you'll have insight into the safety measures that need to be taken before accidents occur. Reading such parenting experts as Dr. Penelope Leach and Dr. Spock can also give you advice on what to look out for when childproofing a home.

When prospective customers call you, the first step is to set up an appointment to walk through their home and point out things that could injure their children. Special attention is paid to the kitchen and bathrooms, since that's where children frequently get hurt. Look around from a child's-eye view: Are there miniblind cords hanging down that could strangle a child, flimsy shelves that could fall on them, or medicine bottles and other poisons within reach? Most childproofing firms offer this initial home-safety evaluation for free. After the walk-through demonstration, parents can decide to install the safety measures you recommend themselves, if they're handy and have the time. If not, they may hire you to provide and install the safety devices on a separate visit. Most of your initial visits will be during evenings and weekends, since that's when parents are most likely to be available. Installation can take place during the day or evening, since it's not as critical that parents be there for that stage.

This business may take several years to develop. Before he started A & H Childproofers, Arvey Levinsohn had been informally childproofing friends' and neighbors' homes. "After a while, I woke up and said, gee, this is a business," he told us. "I run this business from the heart, because I want to prevent injuries to children. Thirteen million children a year get injured, and most of it is needless. My business is built on my doing it right. I don't rush, and I don't try to do ten homes in one day. I do everything myself, and don't hire other laborers. I have nineteen years' experience doing this, and have built a wonderful following of people. Seventy percent of my business comes from referrals from parents in playgroups, neighborhoods, and church groups." Arvey finds the work very satisfying. "The only downside of what I do is that I hear a lot of horror stories," he said. "I often get calls after the fact, when parents are on their way home from the hospital. That's when many people make up their minds to childproof their homes."

TOP TIP: Sell gift certificates for your services, and market them as ideal new-baby gifts.

GETTING STARTED: Before you set up your company, do some research on manufacturers of the best-quality safety equipment and set up accounts with them. You'll also need to acquire some tools for installing the safety devices. Then, volunteer your services to friends, colleagues, and neighbors to gain practice in spotting safety issues and installing solutions. Placing an ad in a local parenting newspaper and putting up notices or brochures at schools, libraries, pediatricians' offices, health-care centers, and community notice boards will help spread the word about your business. Taking out a listing in your phone book is also an effective way to reach new customers. Professionals and two-income couples are most likely to use your services. They're concerned about providing a safe environment for their children, but don't have much time to figure out what's needed and to install the products—and they're willing to pay someone else to do it for them.

THE GOING RATE: Pricing is based on how many safety devices you're asked to install. One customer may request only a few cabinet locks and a toilet lock, while another may want you to install $1,000 worth of Plexiglas around stair railings. Childproofing the average home costs between $180 and $220, which includes several outlet covers, baby gates, and cabinet locks. Owners of larger homes may run up charges in the $500 to $700 range.

INVESTMENT CLUB

"It doesn't take an investment genius to beat professional investors and mutual fund managers," maintains financial writer John Wasik. Instead, success comes with diligence, and all across America ordinary people are forming investment clubs. Pooling their money and their knowledge, and starting out with as little as $10 a month and a few hours of research, these clubs can build lucrative stock portfolios using simple investment rules.

For example, one member of the Mutual Investment Club of Detroit began investing $10 a month in 1940. Eventually he increased the amount to $20. From 1940 to the 1990s his total worth of shares grew to over $500,000 based upon an out-of-pocket investment of less than $10,000!

What's the key to a successful investment club? According to Wasik, author of *The Investment Club Book* (Warner Books, 1995), successful clubs have these three characteristics in common:

1. They save and invest over long periods of time using dollar cost averaging so that all their money doesn't come into the market at one time. They are not looking to "make a killing."
2. They do their research and reinvest dividends and gains to compound wealth over time.
3. Members pool their knowledge and invest in conservative stocks that are likely to grow over time. Pooling money with others also lowers each individual's risk.

Several organizations can refer you to an existing club or help you form one of your own (see below). While membership in clubs is about evenly split between men and women, for some reason clubs consisting of all women outperform clubs consisting of only male members. But, according to the NAIC, co-ed clubs do the best, outperforming both the all-male and all-female groupings. So, when you go looking for members, don't limit yourself!

Likely members can be found at work, in your neighborhood, any fraternal clubs you belong to, or your church or temple. Many clubs get their start in families. Even in a family, however, Wasik recommends a formal partnership agreement to cover such issues as operating procedures, research responsibilities (each individual is usually responsible for researching and tracking only one or two companies), how much each member will invest each month, how to withdraw money, and what happens if a member leaves the club or dies. You will also need to set up a separate bank account to hold and transfer funds and set up a relationship with a stockbroker or direct buying plan.

Perhaps the best part of participating in an investment club is that, once the membership and accounts are set up, you can do all of your work and research at home with the help of a few magazine subscriptions or one night a week at the local library. Must-read publications include *Forbes* (60 Fifth Avenue, New York, NY 10011) and *Business Week* (1221 Avenue of the Americas, 39th Floor, New York, NY 10020) for corporate profiles and industry trends; *Morningstar* (225 W. Wacker Drive, Suite 400,

Chicago, IL 60606) and *Money* (1271 Avenue of the Americas, New York, NY 10020) for mutual fund ratings; and *Barron's* and *The Wall Street Journal* (both at 200 Liberty Street, New York, NY 10281) for investment and business news with complete coverage in every market. Besides trends and profiles, you also use these publications to target companies whose annual reports you decide to request for further analysis.

TOP TIP: Be prepared to be in the club for the long haul. The average investment club member has been investing for over twenty years, for an average return of over 13 percent a year.

GETTING STARTED: Read *The Investment Club Book* and then contact these organizations for help in setting up a club and building a portfolio:

- ◆ American Association of Individual Investors, 625 N. Michigan Ave., Chicago, IL 60611; 312-280-0170. Members have over fifty local chapters, publications on dividend reinvestment programs and low-load mutual funds, and a magazine, all of which are a great help in researching companies. They also offer a home study course and periodic seminars.

- ◆ National Association of Investors Corporation, 711 W. 13 Mile Road, Madison Heights, MI 48071; 810-583-6242. This organization has over ten thousand clubs and regional councils. Education is the main focus and provides an investment advisory service that has beaten the Dow Jones Industrial Average twenty-five times over the past thirty-six years. Perhaps the most valuable publication is their *Investor's Manual,* which explains the fundamentals of stock picking.

THE GOING RATE: Unlimited, but the average NAIC club portfolio is worth about $90,000. The famous Beardstown Ladies' Club, based in Peoria, IL, has an average annual return of 23.4 percent in ten years of investing.

College Application/ Financial Aid Planning Consultant

This is a noble calling for anyone who understands the intricacies involved in applying for college and would like to help guide parents and their children through the process. This business involves advising parents and high school students on selecting a college, filling out the application and financial aid forms, and negotiating the best possible financial aid package when a college offer is received. To be qualified for this job, you'll need to be knowledgeable about higher education institutions and have a thorough understanding of the traditional financial aid options through universities, government loans, and scholarships. You'll also need strong communication skills in order to discuss planning strategies with your clients and clearly explain what they need to do to increase their chances of acceptance and receiving financial aid.

Depending on when they get involved in the process, college consultants offer a variety of services that can range from helping clients study for the SAT or ACT exams, suggesting appropriate colleges, helping to fill out the application, and giving advice and even editorial assistance on the essay component. Consultants also endeavor to keep kids on track through the entire application process, making sure they meet deadlines, pay appropriate fees, and fill out the proper forms.

Your job is to help parents get the absolutely lowest possible price for a college education. Steven H. Williams started his home-based business, Strategies for Higher Education, after having been disillusioned about his own college aid experiences. He knew little about financial-aid planning when he applied to college and felt misled by the advice he received from high school counselors and his college advisers. He was snowed under by student loans after he graduated, and decided that he wanted to spare other people what he had gone through.

Steven told us, "The congressionally approved financial aid system has a tremendous number of pitfalls and potholes parents can fall into. I fill out all the financial aid application forms for my clients. They look simple, but they're not. Making a few common mistakes can sabotage any chance of getting financial aid. . . . I call myself a 'professional nag' because I keep calling my clients and reminding them of deadlines and decisions that they need to make. I also make sure their college selections make sense, both for the kid and for the parents' pocketbook."

TOP TIP: The best way to market your services is to offer free seminars on college application and finanical aid planning at libraries, banks, community centers, and other public meeting places. The most successful seminars are often at libraries, especially when the library publicizes your talk in their community newsletter. Putting a small ad in the newspaper and posting notices at local high schools can help bring out a wide audience for your seminars. Steve found that he was able to generate a lot of good leads by taking out a newspaper ad offering a free report he wrote on the secrets of college financial planning. Steve only knows one other consultant who has a similar business, so this is a good niche business if you have the right skills and knowledge.

GETTING STARTED: Learn everything you can about the financial aid system and how it actually works. You'll need to know a number of colleges' requirements for granting aid, the deadlines for filing applications, and the loopholes that can help your clients get a better chance at receiving a generous financial aid package. The Department of Education will send you free information on college loans if you write and request it, or visit their website at **www.ed.gov** or call 1-800-4-FEDAID, which will fill you in on all the important details. If you also plan to advise parents and high school students on college selection, you'll need to know the strengths and weaknesses of the colleges in your area (and top universities elsewhere). You can learn more about U.S.

colleges and universities by reading the well-regarded *Peterson's Guides*, talking with students who are attending different universities, and by sifting through the colleges' Websites on the Internet.

THE GOING RATE: You can charge between $295 and $995 as a college planning consultant. Your rate will vary according to how many application forms you fill out and whether you also help advise the family on finances alone or also on selecting a college. The whole process can take from two to eighteen months, depending on when parents seek your involvement.

MUSIC TRANSCRIPTION SERVICE

New computer technology has given music lovers another outlet for their creativity. With the right computer and software, musicians can now compose music on their PCs and then transcribe it into printed sheet music. If you discover you're not another Lennon or McCartney, you can still help other people who are prolific songwriters. You'll need an electronic/synthesizer keyboard with MIDI interface (keyboards cost $400 or more), a software program like SongWright (available for IBM compatibles from Michael Hulett, Loudoun Street SE, Leesburg, VA 22075; 703-777-7232), and a computer equipped with a MIDI translator. Other music notation programs include Overture and Songworks, both available through most software stores and direct mail catalogs.

Once you have this equipment, you can offer your transcription services to local folk or rock groups or singer/songwriters who create their own songs but don't know how to write music. You can put their songs together into a printed songbook, including lyrics, which gives them something to sell after their performances. Musicians who are too busy performing to spend time laboriously transcribing their music by hand may also be interested in this service. You'll need an audiotape of the musician's songs and a written copy of all the lyrics. When you plug your keyboard into your computer and play the tune, the software will enter the notes onto staffs on the screen. Then, you can go back and make sure the tempo, key, and notation are true to the original song.

Once you're done, you can give your client a printed copy of all the songs. Then the client can take the originals to a printer to have songbooks put together—or you can provide this service, as well, if you have desktop publishing skills.

TOP TIP: You can also use a word-processing or desktop publishing computer program to create templates for cassette labels and sell them to musicians who've recorded their own audiotapes.

GETTING STARTED: Go to all the folk coffeehouses you can and put up a sign or business card advertising your services. You may also find clients by putting up notices on such on-line services as CompuServe and America Online, or by contacting local guitar shops and music teachers. Have a sample of sheet music and a songbook that you produced ready to show potential clients.

THE GOING RATE: Charge up to $100 for every song you transcribe, or set a flat rate for a group of songs.

ORGANIZATIONAL SKILLS

PARTY PLANNER

Planning and running a children's birthday party usually ranks just below public speaking, death, and taxes on harried parents' anxiety lists. You can help relieve their anxiety (and earn some money in the process) by starting a birthday-party entertainment business.

This has great potential as a growth business due to the increase of working parents, since fewer people have time to organize birthday parties on their own. You can position your parties as an appealing alternative to Chuck E. Cheese or Discovery Zone parties. An at-home party can offer more "quality time" for the children, while you help the parents by taking charge of games, setup, and snacks. You'll need to invest in basic party materials such as paper plates and table decorations, props for games, a small china tea set for tea parties, party-planning books, and craft supplies.

Cathy McDonough started My House Hospitality Co. with a friend, Vicki Kilbane, after noticing how many of her friends dreaded being in charge of birthday parties. She and her partner offer a comprehensive party package: They bring tables and chairs, a floral centerpiece, a variety of crafts and games that go along with the party's theme, music audiotapes, and food and drinks (but not the cake or invitations). Some of the most popular theme parties they offer are carnivals and tea parties (which include a "tea bag" bean bag toss). Each party can include a craft, such as making a hat, a doll, or a windsock—parents can choose which one they prefer. Other party specialists offer parties with a collection of wild animals (iguanas, snakes, and hedgehogs are popular), or science parties that include such entertaining experiments as playing with goop or making a volcano.

TOP TIP: You can expand your business by representing local clowns, jugglers, storytellers, and magicians, and receiving a commission each time you book them as entertainers for one of the parties you've planned. Or, you can sell special goodie bags and craft supplies for parents who would like to run their own parties. Taking a booth at craft shows can be a good way to showcase your creative ideas and sell birthday party supplies.

GETTING STARTED: First, develop experience in party planning, whether it's for your own children or for your local 4-H club, gymnastics center, or Brownie or Cub Scout troops. Then publicize your business through putting up notices on local bulletin boards, taking an ad in your metropolitan area newspaper, and developing good word of mouth. Free parenting newspapers—found in most large cities—are also excellent sources of advertising and publicity.

THE GOING RATE: $95 to $220 (depending on the region you live in) for planning and running a two-hour party. More than eight children can lead to chaos, so try to limit the number of children attending.

WEDDING COORDINATOR

Do you love parties and enjoy organizing all the little details that make a party a success? Then you may be ready to tackle the ultimate challenge for party planners: planning an elegant, memorable, smoothly run wedding. This service is especially in demand by employed women who don't have the time to scout out reception sites or make dozens of follow-up calls to make sure everything's proceeding on schedule.

You may be asked to put together an entire wedding, including finding dresses for the bride, her mother, and her bridesmaids, ordering invitations, choosing a band and DJ, picking a photographer, and finding the perfect wedding cake. You may even be asked to create custom invitations and custom favors, or find someone to write a song to celebrate the event. To book the best locations and better bands and orchestras, you'll need to start planning one to two years in advance of the wedding date. Or, you may be hired simply to attend the wedding and reception and make sure that the right wine is being served, the band is playing the right songs, and that the cake is cut at the right time. This more limited on-site service is for families who would like to save money by planning their own wedding, but want to have someone on hand during the wedding day to handle any problems that might arise, so they can relax and enjoy themselves.

Since there are often last-minute crises in the wedding business, you need to have strong problem-solving skills and be able to keep your head when things go wrong. You might have to cope with a fire at the reception site a few days before a wedding, a florist that doesn't show, or a bridesmaid who badly rips her dress right before she's supposed to walk down the aisle. For that reason, have backup plans ready, whether it's equipping yourself with a sewing kit to make emergency dress repairs or keeping a list of alternate reception sites and flower shops. It's important to be resourceful and quick on your feet and head off potential problems before they occur. That's what you're getting paid for, after all.

TOP TIP: Publicize your business through bridal shops, florists, photographers, and others providing wedding services, and advertise in local newspapers and in the phone book. You can also go after related business by publicizing your ability to plan any kind of party, from anniversary and retirement parties to graduation parties, reunions, and large corporate functions.

GETTING STARTED: You'll need experience in planning parties, whether it's office receptions or private dinner parties, and excellent organizational skills. You should be familiar with a wide range of caterers, cake bakers, florists, bands, and printers. When you attend weddings and catered parties, pay attention, and start making a list of chefs, reception halls, and photographers you can recommend to your clients. Also, consider joining the Association of Bridal Consultants (200 Chestnutland Road, New Milford, CT 06776; 203-355-0464) for up-to-date information on the industry and referrals.

THE GOING RATE: A wedding consultant usually charges a fee of 10 to 15 percent of the total cost of the wedding package she plans, with a 50 percent deposit up front. Some coordinators don't charge their clients anything but receive a commission from the people they recommend. This method means that they are not disinterested, though, and may end up recommending a mediocre DJ because he gives them a hefty payment for referring him. If you are simply hired to oversee all the details on the wedding day itself, you can charge $100 an hour for your services.

Professional Organizer

Here's another way you can profit from your organizational skills: become a professional organizer or "clean desk consultant." Some people are natural-born organizers. They have their lives plotted out months in advance, carry color-coded personal organizers with them, have a place for everything and everything in its place, and feel the urge to turn chaos into order. If you fit this description, you can use this skill to help more disorganized types take control of their messy rooms and of their lives. Professional organizers go into people's homes or offices and show them how to sort through their accumulated debris and decide which items are worth keeping. Then, they set up a filing system and persuade clients to dump or recycle papers and objects that are no longer needed.

This can be a big job, since people generally don't call a professional organizer until their accumulations have snowballed and they can no longer find their floors or desktop. "I walked into a home recently," the owner of an organizing company told a reporter, "and shoes, boots, and coats were all over the living room. What's in the coat closet? Blankets and sheets. What's in the linen closet? Newspapers and boxes of old records." To sort out this kind of problem, you need to be able to patiently go through each item, find a place for it, and teach your customers how to avoid such messes in the future. (Parents could be particularly good at this job, having lots of experience in encouraging children to clean their rooms.)

TOP TIP: Take out a yellow pages listing and advertise in local papers and local business publications. Offering gift certificates and marketing them for birthdays, graduations, promotions, or Mother's or Father's Day can be a good way to call attention to your business. Developing an eye-catching flyer or business card would also be helpful, since you can hand them out at local office buildings and community centers. Since most people never seem to have enough time these days, mention in your flyers and ads that you can save customers' time by helping them manage their homes and offices more efficiently. As another organizer commented, "If you can't find things, if you aren't organized, it ends up costing you time."

GETTING STARTED: Before you begin your business, contact the National Association of Professional Organizers (1033 La Posada Drive, Suite 200, Austin, TX 78752; 512-454-8626) which boasts around eight hundred members. Call their information and referral hot line at 1-512-206-0151 and request a membership packet. NAPO supports its members by giving them the names of people in their area who are looking for a professional organizer, so make sure you get on their referral list.

THE GOING RATE: You can charge $40 to $65 an hour for your services if you specialize in organizing people's homes. Organizers who go to corporate clients' offices tend to charge higher fees, sometimes as much as $450 for a half day or $900 for a full day's work.

REFERRAL AGENCY

What don't we use referral services for? Plumbers, maids, child care, dentists, shopping and errands, elder care, home health care—you name the service and there's a niche for a referral agency to find a reliable practitioner for it.

And the need for such agencies is growing. Most people these days don't have the time to look up, call, and interview three or four plumbers, carpenters, or baby-sitters when they need someone. With tight work schedules and mobile transplanted executives, new folks in town may not know enough neighbors to get a "word of mouth" over the backyard fence. Hence, the need for referral agencies that maintain lists of reliable professionals for home-care needs.

You don't need a background in personnel to run a referral agency, but you do need good interviewing skills to build your stable of referable professionals and good communication skills to service your clients. A peppy, slightly aggressive but positive personality is ideal. Some background in your target area also goes a long way toward establishing credibility; thus, a teacher running a tutoring or baby-sitting referral service sounds more credible to potential clients than a car mechanic trying his hand at the same service.

Your agency can collect fees from your clients, from the referees you list, or from both. You can specialize in one type of service—such as child care—or offer a broad selection. While it's possible to start out with nothing but your home phone and a Rolodex well stocked with business cards, successful referral agencies eventually have to budget for a computer to handle the database, mailing lists, and billings, in addition to a second phone line with voice mail to make sure you don't miss any calls.

The Chore Store Inc., of Atlanta, founded in 1992 by Bonnie Barton and Peatsa C. Wallace, lists over fifty service areas, including chimney sweeps, contractors, and exterminators. The Chore Store uses the dual approach to fee collection: Clients pay an annual "membership" fee that allows them to use the agency as often as they wish. Professionals who wish to be listed with the Chore Store must first pay an application fee and then pass a background check. If they pass and get on the approved referral list, then they also pay back a percentage (typically a 10 percent finder's fee) of any jobs they get through the agency.

The Chore Store is successful, but Wallace told interviewers that they spent way too much in start-up costs due to a wildly expensive advertising campaign in which they mailed out slick, professionally designed brochures to fifty-five thousand local homes. This direct mail campaign cost them almost $100,000, even though their base start-up costs for equipment, software, and inexpensive advertising only came to a more modest $15,000.

While their start-up was expensive, Wallace maintains that it was a strategic move for them: "Because of the bad credibility image that the home improvement business has, we purposely wanted a very corporate, credible, reliable image in all of our advertising materials. We were a start-up, but we didn't want to look like a start-up. And our strategy worked—we projected the right image."

The Chore Store has been so successful that Wallace and Barton now also provide Business To Grow: Home Service Referral Business, a "business-in-a-box" kit for others interested in starting a home service referral company. The kit includes a manual, all documents, and software. This is not a franchise—there is no licensing fee. For information and costs, write to the Chore Store at 280 Elizabeth St., Suite A-114, Atlanta, GA 30307.

At the other end of the spectrum from the Chore Store is the small specialty agency, such as the specialty pet matchmaker referral service run by an Illinois woman. Here are some of the questions she might get asked by clients: What's the best dog for a small apartment? My husband has allergies—is it true poodles hardly shed and are well tolerated by people who otherwise couldn't have a pet? Is there a breed that's safe to have around young children? There are other animals in my house—which breed would integrate best into my menagerie? My great-aunt needs a companion animal, but she's not mobile enough to give it a lot of exercise—should she get a dog or cat or bird?

Enter the dog referral service. People are quite used to using referral services for everything from nannies to plumbers, and expert knowledge in the dog-breeding field can easily be turned into a moneymaking referral service that matches the appropriate breed to the right family.

Most people are attracted to a certain breed of dog because they think it's attractive, or because the neighbor down the street had one when they were a kid. But there are over two hundred breeds of dog recognized by the American Kennel Club, and animal personalities can vary greatly from breed to breed (and even bloodlines within the breed). The wrong choice can make for a disastrous relationship if your dog's personality doesn't fit your family's lifestyle.

A pet matchmaker not only needs extensive knowledge of animal breeding and temperament but good people communication skills, too. A prepurchase recommendation interview with the clients, either over the phone or in their home or via a letter, is essential to establish their lifestyle and home atmosphere. You should also have knowledge of local breeders within a three-hour commute from your home base town (most clients don't want to travel further than three hours).

While most of your work can be done in a home office and via the phone and mail, you should have a computer to keep up your cross-referenced databank of clients and breeders. Be prepared to make site visits to the breeders to check out their facilities, and keep up with the local dog and cat shows to get an idea of what the current popular breeds are and meet new breeders and handlers.

TOP TIP: Find new customers on the local level through ads in community newspapers. Don't overspend on direct mail advertising.

GETTING STARTED: Decide whether you are going to be a general services agency or specialize. Develop a thorough background check process, including credit checks, customer complaints, and litigation checks. Make site visits and compile a database before you advertise for clients.

THE GOING RATE: Depends on how many sources you get income from: clients, referees, or both. Many referral agencies charge $30 to $50 to the client and request a 10 percent finder's fee from the provider. The Chore Store charges a $50 membership fee, a $50 application fee, and a 10 percent finder's fee. In 1995 these fees grossed them $400,000.

EDUCATIONAL AND ENTERTAINMENT SERVICES

◆

WHAT YOU NEED TO KNOW TO GET STARTED

We have all been educators and entertainers at some point in our lives, even if it was only teaching a five-year-old how to tie shoelaces or regaling the relatives with a funny story around the dinner table. You needn't be a certified teacher or professionally trained performer to be good at passing on knowledge of and enjoyment in your craft.

But people who provide education and entertainment services as a business must truly love their craft *and* their clients. An incredible musician who lacks good interpersonal skills will have trouble keeping students. A home preschool provider can have the best projects, books, and snacks on the block, but unless she really enjoys a hectic houseful of children she'll have a nervous breakdown before half of her charges are out of diapers. A brewmeister who spends all his time extolling his own beer and doesn't give his apprentices a chance to savor their own success won't be in business for long. But if you can cover both bases— the craft and the client—educational and entertainment services are some of the most personally and financially rewarding enterprises you can become involved in. You will, in effect, have what the Chinese call "double happiness"—the pleasure of your craft and the pleasure of sharing it, too.

Instruction at home has, of course, a long and venerable history. In fact, home is the original classroom for all of us, the very first learning environment we experience. The home-based preschool industry, which is booming, takes advantage of many working parents' desire to have their little ones educated in a homelike setting. And the warm and personal home atmosphere is one reason why many students do much better with a tutor than in a traditional classroom setting.

In fact, tutors are in demand for virtually every subject and at every age level imaginable. As school budgets are cut and the number of pupils per classroom rises, concerned parents turn to private practitioners to provide enrichment education for art and music and remedial work in core subjects like math and reading. We know of one Connecticut public school district that used a local private science class provider, called Little Scientist, to teach eight science classes in its elementary school. Interest in the field is growing to meet the demand; in 1990 the American Association of Educators in Private Practice had sixteen members—in 1996 that figure had grown to more than five hundred. (The AAEPP can be reached at N. 7425 Switzke Rd., Watertown, WI 53094; 800-252-3280.)

Don't sell yourself short and think that there is nothing for you to teach if your expertise is not algebra or English. Teach what you know. Besides the usual academic subjects, there are unlimited home instruction opportunities for leisure and hobby activities. We found a home brewer, woodworker, and handmade papermaker with successful home instruction businesses; any of these enterprises could stand alone or be profitable add-ons to an existing food or craft business.

The good news about private individual and group music instruction is that the market should expand rapidly over the next decade. One in four Americans plays a musical instrument, but today, according to *American Demographics,* a majority of the nation's school districts either have no music specialist or only a part-time one. Currently, 42 percent of players first learn to play through private lessons. Expect that percentage to grow even higher as the demand for private instruction increases to fill the vacuum of public school education. We profile a piano teacher, because the piano is still—as it has been for many years—the most popular instrument. In descending order, the next most popular are guitars and other fretted instruments (including banjos and mandolins), drums, and then the flute.

One gratifying new development in the music instruction industry is that now people with an affinity for music can become music instructors through a group music program. We profile two, Kindermusik and Musikgarten, which offer training and support for the novice instructor and present a great way to break into the business.

Where, we wondered as we compiled this section, does education end and entertainment begin? Several of the entertainers we profile, such as the touring book reviewer and educational performer, straddle the line between the two. Other performers, such as storytellers, magicians, musicians, and puppeteers, could have been placed under either category, depending on whether they pitch their services primarily to educational institutions, commercial establishments, students, or to private parties. We found a successful puppeteer to profile, but a performer in any of the above-mentioned categories could structure his or her business in the same manner.

A WORD ON MARKETING EDUCATIONAL AND ENTERTAINMENT SERVICES

Whether you call it education or entertainment, all of the businesses in this section are very specific about the markets they pitch to, be it mom-and-tot song sessions, Power Ranger puppet shows, or remedial reading. How can you find out if there's a likely market for your services before you invest money in equipment and advertising? Spend some time researching, first.

Your local yellow pages directory and the U. S. Department of Commerce are your two best inexpensive sources of market data for your educational or entertainment services business. The directory will give you an idea of how many such services are already working in your area. Are there so many that the market is saturated, or none at all (which suggest either no demand or a gold mine waiting to be discovered)? What does your competition charge, and what aspects of their service do they feature in their display ads? The U.S. Department of Commerce's Census Bureau offers several useful publications. (Didn't you ever wonder what they did with all that information they collect in the *other* nine years?)

Ask for these titles:

- *Measuring Markets: A Guide to the Use of Federal and State Statistical Data.* This book will help you find the right publications for the location and subject that interests you.
- *Standard Metropolitan Statistical Areas,* the *Census Tract Reports,* and *County Business Patterns* will give you a wealth of information on population by age, sex, income, ethnic background, value of homes, and number of persons in a home. What is all this data good for? Well, for instance, a puppeteer or home day-care provider may want to search for large numbers of families with young children.

You can also check your local library for a copy of *Do-It-Yourself Marketing Research* by George Breen and Albert B. Blankenship (McGraw-Hill, 1992).

TEACHING AND CHILD-CARE SKILLS

HOMEMADE PAPER WORKSHOP INSTRUCTOR

Papermaking is a creative artistic medium that can be enjoyed by all ages—from preschoolers to their grandparents. People who enjoy this craft and want to help others learn how to make their own paper can offer courses through community centers, park districts, museums, and art galleries, or can offer workshops in their own homes.

Once you've learned this skill and perfected it, you'll need to gather a collection of materials, including small pieces of scrap paper and construction paper, blenders for grinding up the paper scraps with water (garage sales are a good source for inexpensive blenders), several vats, cotton sheeting to place drying paper on, and dried flowers, tinsel, ribbon, and other materials to decorate the paper with. You'll also need to buy or make the molds by stapling wire screens (in different shapes) to wooden frames. Some popular shapes for homemade paper molds include hearts, ovals and flowers—or you could create more imaginative shapes of your own design. You'll want to make a variety of paper styles to show your students.

TOP TIP: Offering a variety of classes can help attract and retain prospective students. We spoke with Phyllis Nelson, who teaches such programs as parent-child classes, papermaking and stenciling, making paper baskets and bowls, making Japanese paper, and even a class on making paper from garden plants such as iris, lilies, yucca, and cattail leaves. Once she began offering classes, positive word of mouth led to other groups calling her and asking her to teach for them as well. Phyllis said that teaching experience and artistic abilities are helpful, as is the patience to see your projects through from start to finish (remember, paper takes twenty-four hours to dry!).

GETTING STARTED: Consult one of the following books: *The Art and Craft of Papermaking* by Sophie Dawson (Running Press, 1992), *Making Your Own Paper* by Marianne Saddington (Garden Way Publishing, 1992), or *The Art and Craft of Paper* by Faith Shannon (Chronicle Books, 1994) and take a course in your community to learn the skills.

THE GOING RATE: You can charge each student $25–$30 a class; eight to fifteen students is a good number. (You can also sell your paper creations at arts & crafts shows, with handmade greeting cards going for $2 to $6 apiece and paper bowls and baskets selling for $25 to $75, depending on their size and complexity.)

TEACHER OF HOMEBREWING AND BEER-TASTING CLASSES

It's not enough to be an enthusiastic beer drinker for this job— you also need to be proficient at the fine art and science of brewing beer. Microbreweries and brewpubs have become increasingly popular over the last few years, and many people would like to be able to create their own fine brews in their basement. In fact, the American Homebrewers Association estimates that 1.5 million Americans are actively brewing beer at home.

Homebrewing and beer-tasting classes have been springing up in order to meet this demand. While these classes are most often held at community colleges, we've also come across some brew-meisters who hold classes in their homes.

Your introductory class should cover basic brewing techniques, how to get started, and beer appreciation—how to judge and evaluate major styles of beer. Your students will need to know the difference between a pilsner and a stout, for example, since it's hard to make a good beer if you don't know what the finished product will taste like. A basic homebrew kit (including a large plastic fermentation bucket, siphon hoses, bottles, a bottle cap-per, and caps) is required, which can be purchased at major sup-ply stores or specialty catalogs for between $50 and $100.

J. Andrew Patrick, a homebrew instructor and proprietor of the Home Brew U. BBS Network (1-847-970-9778), counseled us to beware of state and federal rules regarding brewing. It's illegal to sell your homebrew without a license from the Federal Bureau of Alcohol and Tobacco—though sharing drinks with friends and students is perfectly legal. Make sure everyone in your class is twenty-one, and don't give them so much to drink that they're driving home drunk. He commented, "You're deal-ing with alcohol here, so be responsible. I limit my students to the equivalent of two beers apiece over a three-hour class. We usually give everyone a taste of twelve different beers, and a taste is all you need."

TOP TIP: Join the American Homebrewers Association (PO Box 1679, Boulder, CO 80306; 303-447-0816) to keep in touch with other homebrewers and to receive *Zmurgy* magazine, the trade magazine for homebrewers. Many metropolitan areas also have local homebrewing clubs that you can join to trade brewing tips and techniques.

GETTING STARTED: The first step is to educate yourself about all aspects of brewing. Andrew Patrick told us, "It is a challenging discipline—you don't just drink beer all the time. You have to digest a lot of information to become conversant with it all." Two of the best beginning books to read are *The Complete Handbook of Homebrewing* by Dave Miller (Garden Way Publishing, 1988) and *The New Complete Joy of Home Brewing* by Charlie Papazian (Avon, 1991). Storey Communications in Pownal, VT, offers a good selection of brewing books; you can reach them by calling 1-800-441-5700 or by visiting their Beer Page on the Internet at **www.storey.com.** You can also access two newsgroups dedicated to homebrewing on the Internet: alt.beer and rec.crafts.brewing (the latter offers daily editions of the electronic publication *Homebrew Digest*). America Online includes brewing forums (go to keyword BEER); on CompuServe, check out the Wine + Forum.

THE GOING RATE: Charge each student around $50 per class. (You can cover the material in an all-day Saturday course, or offer three or four shorter sessions.) Six to ten students is a good number. Your fee should include recipes and other handouts.

TUTOR

This is a great way to use your teaching skills one-on-one, without having to put in long days in a classroom. Don't even think about this at-home job unless you've had relevant teaching experience. You'll also need the ability to explain things more than one way when students don't get it the first time, know how to structure lessons individually for each child you tutor, and communicate well with the child's parents and teacher. Make sure you have a supply of up-to-date textbooks in the subjects you plan to specialize in, and a work area set up in a quiet room of your house with a large table, good lighting, and plenty of supplies. Math tutors should stock up on extra protractors, compasses, calculators, and rulers, since students inevitably forget to bring theirs, and reading tutors will need a range of storybooks, workbooks, and flashcards. Workbooks (and other supplies) are available at teacher supply stores, or may be ordered directly from the publishers.

At an initial meeting with a prospective student and his parents, you'll find out what difficulties the child is having in school, ask the parents' permission to contact the teacher, and decide together how many tutoring sessions a week are necessary and how long a session a child could handle. Most students average one hour a week of tutoring per subject, and you can choose any time that fits your schedule best. You'll also need to offer a diagnostic test to help zero in on the child's strengths and weaknesses, so you'll know right away which areas to start working on.

Most importantly, find a way to motivate the kids, since many of them require a tutor because they're not excited about school. Peggy Clark, an elementary school math and reading tutor, has put together a point system that's had good results. She makes a list of small things a child can earn, from candy and gum to pencils, pogs, and books, and assigns a number of points to each item on the list. She awards an agreed-upon number of points each time a child remembers to bring her book, paper and pencils, and any tests that need reviewing, for doing math problems correctly the first time, and for correcting any mistakes on their own. Students receive bonus points for showing initiative and for coming on time (or calling to say they can't make it). Peggy said, "The kids can cash in their points right away or work toward bigger items—I individualize this system, taking into account each student's needs and responsibilities. It's really helped motivate students who are losing interest."

TOP TIP: You can post your business card at local schools' offices and notify school boards in your area of your tutoring specialties, since they often make referrals, or run a classified newspaper ad. Word of mouth also works well once you've developed a name for yourself as a tutor who can help children get up to speed.

GETTING STARTED: Try to find a mentor who's been tutoring for a while to help you learn the ropes. And make friends with the teachers of kids you're tutoring so you can find out about upcoming homework assignments and get access to school materials. Used book sales and teacher supply stores are other places to find a variety of textbooks. Some communities offer "textbook recycling programs" where you can pick up free materials that the school districts are no longer using, so find out if there's a program like this in your area.

THE GOING RATE: $20 to $75 an hour, depending on the region you live in ($30 to $40 is probably the average hourly rate). Tutors charge for the actual time they're with their students, not for their preparation time.

WRITING TUTOR

In addition to freelance writing, good writers can find work by helping college or graduate students polish their writing. (Just because they've reached higher education does not necessarily mean that they've learned to write.) As a tutor, you can help students develop topics for papers and assignments, organize and edit their writing , and compile bibliographies. Sometimes you'll be asked to type their final handwritten version on your computer as well.

You'll need a computer and access to a library for books on writing style—from the ever-reliable *Chicago Manual of Style* to specific books on the students' subject areas. For instance, sociology and art history students will probably need to follow different styles for references. Advertise your service by putting up a notice on the bulletin board at a local university or community college. Once you've begun, word of mouth can quickly bring you new customers.

"If you enjoy working with words and with people, this is a really good job, and you can do it any time of day or night," said Maryann Wegloski Cooke, who has been working with social work and philosophy students. "But some students want me to write their papers for them, which would be wrong. You have to stand firm and place limits on what you will or won't do." Another drawback can be last-minute assignments, when students delay working on a paper until a day or two before it's due. Of course, you could always charge an extra fee for rush work.

TOP TIP: Make it clear up front that you are not a term-paper-for-hire service, or both you and your clients will be disappointed. A simple letter of agreement or contract form will help you avoid misunderstandings.

GETTING STARTED: Upgrade your computer to handle the most popular word-processing programs and exchange files between different operating systems. Then get business cards made up and put them on bulletin boards in the campus lounges, residence halls, and library.

THE GOING RATE: $12 to $15 per hour for this type of tutoring.

MUSIC TEACHER

This is a wonderful job if you'd like to share your love of music with others. Teaching any kind of musical instrument is easy to do in your home, and offers extremely flexible hours. You can choose to teach a few students on the side or take on dozens of students—one piano teacher we interviewed teaches eighty-three students a week at her home! You can also set your own hours. While most schoolchildren need to take lessons in the late afternoon, early evening, or on weekends, you can fill up your days by teaching adults and home schoolers.

As we said earlier, piano is still the most popular instrument for children to learn, so let's use that as our example instrument. You'll need very strong musical skills, of course, and a thorough background in all elements of study, music pedagogy, and performance. You should have a bachelor of arts degree with a major in piano as a minimum. A professional bachelor of music degree with a piano performance major from a music conservatory is preferable for teaching advanced students.

Don't consider this business unless you're skilled at teaching, patient, understand learning theory and motivating techniques, and able to relate well to children, young people, and adult learners as well. You'll need a good, solid piano, and should place it in a quiet room where you will not be disturbed while you're teaching. Buying a used piano is fine, as long as it's been well kept and has the right tonal quality. A good tape recorder will also come in handy. Many teachers ask their students to bring a blank audiocassette to their lessons. You can enhance learning if you tape yourself playing the piece a student is working on, or record two or three different recordings of the piece by different pianists. This helps students realize that there can be several different interpretations of piano classics. When students have prepared polished pieces, the taping gives them a permanent record of their progress.

Joining a network of professional musicians or music teachers can be very helpful for you. It'll give you the opportunity to learn from your peers, avoid isolation, attend seminars and conferences, and enable your students to improve their skills by taking part in national piano-playing auditions. The major associations you may want to join are: The National Guild of Piano Teachers (PO Box 1807, Austin, TX 78767; 512-478-5775; they publish the *Piano Guild Notes* journal) and the Music Teachers National Association (441 Vine Street, Ste. 505, Cincinnati, OH 45202; 513-421-1420, which publishes *American Music Teacher* magazine). Two very useful books are *Guide to the Pianist's Repertoire, 2nd Edition,* by Maurice Hinson (Indiana University Press, 1994) and *How to Teach Piano Successfully, 3rd Edition,* by James W. Bastien (Kjos, 1988). You may also want to stay up to date by subscribing to *Keyboard* (411 Borel Avenue, Suite 100, San Mateo, CA 94402) and *Clavier* (200 Northfield Road, Northfield, IL 60093) magazines.

TOP TIP: Many of the music teachers' associations refer prospective students to their members, so join as many local music associations as you can. You can also attract new students by publicizing student recitals and your own performances.

GETTING STARTED: Most private music teachers begin teaching friends' and neighbors' children, then attract more students through word of mouth. You can post your card or brochure at musical instrument shops, local schools' and colleges' bulletin boards, or take out a small ad in your community newspaper listing your credentials. A highly regarded teacher who has developed a strong following after two decades of teaching piano told us her secret: "Set high standards from the beginning. Your reputation will build, until you can pick and choose your students. It can take years to build your business from the ground up." This teacher also advised, "Take this seriously and treat it as a business. I formalize the program and make it clear that students are expected to take lessons for nine months a year and four to six lessons in summer. They need to pay at the beginning of each month, and can't cancel at the last minute without forfeiting their payment."

THE GOING RATE: Most students take lessons once a week: A thirty-minute lesson is average for beginning students, while advanced students may take forty-five- to sixty-minute lessons. You can charge an average fee of $14 to $16 for each thirty-minute lesson; $18 to $20 for a forty-five-minute lesson; and $20 to $22 for a one-hour lesson. Many instructors offer a discount of $1 to $2 per session if two or more children in the same family take lessons.

KINDERMUSIK OR MUSIKGARTEN INSTRUCTOR

If you love music and enjoy teaching young children, you can set up a business as a licensed Kindermusik Specialist. As the name implies, this music program for young children was developed in Germany, then was brought to the United States in the 1970s. A similar program called Musikgarten was founded a bit later. They both introduce young children to music through singing, moving, listening, and playing simple instruments, and teach note-reading in creative ways.

They've found that the preschool market is one of the fastest growing markets in childhood music education. You can avail yourself of this ready-made entrepreneurial opportunity if you have a solid musical background and training in at least one instrument or voice. A college degree in music would be helpful, but is not required. Since most classes consist of eight to ten children, you'll also need to be skilled at group teaching. And because you'll build your clientele from scratch, you'll need to be a self-starter and be willing to blow your own horn until your classes get rolling.

To learn more about these teaching opportunities, contact Kindermusik and/or Musikgarten and ask for an information packet and their workshop schedules. You can reach Kindermusik International at PO Box 26575, Greensboro, NC 27415; 1-800-628-5687. Contact Musikgarten at PO Box 15514, Richmond, VA 23227; 1-800-216-6864. Both companies offer a certificate program to train teachers in their approach through a series of workshops held at several U.S. locations. They also offer marketing support, complete curricula and lesson plans, tape recordings, instruments, newsletters, and licensing.

The beauty of these programs is that they tell you exactly what you need to do to start up, run, and promote your business. Because they are not franchises, your start-up costs will be minimal. If you can, attend both a Kindermusik and a Musikgarten introductory workshop to help you decide which program you'd like to join. In the Kindermusik program, you need to purchase a license after you've completed your training workshops, and take continuing education programs to keep your license up to date. You can buy all the supplies you need—sheet music, teacher's guidebooks and lesson plans, recordings, a variety of rhythm in-

struments, audiotapes, manipulative games, and brochures—
through the program you've joined.

After that, it's time to choose a site for your classes. Most
teachers begin using a large basement or family room in their
own homes. The disadvantage of using your home is that you'll
have a lot of traffic in and out, and your family will lose some
privacy. One woman taught music classes to two hundred kids a
week, and her house took a beating. It would be ideal if your
house had a separate entrance and separate bathroom for your
in-home "classroom." When your business grows, you could rent
a room from a local church, school, or college to accommodate
larger classes.

Kathy Cathey has taught Kindermusik as part of a college
music program for several years. She told us, "Go in and have a
ball. If you make it fun, you have a much better chance of suc-
ceeding. Talk to as many other music teachers as you can, and
sift out what works for you. You can glean a lot of helpful ideas
from other teachers. The Foundation for Music-Based Learning
also has a wonderful publication called *Early Childhood Connections* (PO Box 4274, Greensboro, NC 27404; 910-272-5303)."
Kathy did give us this caveat: "I would not advise you to go into
it for the money, although your business can certainly be profitable. You really need to love to be with children. Because that's
what will make your program a success."

TOP TIP: Volunteering to offer a free music program at a local
library or children's museum is an effective way to demonstrate
the benefits of your musical approach to parents and their children. Many times you'll hear "Where do we sign up?" at the end
of one of these sample workshops.

GETTING STARTED: After you take several workshops and
become licensed, you'll need to start spreading the word about
your music classes. Some of the best places to advertise are in
school district newsletters and parenting publications. One Kindermusik teacher ran a small ad in a newsletter mailed to parents
of preschoolers and received 130 phone calls soon after! Offering

a variety of class times will also help attract prospective students. Parents of toddlers and preschool children prefer morning or early-afternoon classes, while school-aged children will need to take classes in the late afternoon or early evening. While you may need to set aside one evening or Saturday a week for classes, you have the flexiblity to choose the days that are most convenient for you.

THE GOING RATE: Although Kindermusik and Musikgarten teachers set their own fees, they try to keep their prices reasonable and in line with those of other music teachers. These programs usually offer classes for three separate age groups: eighteen months to three years with parent or caregiver, three-and-a-half- to four-year-olds, and four- to seven-year-olds. A typical fee is $125 for a fifteen- or sixteen-week semester; this includes two books, a cassette tape, and a parent handbook. Many teachers charge up to $200 a semester for classes for four- to seven-year-olds, since their classes are longer and include more hands-on materials and rhythm instruments to take home.

COMPUTERTOTS INSTRUCTOR

COMPUTERTOTS is an international franchised company that teaches young children computer skills—and offers home-based, flexible work opportunities for its franchise owners and class instructors. Founded in 1984 by two mothers with a background in education, COMPUTERTOTS classes reach around forty thousand children a week at over three thousand locations worldwide. In fact, *Working Woman* magazine recommended COMPUTERTOTS as a "best bet in the hot new area of children's services." You would make a good computer teacher if you enjoy teaching, like children, and want to help them become familiar and comfortable with computers, keyboards, and the mouse. Classes are typically held at preschools, day-care centers, and park districts or community centers in four-week sessions from September through May. The thirty-minute COMPUTERTOTS classes are offered for three- to five-year-olds, and Computer Explorers classes are held for six- to twelve-year-olds. Most classes have no more than three to five students, to allow each child the opportunity for lots of hands-on experience on the computer.

COMPUTERTOTS provides its teachers with a computer to use while they are teaching, along with the latest and greatest educational software. You simply need to bring your knowledge and teaching abilities to class. You can bring the computer home between classes, so your children can also benefit from your COMPUTERTOTS connection. One teacher told us, "I wanted to work with children—adults often need to take a child's view in approaching the computer. Children are open and eager to explore, and realize computers won't explode if you press a few buttons. I also like the steady hours and regular source of income."

TOP TIP: COMPUTERTOTS teaching can prepare you for working as a computer consultant for adults. These classes will give you experience in teaching computer concepts and in learning to explain things in a simplified way. Adults need clear, simple explanations as much as children do.

GETTING STARTED: Call COMPUTERTOTS' toll-free line (1-800-531-5053), write to them at 10132 Colvin Run Road, Great Falls, VA 22066, or visit their home page (**www.entremkt. com/computertots/**). The national office can tell you how to get in touch with franchise owners in your area. Then it's up to you to contact local franchise owners and ask whether they might be looking for new teachers. Mention any relevant skills you have: whether you're a computer whiz, or a terrific teacher. Most COMPUTERTOTS franchise owners don't assume that their employees will have a computer background. They prefer to hire former teachers or early-childhood specialists, but will train people they think could make good teachers. Many of their teachers are at-home moms looking for part-time work, college students looking for experience, and retirees. Once hired, teachers are under contract for a year. COMPUTERTOTS provides all the computer equipment, training, and teaching materials they need.

THE GOING RATE: COMPUTERTOTS teachers receive between $10 to $15 dollars an hour for each class they teach.

PART-TIME PRESCHOOL TEACHER

If you enjoy working with children but don't want to spend all your free time taking care of other people's kids, this may be the perfect compromise. This business makes the most sense if you live in a small community with few established preschools. One advantage to running a preschool part-time is that in many states, you don't have to be licensed if you provide care for less than three hours a day (check with your state's licensing office to find out its guidelines for preschools and child-care providers). On the down side, it is very difficult—and extremely expensive—for a home-based preschool teacher to get liability insurance.

You'll need a large comfortable family room or basement filled with art and craft supplies, blocks, educational toys and games, lots of children's books, and such hands-on science tools as microscopes and magnets. Garage sales, teacher supply stores, and educational catalogs are a good source of these materials. Teaching skills, a sense of humor, and patience are also essential. You should also be skilled at communicating with adults as well as children, since you'll have a lot of involvement with parents.

Christine Fletcher, who founded her own at-home preschool a few years ago, counsels, "Don't try this without some experience in group care. You should have a nodding acquaintance with child development and early-childhood education. You should also be good at solving problems, have first-aid training, and know how to make lesson plans—it's not enough to hand each child a box of crayons and consider your job done." Her parting advice: "Don't take too many kids. Be realistic about what you can do. I recommend no more than five to seven children for one adult. If you want to take on larger classes, you'll need to hire an assistant."

TOP TIP: Child-care resource and referral agencies in many communities offer advice and support for both child-care providers and parents. Make sure you're listed on your local CCR&R referral list for parents seeking information on day-care and preschools.

GETTING STARTED: The National Association for the Education of Young Children (1509 16th Street NW, Washington, DC 20036; 1-800-424-2460) is an excellent resource. It publishes a helpful journal called *Young Children* and has local affiliates around the country. *Nursery School and Day Care Center Management Guide* by Claire Cherry et al. (Fearon Teacher Aids, 1987) is a how-to book on starting your own nursery school or day-care program. Make sure you check with county and local municipal ordinances regarding zoning regulations and physical space requirements. You can let parents know about your preschool by sending a press release to local newspapers and spreading the word to friends, neighbors, and acquaintances.

THE GOING RATE: $50 to $60 a month per child for two two-and-a-half-hour classes a week; $75 to $95 a month per child for three classes a week.

BABY-SITTER FOR LOCAL INNS AND HOTELS

Offering your baby-sitting services to inns, hotels, and B&Bs in your community is another way to earn money through part-time child care. Experienced baby-sitters are in great demand by parents who would like to go out in the evening while they're on vacation, and most hotels and inns keep a listing of approved sitters for their guests. The hotel will call a day or so in advance when a guest requests a baby-sitter, and you can decide whether you're available that night. Weekends and holidays can be very busy, especially if you live in a large city or popular vacation spot. Some hotels may require you to be bonded, and certified in first aid.

All that's needed is a love for children and willingness to go play with them at their hotel room; some hotels may give you the option of caring for the kids in your home. You might want to bring along a few toys or games to help break the ice. By sitting down with them and taking a look at the toys together, you can help distract the children from feeling shy or worried about their parents' absence.

TOP TIP: You can offer to provide weekly rates for parents who are visiting for an extended period of time, or for families with summer homes in your area. Many families return on vacation to the same area year after year, and will ask for you by name if they're pleased with the care you gave their children.

GETTING STARTED: Your first step is to call the manager or concierge at local inns and hotels, and getting your name on their sitters list.

THE GOING RATE: This varies from region to region. Many hotel sitters are paid between $7 and $10 an hour, depending on the number of children involved.

ENTERTAINMENT SKILLS

PUPPETEER

This entry demonstrates that it's perfectly possible to have fun and make money at the same time. Most puppeteers develop a business out of a hobby they already enjoy. If you think that you too would enjoy presenting puppet shows, you'll need to construct a portable wooden puppet stage, sew some curtains for the stage, and buy or make some puppets. Marionettes are particularly popular with older children and their parents, because of their intricate detailing and ability to make so many different motions. However, fuzzy hand puppets and rod puppets are especially enjoyed by preschoolers.

The choice of the puppets you'll use will probably be determined by the time it takes to create them. Hand puppets can be constructed very quickly, while a wooden marionette can take sixty to eighty hours to carve, mold, paint, attach strings, and make clothing. It's a labor of love for those with artistic abilities and enough time to create. (If you do make your own puppets, you can add to your business by teaching puppet-making workshops to teachers, parents, and kids in addition to offering puppet shows.)

Once you develop or add to your collection of puppets, it's time to decide on the stories you'll present. Favorite fairy tales, such as "Sleeping Beauty," "Aladdin," "Cinderella," and "The Three Little Pigs" are often chosen, since both children and adults enjoy the familiarity of knowing that good will triumph in the end. Fairy tales also lend themselves to elegant painted backdrops and beautiful puppet costumes, which is part of their charm. You'll need to paint a variety of scenes on cloth or cardboard for the backdrops, or find an artist who can do that for you, write a script, and record some background music and any sound effects your story needs. Since you will bring your show to a variety of audiences at different locations, make sure you can use the family van or another vehicle large enough to transport your stage and puppets. Many puppeteers travel in pairs: usually a man and woman who manipulate the puppets and make all the voices. It's possible to put on a solo puppet show, but you may need to ask a friend or your spouse to record the lines for the opposite-sex puppets ahead of time.

If you're just getting started in the puppetry business, you'll find that The Puppeteers of America is a wonderful resource. This national nonprofit organization is open to anyone who has an interest in puppetry. It offers a variety of hands-on puppet-making workshops, a national puppetry festival every odd-numbered year, and eight regional festivals every even-numbered year, a puppetry store selling hundreds of different books and patterns, and an audiovisual library of performances and workshops for members to rent. The association also publishes *The Puppetry Journal* and the *Playboard* newsletter. To get information on joining, write to: The Puppeteers of America, #5 Cricklewood Path, Pasadena, CA 91107 or call 818-797-5748. Many larger cities have their own puppetry guilds as well.

There's no better way to learn than to attend puppetry workshops and conferences and talk to others already in the field. Jim Malone, president of Puppeteers of America, gave this advice for beginners: "Jump in with both feet. Get real active. Every puppeteer I ever meet is willing to share ideas." He also recommended that you see as many different performances as you can to discover which types of puppets and shows you find most appealing. Some puppeteers develop "variety shows," where one puppet at a time comes forward and tells a joke or sings a song. Others prefer more traditional storytelling performances. Jean

Kuecher, owner of the Marionette Playhouse, is a member of the latter group. She told us, "Your stories should be involving, and people should care what happens to the characters. You can have beautiful puppets, but you won't entertain if you don't tell a good story."

TOP TIP: Send a press release out to local newspapers every time you do a puppet show or workshop at a library, school, or other public place. Many times a local reporter will come out on a slow news day, and you'll gain some wonderful free publicity. These clippings can be added to your promotion packet and can help you get future bookings.

GETTING STARTED: You'll find an audience for your shows by contacting schools, libraries, preschools, and day-care centers, children's museums, local clubs, and Boy and Girl Scout troop leaders. Birthday parties are the other best source of bookings. Taking out a classified ad in a local parents' publication is the most cost-effective way to publicize your children's shows. These ads are usually inexpensive enough that you can afford to run your ad for several months, so people will know where to find you next time they'd like to hire an entertainer for an event. Make sure that you also announce your other programs at the end of each show and hand out a business card or brochure to each adult attending. Puppeteers can be shy and retiring, preferring to remain behind the scenes. But if you want your business to thrive, you will need to step out from behind the stage and do some self-promotion.

THE GOING RATE: Prices will vary depending on where you live. A typical fee is $130 for a performance at a birthday party or child-care center, and $150 for a library, club, Scout group, or other organization. Since many puppeters bring larger stages to schools, which take a couple of hours to set up and dismantle, they charge up to $300 for a school performance. You can charge $150 for teaching a one-and-a-half- to two-hour puppetry workshop at a school, group, or children's museum.

EDUCATIONAL PERFORMER

What can you do if you're a teacher with a passion for King Arthur, or medieval times, or myths and legends from other cultures? You can develop an act and take it on the road. School systems are always looking for well-crafted presentations on a variety of educational subjects for school assemblies. Developing an interdisciplinary program would be a plus, since that's a popular trend in education these days.

Joan Caton turned her interest in Arthurian legends into a thriving at-home business, Caton Enterprises, Ltd., based in Elmhurst, IL. She studied the Arthurian period through a humanities fellowship for high school teachers, and then wove the stories and illustrations into a one-hour presentation, complete with banners, knights and ladies, music, and slides. She developed a brochure with a postage-paid response card and targeted sixty regional schools that might be interested in the program. She got five bookings from her brochure, which she then parlayed into other bookings through the positive word of mouth she'd generated. She's also managed to land some lucrative corporate bookings for company parties featuring a Renaissance dinner.

If you're not the dramatic type, you can develop and sell a curriculum kit in your special interest area. Teachers will pay for the convenience of having complete lesson plans and materials that are ready to use.

TOP TIP: Do a little market research first to make sure you're in a subject area for which there will be some demand. Departments often change themes and areas of specialty study each term. Contact the curriculum director at your school or district level and ask to see a copy of their plan, which is available to the public.

GETTING STARTED: The supplies performers need vary according to their subject. Joan Caton made her own elaborate medieval costumes, suits of armor, shields, and banners for her presentation (she has since rented many of the costumes out as additional moneymakers). Finding a niche of your own is the key to your success. We've come across people who've offered specialty programs on brass rubbing, animal shows, and dinosaur discoveries, and others who satisfy schools' demand for children's programs on substance abuse. Additional skills you'll need include the ability to interact well with people and to convince your clients that your program will make their teaching more effective.

THE GOING RATE: In a receptive urban market, you can charge between $150 to $350 for a single performance, or two back-to-back performances for $500 to $575.

TOURING BOOK REVIEWER

Would you like to share your enjoyment of good books with others? As a book reviewer, you could get paid for presenting readings and reviews of fiction and nonfiction to book groups, libraries, women's clubs, and community organizations. Some reviewers have a background as English or writing teachers and offer literary discussions and critiques. Others put on a dramatic presentation from a first-person point of view, sometimes dressing as the author or a character in the novel.

You can prepare your reviews by choosing some current books or old favorites, reading them carefully and marking up your favorite passages, researching the author or topic, and then writing a script. Audiences enjoy anecdotes and background stories about well-known authors and historical figures, so make sure you include intriguing stories in your presentation. You're likely to attract a wider audience if you have a flair for the dramatic and consider yourself a storyteller rather than a lecturer. Your goal is to entertain as well as to teach people about a particular book.

TOP TIP: Once you've rehearsed a few different book reviews, get in touch with your library to see if they would be interested in hiring you for a daytime or evening presentation. Your library may also have lists of book group leaders in town you can contact.

GETTING STARTED: Talk to managers of local bookstores as well to see if they would like you to do a few book reviews and help bring more customers into their stores. Women's clubs and seniors' groups are also looking for entertaining and educational speakers for their meetings and luncheons.

THE GOING RATE: At the beginning, your fee may be only $25 to $50 per presentation, but you can raise your rates to $150 to $250 if you gain a good reputation as a speaker in your community. Often one good booking will lead to another, as audience members will tell their friends about you, who may then hire you to present your reviews for another organization.

SONGSMITH

If you are an amateur or professional musician and have a talent for songwriting, you can set up a business as a custom songwriter. To succeed, you'll need to be able to create hummable tunes, write memorable, touching, or amusing lyrics, and be willing to rewrite a song several times until your customer is happy with it. Custom songs can be advertised as a unique way to celebrate life's special moments. They are particularly popular for wedding, anniversary, and birthday gifts.

There are two approaches you can take. Rhonda Pawlan, a Chicago-area songwriter who runs her own business called SONGWORKS, explained her songwriting process to us. She writes new lyrics to a popular tune, then provides the lyrics for her customers to sing at weddings, birthdays, and other celebrations. She generally has a one-hour meeting with each customer, asks a lot of questions about the guest of honor, then pieces together a song that is a tribute to that person. If you'd like to do something similar, good interviewing skills are necessary to help you learn everything you can about the subject of the song. So is the ability to match the right words and rhyme scheme to a familiar melody (show tunes are most frequently requested). A sense of humor is also a plus, since the most affecting songs blend sentimental and humorous verses. Many customers will want you to create a cassette of the song as well as a keepsake.

The second approach is to create an entirely original song, with your own tune, and provide it to customers on audiotape. Songwriter Dan Gillogly sells custom songs by placing small classified ads in his local free parenting newspaper. He gives prospective customers a questionnaire, so he can determine their musical likes and dislikes before he begins composing. He asks, "What musical style do you like? Rock, R&B, country, folk, a dance tune, or a ballad? Do you like a fast or slow tempo? Would you prefer a female or male singer?" Then, he asks about the event and the subject of the song. Once he has all the information he needs, he goes off to his home writing studio, creates a song on his computer, modifies it until he feels the song is right, then records the song onto a cassette tape.

If you plan to make your own cassettes, you'll need a quiet room to work in, a computer with a MIDI translator, a synthesizer hooked up to your computer, and a software program that allows you turn your computer into a recording studio. Some popular music software includes Musicshop, Cakewalk, Finale Allegro, Encore, Rhapsody, and Master Tracks Pro. Many of these programs use familiar tape-deck-style controls for quick recording, editing, and playback. You can enter the notes through an electronic keyboard or with a mouse, edit it on screen, then play it back via your keyboard or computer. Make sure you run the songs by your clients before they're completed. You'll also need to buy blank cassette tapes in bulk. A rhyming dictionary is another useful purchase to help inspire you when you're writing lyrics.

TOP TIP: Rhonda Pawlan advised, "Always be as accommodating as possible. Although it's great to have several weeks notice, I've done many rush jobs to please new and repeat customers. I want to keep a positive reputation. For example, I wrote a poem for a repeat customer just last week, in one hour!" Don Gillogly offered this additional advice: "Be patient. It can take time to build up this business. And have fun. If you're not having fun, no one will enjoy your songs."

GETTING STARTED: Musicians who perform at weddings and private parties can mention their custom songwriting services to all of their clients. It can also be offered as an add-on or to close a sale. Word of mouth is usually most effective in drumming up new customers, so you might begin by offering your services for free to people you know until you make a name for yourself. Leave fliers at stores selling musical instruments and CDs and tapes. You could also work through party planners, but you'll need to pay them a commission for referring you. For more marketing ideas, read *Songwriter's Market,* published annually by Writer's Digest, *Making Money Making Music* by James Dearing (Writer's Digest, 1990), and *The Craft and Business of Song Writing* by John Braheny (Writer's Digest, 1988).

THE GOING RATE: It's a good idea to ask for a deposit. You can charge a basic creative fee of $75 to $125 for writing a song, plus an additional $25 to $30 for making a cassette version. You can charge an additional $150 to $300 if you need to hire a professional singer (additional singers and musicians each receive around $100 an hour), or if you're asked to create a more polished version in a recording studio. Some songwriters even offer the option of dubbing the song onto a customer's videotape of a special event. Since rates can vary widely, depending on the area you live in, do some market research to make sure you charge what the market will bear.

SECTION 5

HOUSE
AND
GARDEN

◆

WHAT YOU NEED TO KNOW TO GET STARTED

This section covers businesses that are not only home-based, but also home-centered. The market for all sorts of home-related skills and services is growing; demographics indicate that despite the media's hype of "cocooning," the rise of families where both parents work outside the home, plus longer office hours and commuting times, actually leave people with less and less time to pursue home activities. Of course, they still want their home to be attractively decorated, to have fresh flowers on the mantelpiece, home-baked bread on the table, and the dog trained and walked and relatively free of mud and burrs. If you have the talent and time for the domestic arts and animal husbandry, you have a good opportunity to provide the home touch for people who aren't home all the time.

Anyone who has ever paid a mortgage or rent bill is attracted to the concept of making some real money from their real estate. When you make money from your house and garden you are going back to the original production site—the family farm. Of course, these days a micro farmer may be growing a patch of organic chamomile instead of acres of corn, or hosting garage sales instead of barn raisings, but the pride and pleasure of growing or baking or breeding or improving your home place—all the while making money on it—is hard to beat.

Making money from home and garden can be as low-tech and simple as house waiting and making your home available as a commercial set, or as labor-intensive as catering and gardening. The range of successful activities we profile is quite wide, but, unlike simply outfitting a home office for business services, some of the business opportunities described in this section will require extensive remodeling or customizing of your property. For example, working with animals, whether as a trainer, breeder, or sitter, will require room for kennels and exercise areas. Cooking and catering businesses may (according to their local board of health) have to upgrade their kitchens to commercial grade equipment and safety features. Flower, herb, and produce growers may have to install drip irrigation systems or greenhouses.

What all this means is that you may need access to capital— that is, working money to start up your home and garden business properly. In general, as a small, part-time business operator you should try as much as possible to avoid borrowing money and saddling yourself with debt. Try to make the best use of what you already have on hand. For instance, many rural and suburban homes (and even city homes in residential neighborhoods) have garages or garden sheds out back. If you're interested in breeding animals, consider converting your garage to kennel space instead of building a whole new structure (this will also leave you more room for runs). If you want to try landlording but don't have the capital or skills to renovate part of your home into an apartment, consider renting your shed for boat and trailer storage, instead. If you are considering catering, wholesale to restaurants first, so that you don't have to worry about developing attractive packaging or upgrading your kitchen to public license standards.

HOME CARE AND INCOME OPPORTUNITIES

PUT YOUR HOUSE IN THE MOVIES

Though most Hollywood movies are still made on sound stages, films being shot in other locations need real-life houses, streets, and shops as settings for their stories. Besides films, commercials and print ads are almost always shot locally, and photographers and advertising agencies are frequently on the lookout for a unique background for their work.

What are the film companies interested in? Mostly luxury-type houses. Great kitchens are always in demand, especially for commercials. But don't be discouraged if you don't live in a House Beautiful. If you have something unique and picturesque that oozes charm, like a classic farmhouse with a big porch, a great old barn, a fabulous garden, or even a fishing shack that looks like Captain Courageous lives there, your property has potential as a film or commercial location.

How do art and advertising directors find out about good sites? All states and many municipal governments maintain a "Film Promotion Office" to aid and encourage this type of commercial activity in their area. We recommend you list with both your state (contact the general information operator for your state government) and closest city (contact the general information operator for your city government). To get in the listings, simply take four to six regular color snapshots of the exterior of your house, plus the important interior rooms (kitchen, living room if there's a fireplace, great staircase if you've got one, master bedroom). Send them, along with your name, address, and phone number, to the film offices and request to be placed in their location files.

If a scout for a film or commercial sees your place in the files and is interested, they'll come out and make a new set of photos detailing exactly what they're interested in. You can't guess what will catch their eye. Darcie's dad's old brownstone was used in a made-for-TV movie because the film designer liked the front steps.

TOP TIP: Don't bother "decorating the set" yourself—the crew bring everything they want. For example, the expensive flower arrangement Darcie's folks outfitted the brownstone with was immediately ripped out by the film's set designer.

GETTING STARTED: Order Jim Leonis's guidebook *Filmed on Location: A Guide to Leasing Your Property as a Film Location* (Premiere Publishing Co., 1994).

THE GOING RATE: You may have to wait months or even years to get a nibble, but the wait is well worth it—the typical range of compensation for one day's use of your property is $1,000 to $5,000.

LANDLORD

Are you an empty-nester or young couple with a big mortgage and too much house on your hands for your current needs? Then consider turning those extra rooms into a rental unit that makes you extra money every month.

Besides income, being a landlord brings other benefits. A tenant means that someone else is around to watch the place if you travel or are away on business a lot, and may even share simple upkeep chores such as grass cutting and snow shoveling. Your best candidates for apartment renovation are a basement, attic, garage, or second floor with access to a bathroom and kitchen facilities. If access to a kitchen isn't possible, you can still rent out the space as a small office.

Before starting any renovation, check local zoning and licensing laws to make sure your new apartment can meet code regulations. An easy way to ascertain the market for apartments is to check the local paper and supermarket bulletin boards for "Apartment Wanted" notices. Make sure you jot down the specifics of the "Apartments Available" notices, too, so that you get an idea of the amount you can charge for your flat when it's finished.

According to several experienced landlords we spoke to, the most important part of a successful tenant/landlord relationship is the lease. Make sure you spell out in this document just what your responsibilities—and the tenant's rights—are. For example, who is responsible for the utilities? Is access to the laundry room included? Will pets be allowed? A parking space included? Will the tenant get a discount for shoveling the walk or cutting the grass? When is the rent to be paid, and what is the penalty for late payment? Many bookstores and office supply stores carry blank copies of leases you can purchase.

How much should you spend renovating your extra space into a rental unit? Costs can vary widely, depending on how much of the work you can do yourself and whether you'll have to add a lot of new plumbing. It can be as little as $2,000 to add a small kitchenette to an existing finished basement or as much as $20,000 to add insulation, skylights, and all new plumbing to an attic. But Patrick Hare, coauthor of *Creating an Accessory Apartment,* counsels that few investments can give homeowners "so much gain for their pain," since the income over the years is greater than the cost to create the apartment in the first place. Therefore, set your renovation budget in terms of "time to payback." A one-to-three-year payback is reasonable, but a renovation that costs you five years to recoup in rents is not worth it.

TOP TIP: Make the apartment entrance as separate and private as possible. And, if possible, partition off part of the yard or deck for the tenant's use. That way, the issue of sharing won't come up—remember, you want a tenant, not a roommate.

GETTING STARTED: Check you local zoning and building codes and read these two publications: *Creating an Accessory Apartment*, by Patrick Hare and Jolene Ostler (McGraw-Hill, 1987), and *The Consumer's Guide to Accessory Apartments* (Publication D-12775) from AARP, 601 E. Street NW, Washington, D.C. 20049 (202-434-2277).

THE GOING RATE: $100 to $1,000 a month, depending on location, size, and demand.

Rent Out Your Residence Short-term

Your home, boat, or vacation home can be an easy source of tax-free income if you rent it out for fourteen days or less during the course of the year. Income you receive for a rental period of two weeks or less is completely tax-free; in fact, as Ernst & Young partner Sylvia J. Pozarnsky told *Bottom Line*, you don't even have to report this income to the IRS, and there is currently no *dollar limit* on the amount of income you can receive in this way, as long as the *time limit* is met.

While this might not sound like an immediate opportunity for a windfall, think again. Do you live near a major vacation site, theme park, or annual event? Rent out your home for the high season and use those two weeks for your own holiday. People with homes to rent for the Indianapolis 500, Superbowl, Olympics, or Kentucky Derby can command top dollar for a convenient set of digs during these high-profile events. Folks who live near a national or state park, a Renaissance Fair, fishing derby, pro golf tournament, or outdoor concert series also have a very valuable real estate location.

The size of your home doesn't matter. Families will want several bedrooms and baths, but a single or couple might be just as happy to rent your studio. Even a boat can qualify as a residence, as long as it has sleeping quarters, a kitchen, and toilet facilities.

TOP TIP: Move valuables and breakables to a friend's house or a locked storage room to give you peace of mind when you're gone, and book only through an agency that will screen clients for you.

GETTING STARTED: Check your local yellow pages or state and county tourism bureaus to find a vacation leasing company to list your residence or boat.

THE GOING RATE: $100 to $1,000 a week, depending on your residence and the desirability of the event. The booking agency can give you pricing guidelines for your area.

RENT OUT OTHER STRUCTURES

You don't need to renovate your house or leave town to get a taste of landlording income. Depending on where you live, other structures on your property may be in high demand. If you live near a commuter line or in a densely populated part of the city, your garage or even the parking space in your driveway may be a very rentable item.

In some cases, you can just rent your raw space, without even a structure. People who own campers, trailers, and boats are often in need of off-season storage for their big toys, either because they don't have enough room themselves or because their neighborhood zoning prohibits storage of such big items on the street.

While your on-site presence can offer extra security and peace-of-mind to your clients, make sure they don't abuse your home-owner's rights by showing up at all hours of the day and night. One baker we spoke to rented out space in his yard to several local boat owners. The extra money was welcome, but inebriated boaters pulling into his driveway at all hours of the night proved too disturbing for a man who had to be up at 4 A.M. After laying down strict rules on hours of access he lost about half of his customers but regained his sleep. Next year, he is considering offering only winter storage.

Specifics as to hours of operation, when rent is due, liability, and exactly which space you are renting out should be spelled out in a contract. One trailer yard owner recommends that the contract should have a special provision that makes the car/boat/trailer forfeit if the rent is more than three months overdue. Stop in to your local library or quick copy shop for a book of simple business forms.

You'll also want to tidy up your property to make it look attractive and secure. A fresh coat of paint, new locks, and a few flowers around the garage will cost under $50 and will do more to help your sales pitch than anything else. If your driveway is asphalt or concrete make sure it's patched and sealed, and if it's gravel get a new load spread hard and even. Keeping your driveway in good repair is as important to you as to your client.

TOP TIP: Unless you have a very large yard with many spaces to rent, an expensive yellow pages ad will be a waste of your money. The best way to rent a garage is word-of mouth—tell everyone you know, even people you meet on line at the grocery store. You can also advertise for clients cheaply in local weekly papers and on the bulletin boards of marinas, train stations, and campgrounds. You can also leave your business card with local garages and car dealerships.

GETTING STARTED: There is usually no problem with renting out your garage, but if you are going to be storing boats or trailers on your property check your local zoning laws to make sure such storage is a permitted use.

THE GOING RATE: Varies with demand. Set your prices at about two-thirds of local commercial parking lots and storage yards to be competitive if demand is low; if demand is high you can charge as much as 90 percent of commercial rates.

INTERIOR DESIGNER

Interior designers identify design possiblities for interior spaces, from one room in a small home to entire office complexes. They develop complete design plans for their clients, create a budget, and choose a color scheme and style that complements the building and make the rooms seem inviting, beautiful, and comfortable. They also need a grasp of mechanical requirements and building codes, a knowledge of heating and ventilation systems, lighting, window treatments, fabrics, furniture placement and floor plans, wall and floor coverings, storage requirements, and other practical details.

Before you consider this business, you should ask yourself these questions. Do you have strong visual skills and a well-developed aesthetic sense? Do you understand how to work with colors, light, and space? Do you have good interpersonal and communication skills, which will help you in discovering your clients' design preferences? And do you have a knowledge of business and marketing? Each of these skills is important if you plan to run your own interior design business. You'll also need to decide early on whether you'd like to specialize—in kitchens and baths or commercial work, for example—or whether you'll be a generalist.

You'll need to gain as much practical experience as possible before you can think about going out on your own. Working in a furniture store or design studio can help you develop that invaluable hands-on experience. Reading *Marketing Basics for Designers: A Sourcebook of Strategies & Ideas* by Jane D. Martin and Nancy Knoohuizen (Wiley, 1995) can give you helpful marketing strategies for building a successful private practice. Then set up your home studio by buying a drafting table and drafting tools (if you don't already own them) and making room for product catalogs and samples. A computer is handy for invoicing and business correspondence, although some designers make do without one.

Developing a portfolio of rooms you've designed (or sketches of design ideas) is an important first step to show potential clients. You can stay on top of trends, new products, and creative decorating ideas by visiting your local merchandise mart and reading *Architectural Digest, Interior Design, Interiors,* and other professional and consumer magazines. Once you're established, referrals by past and present clients is the best way to bring in new clients. A listing in the yellow pages is also a worthwhile marketing expense. Visiting local real estate agents, home furnishing stores, wallpaper and paint stores, and other decorating outlets and letting them know about your business can be a great way to get referrals.

TOP TIP: Consider going into business with a partner. Lisa M. Knowles told us that her move from full-time interior designer to part-time home-based designer was made much easier by teaming up with a partner. Lisa told us, "We both work separately but share fifty-fifty in office expenses, including phone, fax, bookkeeping, and invoicing. A partner can give you good feedback and help handle projects when you're swamped. Having a partner also helps bring in more clients, since there are two of you out there."

GETTING STARTED: Most designers have a four-year university degree in interior design. If you didn't study this in college, there are other alternatives—you can take a home study course. Contact Sheffield School of Interior Design (211 E. 43rd

Street, NY, NY 10017; 212-661-7272) for information on their program, which has trained thousands of designers through correspondence courses since 1985. Several states also require a license, which means taking a two-day exam. Contact the National Council for Interior Design Qualification (914-948-9100) to learn more about their NCIDQ exam.

Joining the American Society of Interior Designers (608 Massachusetts Avenue NE, Washington, DC 20002; 202-546-3480) is also a good idea for designers who've had several years of experience. Members gain access to their local chapter meetings and workshops, can network at the annual national conference, and receive the association's bimonthly magazine, *ASID Report*. The ASID runs a Client/Designer Selection Referral Service, which can help send potential clients your way. Ask for their *Interior Design Career Guide* booklet, which offers basic information on the profession, educational requirements, employment prospects, and compensation.

THE GOING RATE: $60 to $150 an hour is what you can charge if you're an experienced interior designer. If you're just beginning, expect to receive $35 to $45 per hour. Some designers charge a percentage of the final cost of the project instead of an hourly fee.

DECORATING CONSULTANT

If you have a good eye for interior design and color coordination but don't want to be a full-time interior decorator, you could market yourself as a "visual coordinator," "home accessorizer," or "architectural color consultant." Whatever your title, you could go into people's homes and help them improve the look of their rooms by suggesting new colors for walls, adding colorful pillows, or moving furniture around.

Thia Bruno went into business for herself as a visual coordinator after several years spent rehabbing old houses and working in real estate. Her friends used to come over, look at her house, then ask her to help them give their homes a new look. She's built up a large clientele all through word of mouth. She told us her decorating philosophy: "I think your house should be you, not me. I don't believe in getting rid of people's favorite photos or knickknacks. Many decorators hate people's treasures, but that's what makes a house a home, and makes it wonderful. People think you have to spend a lot of money when you redecorate, but it's not true—you don't have to be rich to have a pretty or charming house."

Like Thia, you could differentiate yourself from other decorators by helping clients make their houses look good—without having to take out a second mortgage or raid the kids' college funds. Some inexpensive ways to "dress up" a home are arranging the furniture by putting it on angles, hanging pictures at the right height, and adding such designer touches as a small table with a beautiful bowl on it or a large plant. You can also recommend such quick fixes as repainting kitchen cabinets instead of replacing them and adding ceramic handles, or repainting furniture that's getting old and tired looking with shiny lacquer paint.

You'll need a strong visual sense and the ability to look at a room and figure out some ways to improve it. You should be good at working with people, and able to make yourself available some evenings and weekends. You'll need to know where to go to get the best selections of paint, wallpaper, and curtains. Most importantly, be flexible, open-minded, and don't impose your tastes on other people.

TOP TIP: Take out a classified newspaper ad, and tell everyone you meet about your new business. Then, visit local Realtors' offices with your portfolio. Let the Realtors know that you're available to help them rearrange a house to help it show well (this can be accomplished by adding candles, pictures, and books and by changing room layouts to make the house look warm and inviting).

GETTING STARTED: Get some experience working for a designer or take a course on home decorating. Pay attention to the decorating ideas and little touches shown in *House Beautiful* (1700 Broadway, New York, NY 10019), *Victoria* (224 W. 57th Street, 4th Floor, New York, NY 10019), and *Metropolitan Home* (1633 Broadway, 41st Floor, New York, NY 10019). After that, put together a portfolio of different decorating ideas, either photographs you've taken of interiors you've designed or clippings from magazines, to show potential clients.

THE GOING RATE: You can charge up to $100 to come out and walk through a house, discuss your clients' preferences, then come back with a decorating plan. You may be hired to redesign one or two rooms, or an entire house. A detailed plan includes wall colors and coordinating colors, kitchen tiles, additional furniture they could use, and advice on rearranging their rooms. The homeowners could then do the work themselves, or you could recommend a few painters and wallpaperers. Additional visits can be billed at $50 per hour, if they'd like you to come back with more ideas. If you're working for a Realtor, you can charge a $150 fee for an hour or two of improving a house's interior before an open house.

Neighborhood Concierge

A neighborhood concierge can also be called a "house waiter"— but this type of waiter doesn't serve food but waits for repair services, delivery trucks, contractor estimators, and meter readers to show up at homes when the owners cannot be home themselves.

As anyone who has ever waited for the washing machine repair person or window installer knows, waiting for a repairman usually means at least a half day of work lost. Many people are willing to pay someone else $6 to $10 an hour to be their stand-in at home so that they can go to the office. You can wait in the client's home or, if you are only servicing your local neighborhood, have the repairman or delivery person come to your home first. If the package is small, it can be delivered directly to your house. Clients deposit their keys with you to let the delivery service in with larger items, such as furniture and appliances. A neighborhood concierge service could also be easily developed in a condo or apartment building that doesn't have a doorman.

Being a neighborhood concierge certainly doesn't require any high-tech skills, but you must possess something that no school can teach—a sterling character. If people are to trust you in their homes or with their keys or precious package, your character must be beyond reproach.

One California concierge cautions that good waiters must be very patient and dependable. "I'm sedentary, love to knit or even do quilting while I wait." She doesn't do housework or child care, and charges $10 a hour to her mostly DINK (double-income, no kids) clients.

To get started, first identify a neighborhood in need of concierge services. Then, place flyers on all the doors of the neighborhood. Also send them to local repair services and delivery departments of local appliance and furniture stores in order to get referrals from them. A typical ad, which could appear in the weekend classifieds of the local paper, would be, "I'm dependable and patient. I'm good at waiting for you. I will wait in your home for $10.00 an hour for repair or delivery persons and sign for your delivery."

TOP TIP: Schedule only one client a day, since plumbers who say they'll be there at 10 A.M. may run into an emergency and not show up till well past noon.

GETTING STARTED: Invest $40 or so in a hundred flyers to drum up local business. Leave flyers on neighbors' doors and with local repair and delivery services who may want to recommend you to their clients. Prospective clients may want to meet you in person first. If so, be prepared with a conservative outfit, thick novel, and written character reference from a previous client, local clergy, or school principal.

THE GOING RATE: Charge a minimum of two hours and make $20 to $70 a day.

FOUND YOUR OWN MUSEUM

Collectors often yearn to share their glorious collections with the world—or at least with people outside their immediate family. If you have developed an impressive collection of paperweights, dolls, toy soldiers, quilts, music boxes, puppets, or any other possible collectible, consider starting a museum in your home.

You probably already have much of your collection on display anyway. You'll just need to invest in additional shelves or display cases and set a room or two aside for your mini-museum; basements or family rooms are usually the obvious choice. Make sure items are clearly organized (perhaps by date of manufacture) and labeled, and that there's enough room between the exhibits for people to walk around. You'll also want to insure your collection for any damage or theft that might result from opening your home to the public.

Take a look at the *Directory of Unique Museums*, edited by Bill Truesdell (Oryx Press, 1985) or a similar reference book to see if there are similar museums in your area. This book includes an astonishing variety of specialty museums, including museums devoted to collections of nuts, cookie jars, antique dollhouses, seashells—even tattoo art and barbed wire—so it may encourage you to elevate your collection to museum status as well. We've recently come across a museum devoted to images of the tooth fairy, the Banana Museum in California, which includes over fifteen thousand different banana items, and the Boston Museum of Bad Art.

TOP TIP: You don't need to open your doors all the time. Many small museums are only open three mornings or afternoons a week, and some are viewed by appointment only. Publicize your museum through collectors' publications and your local newspaper and chamber of commerce.

GETTING STARTED: Check with your local zoning board regarding any necessary permits.

THE GOING RATE: Admission charges vary between $2 and $7, depending on the size and uniqueness of your collection. Children are usually free—but if you collect fragile glass sculptures or other delicate items, you may wish to deny entrance to children under twelve years old.

COOKING AND CATERING SKILLS

COOKIE AND BREAD BAKER

Baking may be a traditional activity, but it's also a fast-growing, moneymaking opportunity of the '90s. For a start, who has time to bake from scratch anymore? Working parents are more likely to buy three dozen cookies or cupcakes for parties or school treats instead of taking the time to bake their own. And the dizzying proliferation of coffee and bagel shops has been accompanied by strong sales of homemade muffins, scones, brownies, cookies and other delectable treats customers consume along with copious cups of coffee.

You're right for this business if you are an accomplished cook, enjoy turning out large quantities of your favorite foods, and have a large enough kitchen to be able to cook in bulk. You'll need at least one large oven (two would be even better), an industrial-sized mixer (a bread machine would also be useful), a cupboard full of baking sheets, pans, baking racks, and other kitchen tools, storage space for basic ingredients and hundreds of pounds of flour, and dozens of cookbooks and favorite family recipes. You may also want to subscribe to the trade magazines *Bakery Production and Marketing* (1350 E. Touhy Avenue, Box 5080, Des Plaines, IL 60018) or *Cooking for Profit—The Business of Food Preparation* (PO Box 267, Fond du Lac, WI 54936).

Before becoming a kitchen entrepreneur, it's a good idea to polish your skills by taking cooking classes at a community college, chef's school, or adult education center. Once you've mastered the basics and the finer points of baking, pastry making, and cake decorating, decide which kinds of baked goods you'd like to sell. Do you want to focus on chocolate indulgences or heart-healthy breads? Are you partial to making dinner rolls or cinnamon rolls? Would you like to churn out wedding cakes or mounds of cookies? You may want to start with just a few items, then expand as you learn what your customers are craving. After you've chosen your specialties, create a flyer listing your foods and prices, and then distribute them to friends, neighbors, coffee shops, and apartment buildings. One woman found that her neighbors were eager to buy her fresh-baked bread. She ended up delivering several loaves a week to many of her neighbors, who stopped buying bread from grocery stores or other outlets.

TOP TIP: Don't forget to send out special mailings to your customers in early November, since Christmas cookies, braided bread, gingerbread houses, cranberry, pumpkin, or nut breads and other festive items (even fruitcake!) sell particularly well during the holidays. Sales calm down in January, when everyone is dieting, but pick up again in time for Easter.

GETTING STARTED: Before you start your business, enroll in a "Food Sanitation" course at your local community college to be sure you're handling foods properly. Make sure your kitchen meets local board of health regulations for your scope of operation. Then, keep your eyes open for possible places to sell your goodies. Ann Fackler's home business, Annie's Kitchen, took off after she decided to target hungry students and grad students at a nearby college. Once a week, she took a picnic basket filled with sandwiches, brownies, and muffins to the college, and they sold like the proverbial hotcakes. She took her basket along to her health club and found that her whole-grain breads and muffins were a hit there as well. After a while, word began to spread throughout the college and the town, and people began to call up asking for food for their parties, piano recitals, weddings, and other events. Ann commented, "The nice thing about doing weddings is that all of a sudden, two hundred people know about you. It's a wonderful way to get known as a professional." By putting a lot of energy into marketing her food, Ann gained tremendous exposure in the community and a thriving business.

THE GOING RATE: Varies depending on the quantity ordered, and whether you're selling to individual customers or to stores. Generally, loaves of bread sell for between $2.50 and $4, muffins for 75 cents to $1.50, cinnamon rolls and scones for $1 to $1.50 apiece, teabreads for $2.50, and cookies for 50 cents to $1 apiece. Cakes and coffee cakes can sell for $6 to $16 apiece.

GOURMET JAM AND SALSA SELLER

Avid gardeners who find that the bounty from their garden threatens to take over the neighborhood might want to consider preserving and selling their produce. Jams that are low in sugar are currently popular, from such staples as raspberry, blueberry, apple rhubarb, and strawberry rhubarb to such out-of-the-ordinary flavors as gooseberry or sweet pepper and jalapeño jam.

Fresh-tasting salsas without preservatives also sell well; offering salsas in clearly marked jars labeled "mild," "medium," and "explosive" will help your customers choose the variety they prefer without experiencing any unpleasant surprises. You can profit from your culinary skills by selling your goods at farmer's markets, roadside stands, delis, craft fairs, and holiday bazaars, and by selling to local caterers, restaurants, groceries, and gourmet food stores.

TOP TIP: If you don't garden, getting produce at a price that will leave room for your own profits may present a problem. Your operation will probably be too small to establish an account with a wholesale distributor, but perhaps you can make an arrangement with someone who does have such an account (like a local grocery store or café) to add on to their order and buy a case or two at a time at wholesale price.

GETTING STARTED: *Marketing a Family Recipe Business Guide* (text plus financial software) from Entrepreneur, Inc., PO Box 19787, Irvine, CA 92713 contains step-by-step instructions on how to market a family recipe. It includes information on how to start from home or rent a USDA-approved kitchen, how to get your product on retail shelves, and evaluations of which foods are currently most popular. *From Kitchen to Market: Selling Your Gourmet Food Specialty* by Stephen F. Hall (Upstart Publishing Co., 1992), is another helpful guide to reaching gourmet store shelves. As ever, check with your town's board of health to make sure your business meets their health requirements.

THE GOING RATE: The retail price of eight-ounce jars of homemade jam is around $5 apiece, and sixteen-ounce jars of salsa also sell for $5. Offering gift baskets with a few of your items packed in an attractive woven basket would enable you to charge a higher price. Gift baskets can be priced as follows: basket with any one item: $6; basket with two items: $15; with three items: $20; with four items: $25; and with five items, $30.

CHOCOLATIER

This may not be the ideal job for a chocoholic, unless you need to gain thirty pounds. It's more suited for cooks who enjoy the creativity of making—and selling—their own chocolate creations. The first step is to take some classes in desserts and chocolate making and perfect your skills by practicing at home. You can find these classes through your local community college or cooking specialty stores. Buy several reputable specialty cookbooks so you'll have plenty of recipes to try. Next, you'll need to come up with a unique product if you're going to survive in the food industry.

One chocolatier we interviewed decided to concentrate on "chocolate boxes." No, they're not traditional cardboard boxes containing chocolate creams. Instead, she creates molded boxes of chocolate, fills them with hand-made chocolates, and tops the whole creation off with a chocolate bow or candied flowers. She even offers a hand-woven chocolate basket filled with hand-dipped strawberries. Because she has a special product that no one else has developed, she's been successful in selling her creations primarily through word of mouth, though she's also beginning to offer her wares through bridal consultants and party planners.

Most of the cooking supplies are ones most people already have—including plenty of bowls and mixing spoons, a stove, and a microwave for tempering the chocolate—though you'll also need a supply of molds, fresh ingredients, and boxes or baskets in which to package your creations.

TOP TIP: An accomplished chocolatier gave us this advice: "You better not mind a mess if you go into this business. The other problem is that it's a very seasonal business. When you're busy, you're extremely busy. At Christmas, I can work 120-hour workweeks. Then in January, it all comes to a complete halt. I use that down time to experiment and develop new ideas for the next busy season."

GETTING STARTED: Contact your local board of health to see if you'll need a license or commercial kitchen certification. Then test all your new chocolates on family and friends (they'll be thrilled to serve as taste testers) to see which ones are the favorites. Include the most popular chocolates in your brochures. You can sell your chocolates at craft fairs and holiday bazaars, through local specialty shops, gourmet stores, and coffee shops, and through direct mail.

THE GOING RATE: Chocolate prices vary dramatically, according to the size and complexity of each item. Little party favors sell for $1 apiece, for example, while elaborate chocolate baskets or arrangements of truffles can sell for $75 to $100 apiece.

OFFICE AND NEIGHBORHOOD CATERER

Many people who enjoy cooking dream about becoming caterers and developing elegant little canapes and ice sculptures for large office parties. If the thought appeals to you but you're not sure your kitchen is big enough for you to whomp up meals for two hundred people, consider trying more limited catering jobs.

Remember the sandwich man in the old Dick Van Dyke show who came around to peddle his wares? You can offer a similar service in your own—or a friend's or neighbor's—office. You could begin by offering a limited menu for a catered lunch three days a week. Each week, send around a menu to everyone in the office and get their orders for the following week. Once you have a count, you can shop for all the ingredients at the weekend and begin creating some of the foods that require advance preparation. Some of the favorite lunch choices you could make are taco or chicken salads, homemade soup and bread, lasagna, gourmet sandwiches, and fruits or desserts. You'll also need to supply good-quality disposable dishes and plastic plates and bowls for reheating in the microwave. You probably already have most of the kitchen equipment you'll need.

If your colleagues' mouths water at what you or your spouse bring to work and if they often ask for your recipe (or a taste), you're on the right track. You can branch out by preparing boxed lunches for schoolchildren and company picnics. Do keep in mind that catering is very labor-intensive for the amount of money you make, so it's not for everyone.

You could also start a catered dinner service for your neighbors. You'll need to ask about the family's special dietary needs and food likes and dislikes, and then come to an agreement on how many meals a week you'll deliver. Let them know that you can create low-fat, diabetic, or kosher dishes, if requested. A meal usually consists of a main course or casserole, vegetables or a salad, and sometimes dessert. You'll shop for the ingredients, cook the meals at your home, and then deliver them before dinnertime. You don't have to be a gourmet cook to provide a valuable service—home-cooked meals "like Mom used to make" are what most people are looking for. Your best bets for customers are two-career couples and people who don't like to cook and are getting tired of eating out of boxes. You could charge around $25 per meal (which serves two to four people), or base your prices on the costs of ingredients plus 30 percent. Make sure you charge an advance deposit of 30 to 50 percent so you can pay for the ingredients you'll need.

TOP TIP: Handing out flyers with coupons, sending menus to local organizations along with a letter of introduction, and word of mouth are your best bets for publicizing your catering business.

GETTING STARTED: Check with your local board of health regarding kitchen requirements and zoning permits.

THE GOING RATE: You can charge $5 to $10 per meal, depending on the city you live in and the cost of nearby restaurants.

You will probably make money on some meals, and lose it on others after you subtract the cost of ingredients that week.

SKILLED AT CARING FOR ANIMALS

Pet-Sitter

This is a wonderful job for animal lovers who enjoy getting paid for caring for and playing with other people's pets. It's a growing field, since more than 60 percent of all U.S. households have pets, and more owners are employed outside the home these days. Most pet-sitters have already cared for friends' pets informally before they decide to make it a business. Dogs and cats are the most common pets that need care when owners are away, but you'll occasionally be asked to take care of rabbits, guinea pigs, hamsters, birds, or tropical fish. It's a good idea to visit the animals before you take the job, and make sure you're shown where their food, toys and supplies are. It's also wise to require owners to write notes to their vets before they depart stating that you have permission to seek medical care for the pets in an emergency but that the owners are responsible for payment.

You can decide whether you care for the animals in their own homes or in your house. Hazel H. Valentine (known as the "Paw Holder" to her clients) has been pet-sitting for eight years and has found that "it's easier on the animals to be in their own homes—they already know the house rules and have food and water they're used to. I follow their regular schedules as closely as I can."

Pet-sitters spend an average of forty-five minutes to an hour per visit, during which they exercise, brush, and feed the pet, clean up the litterbox or any accidents, and provide petting and playtime. This can be great fun or a trial, depending on the pet's personality. Pet-sitter Lucinda Michaelis told us about her first dog-sitting experience in her home. Within the first few hours, the dog had chewed up her baby's pacifier, knocked over the baby, chewed on some pillows, and swallowed an entire child's sock. The only thing he did not get into was the garbage pail, which was in plain sight in the kitchen. The lesson is: You need a sense of humor and patience as much as you need affection for animals. You should also write up a report of each visit to keep the owners informed.

TOP TIP: Developing a brochure explaining your services and fees will help bring in new clients. Then, tell every pet owner you know about your services, and leave your business card or brochure with local vets, veterinary hospitals, and pet supply stores. Distributing your flyers at apartment buildings that allow pets is also a worthwhile marketing idea.

GETTING STARTED: Read *Pet Sitting for Profit: A Complete Manual for Success* by Patti J. Moran (Howell Books, 1992) to learn more about this business. Many two-career couples need their pets cared for every day while they're at work, so spread the word that you're available for daily visits. And, consider joining a professional association for pet sitters: NAPPS (National Association of Professional Pet Sitters, 1200 G Street NW, Ste. 760, Washington, DC 20015; 202-393-3317) or PSI (Pet Sitters International, 418 E. King Street, King, NC 27021; 910-983-9222). Both associations offer phone referral services, networking, access to bonding and insurance, and helpful newsletters.

THE GOING RATE: $6 to $10 for one visit a day; $12 to $15 for more than one visit per day. Most pet-sitters average around

$10 per visit, although many charge $2 to $3 per day for each additional pet. Cats usually require only one or two visits a day. Dogs usually need three to four visits daily, and puppies, until they are housebroken, may need visits more often. Some sitters will also stay with a pet overnight.

Dog Trainer

There's no better home business for a dog lover. But loving dogs and understanding your own pets is not enough. "Say you have Rottweilers—that's the breed you know how to train," said Pat Carr, owner of the Carvilla dog-training school. "That doesn't mean you know how to train a sheltie. Their characteristics are very different—it's not enough to say that a dog is a dog." Carr went on to say, "This is a rewarding career, and a lot of fun if you really enjoy animals. But it does take time to become knowledgeable. Dog training is not the no-brainer many people think it is. A lot of people have no idea how a dog is motivated—they think of dogs as little humans in furry suits." In fact, dog trainers are actually teaching *people* how to train their dogs, not teaching dogs, so you need to know how people learn. Once you've gained an education in dog training, you'll need to find a good place to hold your training classes. You can use your large basement or fenced-in backyard, but you'd only be able to teach one to three dogs in that setting. If your business expands, you could consider renting some space to hold larger classes.

There are several helpful associations specifically for dog trainers you may want to join. The Association of Pet Dog Trainers (PO Box 3734, Salinas, CA 93912-3734; 408-663-9257) is highly recommended by the trainers we spoke to, and offers an excellent annual conference with dozens of educational seminars and workshops. There's also the National Association of Dog Obedience Instructors (PO Box 432, Landing, NJ 07850) and the American Dog Trainers Network (161 W. 4th Street, New York, NY 10014; 212-727-7257). The ADTN provides information, tips, and references about dogs to the general public, along with a list of reputable trainers across the United States. Make sure you're put on their trainers' list so you can receive referrals from their organization.

TOP TIP: You can find customers by calling on local vets and animal hospitals and asking if you could leave your brochures or business cards. Leave brochures at pet supply stores, take out a yellow pages listing, and consider an ad in the local paper. If you're doing your job right, you should get referrals from people who've previously taken your classes.

GETTING STARTED: Take a few dog-training classes through your local dog-training school, dog club, or park district. Buy and study some dog-training videos from one of the top dog supply catalogs (R.C. Steele: 1-800-872-3773 or Foster and Smith: 1-800-826-7206). Then, practice training your own and family members' dogs. After that, unless you have a great deal of experience in training different breeds of dogs, consider finding an experienced trainer and offering to work as an apprentice for little or no pay. (Asking veterinarians for dog trainers they would recommend is the best place to start.) As an apprentice, you get to hang around and see how that trainer achieves results.

Just make sure that you don't ask a trainer in the next town, since you would end up as their competitor. Instead, find a trainer who lives at least an hour away in order to learn your trade. Going further afield can also help you learn training techniques that may not be taught in your community, so you have something new to offer when you start your business. When you do find a good trainer who is willing to act as your mentor, plan to apprentice yourself for six months to a year, if possible, in order to develop your skills and find out whether this is really what you want to do.

THE GOING RATE: The average rate for teaching obedience training classes is $50 to $75 for six one-hour lessons. Beginning trainers may charge only $35 for their classes, while top trainers in urban areas can charge up to $250 for the same number of sessions. Some families would prefer that you come to their home and conduct a private dog-training class for them. Most trainers charge around $50 an hour (or more, depending on the travel time involved) for personalized in-home training.

PET BREEDER

Knowledgeable animal people can make very good money breeding dogs and cats for the pet and show market, but be warned— the related fees and maintenance costs can really add up and cut into your profits.

We've all seen the classified ads or supermarket notices for $500 German shepherd puppies or $400 Maine coon cats and thought, "Gee, what an easy way to make money with your pet." But according to professional breeders, a responsible breeding program is not so easy to set up or maintain.

Your first setup costs will be for the kennel or cattery environment. You'll need indoor and outdoor (not necessarily outdoor for cats) runs, a birthing area that can be sterilized, and sound insulation (or very tolerant neighbors).

Then you'll need the proper animals. A cute bundle of fur from the local pet store has virtually no potential as a profitable breeding animal, even if it is AKC registered. This is because show-quality animal breeders and buyers all know the best bloodlines, which you will not get for $39.95 in a pet shop. So, to start your breeding program you should budget around $1,000 for a suitable animal. Show fees and the related transportation costs for getting your animal known can add up to another $2,000 a year, depending on whether you have the skill to show your animal yourself or pay a professional to present it.

If you have a female, expect to pay $400 to $1,000 in stud fees to get her bred. If you have a male, what you charge will directly relate to how well he does in the shows you attend.

Then there are the vet's delivery charges for the pups, plus

their first set of shots, worming, and, if necessary, tail or ear surgery. This can add up to another $125 per animal before it is
anywhere near ready to be sold.

As you can see from the above, it is quite easy to be $5,000
out of pocket before you even get to your first litter. However,
once your animal's reputation is established and your physical
setup is in place, your operating costs should go down while the
profits go up.

Professional breeders suggest following the show circuit and
the breed you're interested in for a year before taking the plunge
into animal breeding. Also, check your local regulations regarding
breeding operations. Many municipalities effectively regulate animal breeders through ordinances that limit the number of animals any one household can have; others strictly enforce noise
and nuisance ordinances. You may or may not need a business
license; Chicago, for instance, considers your breeding operation
a hobby as long as you advertise your pups in the personal classifieds or through bulletin boards. If, however, you advertise in the
yellow pages or a display ad you are considered a business and
must get licensed. Similarly, the IRS may or may not consider
you a hobby depending on how often you make a profit. It is a
good idea to always maintain separate and business-like records
of costs, expenses, and transactions, in case your status is ever
called into question.

TOP TIP: Consider breeding as an add-on service to some
other animal-related business you already run, such as grooming
or training.

GETTING STARTED: Contact the American Kennel Club
(51 Madison Avenue, New York, NY 10010) at 212-696-8200
and request their Dog Buyer's Education packet, along with the
confirmation and obedience specifications for the breed(s) you
are interested in. If you are new to the show circuit find events
you can attend through *Cat Fancy* or *Dog Fancy* magazines (Box
6040, Mission Viejo, CA 92690). You can also contact the national office of the Professional Dog Handlers' Association at

301-924-0089 for a list of members in your area or the area in which you will be showing.

THE GOING RATE: Profit potential varies greatly by breed and the number of pups in each litter. You can't predict how prolific your female will be or how many of her pups will be of show or just pet quality. Also, prices for pups will vary as the popularity of certain breeds waxes or wains. Consult other breeders in your area to fix your prices. In addition, if you have a good female, plan on breeding her no more than twice a year with an occasional year off, so that you don't wear her out.

BEEKEEPER

If you enjoy nature and are interested in insects, you may want to consider owning an apiary. No, an apiary is not a home for apes, it's a place where bees are kept. Beekeeping is an ancient art—did you know that Artistotle kept bees?—that is still alive and well, since honey is a delicacy most people enjoy. It's also an appealing business because the bees tend to themselves. As long as you manage their health (medicate them regularly to avoid the mites and bacterial infections they're susceptible to) and give them plenty of room to grow, they'll do all the work for you. One hive can produce an average of sixty to a hundred pounds of honey a year, depending on weather conditions.

You can start with a couple of hives and three pounds of bees per hive (yes, they do sell live bees by the pound!). Hives with wooden frames can be purchased from the following mail order companies: Dadant (51 S. 2nd Street, Hamilton, IL 62341; 1-800-634-7468), Brushy Mountain Bee Farm (NC, 1-800-BEESWAX [233-7929]) and Mann Lake Supply (Hackensack, MN, 1-800-233-6663). You can also order a smoker, bee suit, hive tools, and honey jars from these companies' catalogs. They'll ship you a box of bees, and the all-important queen bee in a separate box. The initial investment for two hives and two bee

colonies will come to about $500. This doesn't include a honey
harvester. A large stainless-steel honey extractor costs between
$500 to $600, so you may want to start with a less-expensive,
messier hand extractor for the first couple of years—or search
the want ads for a used large extractor.

You don't need a degree in entomology to succeed at beekeeping, but you do need a lot of patience, since you won't be able to
harvest any honey until you've had the hive a year. You'll also
need to be able to lift heavy trays of honey—some can hold as
much as sixty pounds of honey—and you shouldn't be too squeamish about getting stung (or allergic to bee stings). Your neighbors might complain about your keeping bees near their houses,
so it's a good idea to check local regulations to see if beekeeping
is permitted in your town. If you have a large operation, the
board of health may want to come out and regularly inspect your
extraction practices, so staying small has its advantages.

If you do end up with extra hives, you could make money
renting some beehives to nearby farms to add in pollination.
Pumpkin farms, berry farms, cucumber growers, and orchards
often need help with pollination, so you can rent them extra hives
and charge $50 or more per hive annually.

Regional associations like the Central Illinois Beekepers
Assocation are found throughout the United States, and are a
useful way to meet and learn from other bee enthusiasts. Susan
Sheridan has kept bees for a few years, and counsels, "Try to join
a bee association—it's nice to have someone with more knowledge helping you out if you're a beginner. Some associations have
extractors for their members to share. And don't let early failures
put you off. Your bees might fly away, and you may have trouble
with bees not surviving the winter. It can be discouraging, but
you'll learn a lot if you persevere."

TOP TIP: Andrew Blum, a long-term beekeeper, said, "I buy
cool-looking jars in different shapes from distributors who advertise in the beekeeping magazines. You can make more money by
putting these gourmet honey jars in a gift basket with artificial
grass, crackers, and a bow. By jazzing it up, I can sell my honey

to antique shops and gift shops, and make about $2.50 a pound wholesale." If you sell the baskets directly to consumers, you can charge $4.50 to $7.50 per gift basket.

GETTING STARTED: Prepare yourself by taking a class or reading up on beekeeping before you set up your hives. *A Book of Bees* by Sue Hubble (Random House, 1988) is a well-written and useful reference book, as is *Beekeeping: A Practical Guide* by Richard E. Barney (Garden Way Publishing, 1993). Relevant magazines include *American Bee Journal* (published by Dadant, 51 S. 2nd Street, Hamilton, IL 62341; 217-847-3324) and *Bee Culture* (Box 706, Medina, OH 44256). You could also join the American Beekeeping Association (PO Box 1038, Jessup, GA 31545; 912-427-8447) or the American Honey Producers Association (PO Box 584, Cheshire, CT 06410; 203-250-7271).

THE GOING RATE: You can put your honey into jars, add an elegant handwritten or printed label, and sell it for about $1.50 a pound at local farmer's markets. You could also sell beeswax to craft stores and crafters who use it for candlemaking, or sell your own homemade candles. Beeswax sheets sell for between $2.75 to $6 a pound, and hand-dipped candles can retail for $7–$20 a pair.

GARDENING SKILLS

GARDENING TEACHER

Here's a creative way to use your love of gardening to make some money: offer gardening seminars in your own backyard. You'll need to have an extensive garden with a variety of different plants, a lot of gardening tools, and the ability to teach basic and advanced gardening tips to your students.

You can offer a class each month on a different aspect of gardening—including planning your flower beds, learning about perennials, preparing the soil, learning what's a weed and what isn't, creating an English garden, caring for roses, bulb planting and the like. Students should come prepared for hands-on experience—they can learn quickly by actually working with you in your garden during the class (and your garden will benefit from all this extra labor as well!). You can also offer workshops on drying flowers and leaves, and creating decorative arrangements from dried flowers.

Julie Reasor Fischer calls her business The Cottage Gardener. She has run these seminars from her garden for three years and attracts a hundred students each year. She illustrates her talks by taking students through the garden and showing them her plants at different stages of development. She had previously worked at a local garden center and designed gardens for customers. Fischer told us, "My philosophy is that gardeners are givers. I enjoy giving away anything I can divide from my garden, and send my students home with at least ten cuttings of their choice. My best advice to other gardening teachers: Don't pretend you know something you don't. It's fine to say, 'Let's look it up.' That's another thing I like about gardening—you never quit learning."

TOP TIP: Giving talks and slide shows to women's groups and gardening clubs is a fruitful way to get the word out about your classes.

GETTING STARTED: Take some basic horticulture classes from your local community college or botanic garden. Getting a job in a garden center can also teach you a lot in a short time, and some teaching experience (in any field) would be helpful. Then, publicize your classes through word of mouth and by sending personalized letters to former students and potential students.

THE GOING RATE: You can charge around $35 for a three- to four-hour class (this price includes a folder full of handouts and sending students home with several plant cuttings or seedlings). Offering a five-hour class with luncheon enables you to charge $50 per person. You can also provide private garden consultations for $40—many class participants will request a follow-up consultation at their homes after they take the class.

Specialty Plant Nursery

Gardening is one of the fastest-growing businesses in America, but most of us don't have the acreage required to cash in on the craze with a full-service garden center. However, even a suburban gardener with a twenty-foot border strip and a green thumb has enough space for a nice little microbusiness specializing in hosta, daylillies, or irises.

All three of these plants are popular, expensive, easy-to-grow and—most important—easy to propagate through clump division with a shape spade or knife. The arithmetic is easy: buy ten plants each of several colors the first year, let them grow one year, divide in the fall to double your stock, and start selling.

For irises you'll need a sunny spot, but hosta and daylillies can both take some shade. Unlike a private garden, your plant nursery should be laid out in straight rows to facilitate weeding and feeding. (It's a good idea to start a compost pile to provide high-quality fertilizer for yourself at a low cost.)

We spoke with Jean Frame, who has been running a daylilly business out of her backyard for eight years. "First I had all sorts of perennials, which I was selling for $2 a plant, but the costs of keeping the beds stocked and tidy was wiping out all my profits. Also, I'd have a lot of stock left over at the end of each season, so that with each successive year my garden was more and more full of the plants that nobody wanted. It was getting terrible. But the part of my business that was going well was a small strip of daylillies that I had put in more as a border for myself. People always wanted them, and I'd just go over to the border, lift out a clump with a spade, put it in a plastic bag, and make my sale.

"Finally my husband suggested we specialize in just the daylillies. I bought new stock through mail order to make sure I'd always have early, mid- and late-season bloomers, and to offer more of a color variety. I also learned to clip pictures from ads and magazines to show what the mature plant will look like. I put these pictures in a plastic sleeve and stake them at the front of each row, so that people who don't know the name will still have an idea of how the plant looks.

"I don't do any mail order myself. We live about ten feet off a major road, so I just have my sign out there: 'Daylilly Nursery—Public Invited.' I have an open house every July for which I take out some local ads, and I also take a table at my town's summer fair. I try to keep my prices about half that of the big commercial centers, which sell average daylillies for $6 a pot and rare varieties for $12 or $15. Of course, I don't have the cost of the plastic pot."

TOP TIP: Have your varieties clearly labeled and illustrated, with information on cultivation for the novice gardener.

GETTING STARTED: Gardening is a seasonal business. It will take a least a year for your plants to be at division size. Use that time wisely to make sure you have good signage, packaging, and a spot for customers to park and load up. Start doing early advertising for your plants by writing a gardening column for your local paper, or giving a talk at the library, school, or senior center.

THE BOTTOM LINE: Underprice local commercial nurseries by at least 25 percent; if your plants are exotic or rare consider selling them mail order and through advertising in *Fine Gardening* (63 S. Main Street, Box 5506, Newton, CT 06470) or *Garden Design* (100 Sixth Avenue, 7th Floor, New York, NY 10013) magazines.

SPECIALTY GOURMET FOOD FROM YOUR GARDEN

The specialty gourmet food industry is generating revenues of almost *$10 billion* a year, and many entrepreneurs with a good recipe and big dreams would like a piece of that action. But beware—the experts, such as Stephen F. Hall, author of *From Kitchen to Market* (Upstart Publishers, 1992), warn that you can expect start-up costs of $25,000 to $100,000 each year for three to five years to get one product produced, packaged, labeled, advertised, promoted, and onto store shelves nationwide. And even then, three out of five products will be ultimate failures.

Microbusiness owners with more modest ambitions can place specialty products locally with a great deal more success for a great deal less money if they exploit the very factors that make them small—"home grown," "fresh," and "handmade."

Unless you live in a climate where you can grow fresh produce year-round, or have access to a greenhouse, growing year-round fresh produce for local stores and restaurants is probably not practical. But providing dried spices, sauces, and condiments is within your grasp. These products also have the advantage of a long shelf life.

Home-grown sauces, spices, and condiments can be marketed through farmer's markets, flea markets, roadside stands, gift shops, tourist centers, and—if your land has been free of pesticides for five years—through organic health-food stores.

And here's another advantage to staying small—federal regulations for food product testing and nutritional labeling don't apply to coffee, tea, spice, and products whose real annual revenues are less than $500,000. Being an exception to the Nutritional Labeling and Education Act (NLEA) is important to the small-time operator, because a workup from a food laboratory for a single sample compliance can easily cost over $600!

One of the easiest gourmet condiments to make is herb vinegar. Unlike jam, jellies, and sauces, it doesn't even need cooking or expensive sugars. You can make it all year with nothing more than vinegar and plants collected from your garden or sunny windowsill.

The most popular flavors are basil, thyme, tarragon, and rosemary—but don't be afraid to experiment with other flavors, too. Pick the herbs when they are flowering. Label a paper bag with the name, place the herbs in a bag, and seal them off with a twist tie or rubber band. Hang the bags from a hook or clothesline inside to dry and use as you need them.

You'll also need good-quality wine or apple cider vinegar and a supply of bottles with nonmetal caps or corks (the metal caps will react with the vinegar). Using a ratio of four tablespoons of herbs to four cups of vinegar, let your mixture sit for a month. After thirty days, strain out the herbs, place several whole fresh sprigs in the bottle for the nice visual effect, pour the beautifully flavored liquid back in, and recork the bottles. Voilà, gourmet herbal vinegar!

TOP TIP: Spend a lot of time—and money to a professional graphic designer if you don't have any artistic talent yourself—to get an attractive label. Every gourmet food distributor we spoke to stressed the importance of the label in attracting the customer and in making the retailer willing to carry the product.

GETTING STARTED: Make up a small sample batch of about six bottles and scout local and gourmet food stores to see how many varieties of your garden product they are already carrying. If they already have three or more, the odds of them finding room on their shelves for you is much less likely. You should then concentrate your marketing on other outlets, such as farmer's markets, fairs, and roadside stands. For more information on developing and marketing your gourmet garden product, read Stephen F. Hall's *From Kitchen to Market.*

THE BOTTOM LINE: Your costs will be more in the packaging and labeling than in the product. Set your retail price high enough that the store owner's 50 percent discount won't leave you without a profit.

Make Potpourri and Other Fragrant Concoctions

If you don't have acres and acres of land for an old-time Victory Garden, you can still reap a profit from a few square feet of growing space if you concentrate on the herbs and flowers used to scent potpourri, toilet waters, sachet, and soap. The investment in materials is low, and most of your product preparation can easily take place in an average-size kitchen equipped with no more than a shelf, stove, and table or counter work space.

While almost any plant or flower can be used to create a scented delight, the most popular ones are roses, lilac, lavender, jasmine, and honeysuckle. Among the herbs balm, lovage, pennyroyal, sage, rosemary, chamomile, and peppermint are extremely easy to grow and the most in demand for teas and sachets.

After you have your plant ingredients, the next step is to dry them, either by placing them in a sunny window or placing them in a paper bag strung up on a clothesline or curtain rod. Don't ever use a plastic bag—your flowers will wilt before they dry!

The next step is to find—or create your own—recipe for a delightful mix. We recommend that beginners follow one of the recipes from David Webb's *Making Potpourri, Colognes and Soaps* (TAB Books, 1988) or Anne Tucker Fettner's *Potpourri, Incense and Other Fragrant Concoctions* (Workman Publishing, 1977) until they develop enough of a nose to strike out on their own. Both these books also contain a wealth of tips on preservatives, fixing agents, and more complicated recipes for making perfume and candles.

Besides flowers and herbs, you'll need to decide on what kind of container you want to use for your concoctions. The simplest container is a bag made from scrap fabric and tied off with an attractive ribbon. Yard sales, thrift stores, and manufacturers' closeouts are good sources for old glasses, boxes, and medicine bottles to use for hard storage. Almost anything has the potential to be a container—Anne Tucker Fettner suggests seashells large enough to hold potpourri or sachet under a plastic-wrap seal.

Most of the tools required to make scented products are easy to purchase from your local supermarket or five-and-dime store. At a minimum you will need:

- ◆ Mortar and pestle for grinding herbs and spices.
- ◆ Tea infusers or tea balls to separate solids from fluids.
- ◆ Scale to weigh ingredients.
- ◆ Eyedropper to measure out oils.
- ◆ Several wooden stirring spoons.
- ◆ Measuring cup and measuring spoons for accurate ingredient measurement.
- ◆ Several large jars with tight-fitting lids to store ingredients.

While most of the ingredients you'll need for making fragrant concoctions are readily available at local stores, some items, such as potent oils or fixatives (to make the scent last) may have to be ordered from these specialty suppliers:

Edmund Scientific
101 E. Gloucester Pike
Barrington, NJ 08007
(Glass containers, bottles, perfume-making kits)

Indiana Botanic Gardens
PO Box 5
Hammond, IN 46325
(Oils, resins, bottles)

The Soap Opera
319 State Street
Madison, WI 53707
(Oils, books)

Where are the markets for scented products? While most large chain stores sell potpourri, candles, and sachet, these types of retail establishments usually require large volume and product uniformity. A small producer such as yourself will do better placing products on commission at local individually owned gift, craft, bed and bath, and art stores. Summertime farmer's markets, craft fairs, and flea markets are the best places to sell, especially if you can get a table in the same location every time and develop a steady clientele.

TOP TIP: According to David Webb (author of *Making Potpourri, Colognes and Soaps*), the key concept to marketing your scented products is "making the package fit the market." In his experience, people are willing to pay a premium for fancy packages, but don't expect to find those packages at a flea market. Therefore, save your expensive containers for your retail clients, and sell the more inexpensive fabric containers at the flea markets and craft fairs.

GETTING STARTED: Scout sources for plant materials and containers. Before investing the time and money to get a garden plot going, you could make up a few test batches from herbs and flowers gathered from a friend's garden or discount nursery product just past its prime.

When you are ready to plant, you can keep costs down by joining a seed swappers club, such as the one sponsored by *Organic Gardening* magazine. Send your name, address, and the varieties you're offering or seeking to:

Seed Savers/Seed Sharers
Organic Gardening
33 E. Minor Street
Emmaus, PA 18098

THE BOTTOM LINE: As a rule of thumb for direct sales, your final asking price should be twice the cost of your materials (to cover resupply costs) plus about 40–50 percent additional markup for your actual profit. Thus, a $2 investment in materials and containers should result in a $6 product. The more you grow and develop yourself, the less your restocking costs will be.

BUYING
AND
SELLING

◆

WHAT YOU NEED TO KNOW TO GET STARTED

As varied as your talents may be, few small business owners are expert in all areas of their enterprises—procurement, production, marketing, finance, and so on. If, however, you have expertise in the area of sales, you have a skill that is always in high demand. In fact, good salesmanship is so highly prized that many businesses will actually help you set up your business in order to pitch their products.

This field is commonly known as home sales or home party sales, and Avon and Mary Kay Cosmetics are two internationally famous names that immediately come to mind. But cosmetics and personal-care products are not the whole story in home sales: Manufacturers of clothing, cookware, toys, and vitamins are also eager to set up "consultant" relationships with would-be supersellers.

Here is how most home party plans work: You contact the manufacturer of the books, toys, cosmetics, or cookware and ask to be a rep. They sell you a demonstration kit of their merchandise (depending on the product, a demo kit may cost from $100 to $500), which you then schlep around to other people's houses, street fairs, malls, park district picnics, and wherever else you think you can find clients. You do your demos and write up your orders right on site—there is very little follow-up paperwork at home. You send the order to the manufacturer, who then ships the merchandise directly to the client. A percentage of the sales—

usually ranging from 15 percent to 40 percent, depending on the line—is returned to you from the manufacturer.

Many of the companies offer additional incentives for their reps (or "consultants," as many prefer to be called). For example, consultants for The Pampered Chef can earn all-expense-paid family vacations to Walt DisneyWorld.

Most of the home party reps we spoke to are obsessed with finding new party sites to demonstrate their products. After your first circle of friends is exhausted you have to network aggressively to break into new circles of clients. Usually the manufacturer helps you by offering an incentive of free gifts for the person hosting the party. In effect, you have to pitch twice—once to get the party site, and again to move the merchandise.

If you have a classic sales personality—gregarious, peppy, with a positive drive to succeed—this aspect of home party sales will probably be catnip to you. If you are primarily attracted to the products themselves and are of a retiring personality, watch out—you may end up buying so many additional "add-ons" to your demo kit that you never make a profit! We spoke to several disillusioned home sales reps who actually ended up losing money. They fell into the trap of adding and adding to their demo kits in the hope that a fabulous kit would boost sales, when in fact what they needed were better selling skills themselves.

Assuming that you're the right personality type, contact the product manufacturer of your choice. It helps to be truly interested in or have a background in the product you are repping—it lends credibility to your demos. It helps if a mother or a teacher can point to a certain toy and say, "This one is perfect for small-motor skills development in three-year-olds," or for someone with a background in catering or cooking classes to be able to say, "This is exactly the right weight pan so as not to scorch your roux."

Be prepared to spend a lot of time out of your home on weekends and evenings working your party circuit. Word of mouth is best, but some reps also take out small ads in neighborhood papers, pass out flyers at shopping malls, and hand out hundreds of business cards. In many of these plans there is also a lot of emphasis—and incentives in the form of a better percentage deal from the company—to actively *recruit* additional reps. But be warned—the incentive may not be worth it if the company doesn't protect your territory. A new rep in your area may mean fewer sales for you, even if the percentage is higher. In summation—and we cannot stress this strongly enough—this type of business is good for the person with the right personality, but can turn into a money pit for someone without sales skills.

Perhaps you have made an honest assessment of your talents and come to the conclusion that your skills lie more in the area of buying than selling. Don't despair—there is a need in the marketplace for people with that talent, too. While you love to shop, there are many for whom it is anathema. Others would like to shop for personal or business gifts but simply don't have the time. The demand for this type of service is growing and shows no sign of letting up. Shoppers have found that buying gourmet food and small gifts in a beautifully wrapped basket is a convenient, easy way to send presents for birthdays, anniversaries, holidays, and other special occasions. Corporations also turn to gift basket companies when they want to send Christmas and Hanukkah gifts to their best customers and favored employees. We profile two successful gift-buying services, one that specializes in baskets and another, more general service, to give you an idea of the variety available in the buying, as opposed to the selling, field.

HOME PARTY SALES

A lot of people have made a lot of money working the home party sales circuit. The *Wall Street Journal* reports that home party sales rose 20 to 30 percent in 1996, citing "a captive audience, low marketing costs, and an aura of social pressure that can be lucrative for purveyors." Purveyors can sell everything from lingerie to lettuce spinners, but the first thing you have to realize, according to Charlotte, a veteran Discovery Toys and Tupperware rep, is that "this is not really an at-home business; sure, you're working out of a home—but that home is rarely yours!"

There *are* two ways around the out-of-your-home aspect of the home party sales business. The first is if you choose a company that also does catalog sales, such as Discovery Toys and Avon. Then you can simply make your catalog distribution runs once or twice a month and pray that the orders come in. The second way to get out of going to other people's homes is to use the party sales as an adjunct or add-on business to an event that is already happening in your home. For instance, a logical add-on for someone running a home day-care or baby-sitting service would be Discovery Toys. A good adjunct for someone running cooking classes in their home would be Tupperware or Alfa Metalcraft, especially if you actually use the pieces in your classes. And a good add-on for someone doing massage therapy or haircuts would be Oriflame cosmetics or Shaklee health-care products.

TOP TIP: Make an honest evaluation of your sales skills, then choose a company that produces something you know about in an area in which you already have some credibility.

GETTING STARTED: Evaluate the company carefully. Is it well established with a reputation for treating the reps fairly? Do they pay promptly? Does the demonstration kit include marketing aids and training for you, or is it just a way for the company to sell more products? Once you have targeted one or two companies you are interested in repping for, you can test the waters by offering to host a party for another rep.

THE GOING RATE: Unlimited. Start-up costs usually average $100 to $400 for demonstration kits; figure another $50 to $100 for business cards and flyers.

Below is a list of some of the most popular nationwide companies that use home party reps. If you think home party sales is for you and would like to give it a try, contact the home office.

Alfa Metalcraft Corporation of America
6593 Powers Avenue
Jacksonville, FL 32217
(Cookware)

Amway Corporation
7575 Fulton Street East
Ada, MI 49355
(Cookware, cleaning supplies, cosmetics, and more)

Avon Products
638 Otis Place NW
Washington, DC 20010
(Health and beauty products)

Cameo Products
PO Box 590388
Orlando, FL 32859
(Craft kits)

The Creative Circle
15711 South Broadway
Gardena, CA 90248
(Needlework kits)

Creative Memories
2815 Clearwater Road
PO Box 767, St. Cloud, MN 56302
(Photo albums and scrapbooks)

Discovery Toys
2530 Arnold Drive
Martinez, CA 94553
(Educational toys, games, and books)

Doncaster Direct Sales
Oak Springs Road, Box 1159
Rutherfordton, NC 28139
(Women's clothing and accessories)

Herbalife International
Box 80210
Los Angeles, CA 90009
(Health foods, fitness and nutritional products)

Highlights Express
Box 810
Columbus, OH 43216
(Toys, book, games, videos; affiliated with *Highlights for Children* magazine)

House of Lloyd, Inc.
11091 Grandview Road
Grandview, MO 64030
(Christmas accessories, gifts, and toys)

Jafra Cosmetics
Box 5026
Westlake Village, CA 91359
(Natural cosmetics and skin-care products)

Kitchen Fair
Box 100
Jacksonville, AR 72076
(Cookware and kitchen accessories)

The Longaberger Company
95 N. Chestnut Street
Dresden, OH 43821
(Baskets, decorations, house and kitchenware)

Mary Kay Cosmetics
8787 Stemmons Freeway
Dallas, TX 75247
(Cosmetics)

McConnon & Company
McConnon Drive
Winona, MN 55987
(Household and animal health products; farm line products)

Orilflame International
76 Treble Cove Road
North Billerica, MA 01862
(European cosmetics and skin-care products)

The Pampered Chef
350 S. Rohlwing Road
Addison, IL 60101
(About 25,000 "consultants" sell cookware through low-
pressure kitchen shows)

Tupperware Home Parties
Box 2353
Orlando, FL 32802
(Food storage containers, cookware, and toys)

Usborne Books at Home
Box 470663
Tulsa, OK 74147
(Children's books sold through four avenues: home party,
fund-raisers, book fairs, and direct sales.)

Watkins
Box 5570
Winona, MN 55987
(Food, health, and cleaning products)

The West Bend Company
400 Washington Street
West Bend, WI 53095
(Cookware and electrical appliances)

GIFT-BUYING
SERVICE

Do you love to shop? If you enjoy looking high and low for
unique gifts and finding the best deals, this could be the ideal
business for you. You can begin by providing this service for individuals, and then branch out by contacting local companies.
Busy, time-stressed working parents could use your service to buy
birthday, wedding, shower, Christmas, and graduation presents.

Ask your customers to describe the recipient and the type of gift they're looking for, how much they'd like to spend, their color and fabric preferences, and any gift ideas they might have. By providing speedy, convenient service, listening carefully to your customers' wishes, and coming up with presents that meet customers' needs, you'll attract a lot of repeat business. You can also provide gift-wrapping services for a small additional charge.

You'll need to buy the gifts wholesale in order to make any money yourself, so explore all the options in your community. You'll find this business easier if you live near a merchandise mart or have access to outlet malls that offer designer and brand-name goods at discount prices. If you do, you should be able to add your markup and still save your customers some money on retail prices. To get more gift ideas, visit gift trade shows and stationery shows, and get on as many catalog mailing lists as you can so you have a wide range of merchandise to choose from. Since your customers could pick up the phone and order gifts from a catalog, make sure you know where to buy unusual gifts that they would not be able to find for themselves. Some personal shoppers specialize in infant, toddler, and children's gifts. They focus on finding special shower and party gifts, baby bedding, and nursery furniture. If this angle interests you, test the waters by taking out an ad in a local parenting paper and posting notices at daycare centers, children's shops, and local bulletin boards.

After you've gained experience in gift buying and have established accounts with catalog houses and gift wholesalers, you can sell gifts, premiums, and incentives to local corporations. This is a fun and potentially lucrative business, and is especially appropriate if you have experience in merchandising or retailing. Companies are always seeking ways to keep their names and logos fresh in their customers' minds. They're often in the market for buying such giveaway promotional items as personalized keychains, pencils, calendars, matchbooks, notepads, or shopping bags. To succeed, you'll need strong selling skills, the resourcefulness to find new suppliers of imprinted merchandise, and the ability to fill large orders and meet your deadlines. Ordering items in bulk and getting them printed can take as little as five to ten days or as long as three to four weeks, so encourage your clients to give you as much lead time as possible.

Once a company comes to you with a request—for example, they may want to give away a thousand items with their logo on it at a trade show, and want to pay no more than fifty cents per item—it's up to you to present several different possibilties, such as refrigerator magnets or penknives. Some companies may also seek high-end gifts for their best customers or salespeople, so you'll also want to find manufacturers that can print logos on leather briefcases, crystal, glass paperweights, scarves, baseball caps, and jackets.

TOP TIP: To help get your business off the ground, volunteer your shopping services for friends, colleagues, and neighbors. Advertising in the yellow pages and in local newspapers' holiday gift guides and taking part in chamber of commerce business showcases can lead to good visibility in your community.

GETTING STARTED: Read *Incentive* magazine (355 Park Avenue S., 5th Floor, New York, NY 10010) and go to plenty of premium shows and gift trade shows to get ideas, buy samples, and discover new vendors. You'll want to pick up every catalog imaginable so you can offer a wealth of creative, out-of-the-ordinary gift ideas when clients call. To develop corporate business, send a flyer to a variety of companies in your area, and then follow up with a phone call and personal visit to explain the benefits of your buying service.

THE GOING RATE: Ask for a 50 percent deposit once you receive an order. You can add a fair markup on everything you purchase, making sure that you continue to offer competitive prices to your customers. Offer your corporate quantity discounts depending on the size of their order.

GIFT BASKETS SELLER

The gift basket business is thriving. Shoppers have found that buying gourmet food and small gifts in a beautifully wrapped basket is a convenient, easy way to send presents for birthdays, anniversaries, holidays, and other special occasions. Corporations also turn to gift basket companies when they want to send Christmas and Hanukkah gifts to their best customers and favored employees. If this sounds like the kind of business you'd enjoy, do some research by talking to owners of gift basket companies and reading *How to Find Your Treasure in a Gift Basket* by Ron Perkins (R. Perkins, 1991). Then, visit your city's merchandise mart and attend one of the gift shows that take place in major cities throughout the United States (call George Little Management, Inc., at 1-800-272-SHOW [7469] for a list of show times and locations). This is the perfect place to find suppliers, learn what other basket companies are doing, and get ideas for your own baskets. Reading *Gift Basket Review* magazine (Festivities Publications, 1205 W. Forsyth Street, Jacksonville, FL 32204) is also helpful when you're starting out in the business, since it includes lists of hundreds of suppliers of food items, baskets, shrink-wrap machines, and other necessities.

After you've done your homework about the industry, it's time to order some baskets in bulk and buy a shrink-wrapping machine, ribbons, tissue paper, cellophane, boxes, and tape. You'll need one or more large freezers if you plan to sell fresh baked goods or chocolates, plenty of space in a basement or garage to store your food inventory and baskets, and a large table or workbench. The next step is to decide on the contents of your baskets. The most popular baskets are gourmet food baskets (containing fine cheeses, wine or champagne, and other delicacies), new baby gifts (may include hand-painted bibs or T-shirts, blocks, picture frames, and bottles filled with jelly beans), tea or coffee baskets, and chocolate-lover's baskets. The secret is to find unique products to put in your baskets to help you stand out from the competition. Since a lot of gift stores offer similar, mass-produced baskets, you can carve out a niche by offering plenty of handmade items. Jodi Norgaard's Basket Expressions business took off after she started recruiting local people to make homemade chocolates, brownies and cookies, rich tea breads, toffee, chocolate-dipped cookies, and apricots. She also found several crafters to handpaint picture frames and create baby clothes, handmade Christmas ornaments and stockings, and other items for her company. Since many of these gifts cannot be found anywhere else, her customers keep coming back.

While you can sell gift baskets year-round, this business gets especially crazy before Christmas. Jodi has been able to run her business on her own most of the year, but finds that she needs to hire seasonal workers from early November through the end of December. She and her staff of ten have been known to assemble three thousand baskets in four weeks during the holiday rush. Jodi has found that being a perfectionist and detail oriented has helped her in her business. She told us, "I'm picky about getting bows right. I won't let one basket go out if it doesn't look good, not one. I've had employees redo them over and over again until they're right." She's also found that it's important not to invest in too much inventory at a time, since you run the risk of having the food grow stale before you can sell it.

TOP TIP: Since corporations can give you reliable, volume business, spend some time and energy targeting local companies and real estate agents. A sales background will come in handy here, since making sales calls in person will bring in the most business.

GETTING STARTED: Develop a brochure listing several different kinds of gift baskets. Use your imagination: Along with birthday and holiday baskets, you can include get-well baskets, baskets for golfers, sibling baskets (books and treats to keep big brothers and sisters happy when a new baby comes along), romance baskets, Easter baskets (of course), potpourri and housewarming baskets, and regional specialities appropriate to your location—from southwestern salsa to Chicago pizza. Give customers a list of ideas to choose from, and let them know they can mix and match items to make a customized basket of their choice. Once you have developed your own mailing list of customers, send out a brochure every year or two, and a holiday brochure each fall. You may also want to place a small ad in your newspaper's holiday buying guide, take out a yellow pages listing, and increase your recognition in the community by donating baskets for school and charity fund-raisers.

THE GOING RATE: From $15 to $150, based on the size of baskets and the cost of the enclosed gifts. Some gift companies set their prices by doubling or tripling the cost of the basket and its contents. Be flexible in helping customers create or modify baskets that fit their budgets. You can offer UPS shipping or delivery for an additional fee.

SELLER OF PRODUCTS WITH UNIVERSITY LOGOS

There's a huge market out there for merchandise with university and sports team logos on them. In fact, some people feel naked if they're not wearing something proclaiming their allegiance to their university or favorite team. You can start a business meeting the demand for old school ties, scarves, jewelry, tote bags, umbrellas, T-shirts and sweatshirts, and other products if you enjoy sales and are determined to turn your ideas into reality. To begin with, target a particular college or university. It makes sense to start with the university you attended or a college in your town. You'll need to get approval from the university's licensing department before you can sell any products with their logo on it, and they are more likely to approve your use of their logo if you have an affiliation with the institution.

Then, take a look at the products the university sells to students and alumni, and see what's missing. What items can you sell that aren't currently available? Janet H. Cowel and Sherry Nelson, two active Northwestern University alumna in Wilmette, IL, founded their business, Hollgraham Designs, in November 1995 after they noticed that no one was selling jewelry sporting the popular Northwestern Wildcats logo. They knew that Northwestern had a large number of active, enthusiastic alums, and thought that there was a pent-up demand for university jewelry.

To test their idea, they commissioned a friend who was a jeweler to make fifty pairs of earrings and brought them along to sell in the alumni tent at a home football game. The earrings sold so quickly the partners realized that they needed to find a jeweler who could create jewelry in much larger quantities than their friend could. They found a wholesaler in Chicago who could produce their jewelry quickly in volume, and began offering earrings, pendants, pins, charms, lapel pins, necklaces, bracelets, and money clips, in 14K gold and sterling silver. When the Wildcats had a championship season and managed to make it to the Rose Bowl, their business took off. Even if the university you select has less-than-stellar sports teams, your products can sell well if you come up with a good idea, produce high-quality items, and have the support of the university.

When asked for their advice for other entrepreneurs, Sherry and Janet told us, "One of the nice things about this business is that there's not a lot of overhead. We got a business line, insurance, and arranged to accept credit cards right away, but we don't have to rent out a storefront. Our inventory is our major expense, and we had to guess at Christmastime how much we needed. We've found that we've needed to have a lot of motivation, perseverance, and people skills to get our business going. People told us that if we'd known more about this business, we never would have gotten started. As it is, we've learned about the jewelry business as we've gone along. We've also discovered that alums are our best market; although we tested the student market, too. You can't be everything for everybody."

TOP TIP: You can sell your products through direct mail and telephone orders, at university sporting events and alumni gatherings, as well as selling them through the college bookstore and other retail stores near the campus. Promote your products by taking out ads in alumni magazines and student newspapers.

GETTING STARTED: Begin by submitting your idea and a sketch to the university's licensing department. Universities are very particular about granting licensing privileges, so make sure that the logo on your proposed product is presented accurately and attractively. Becoming licensed also means that you'll need to pay the university a royalty (around 7½ percent) on every item you sell. Once you're officially licensed, you'll need to find a manufacturer that can produce the items for you. Lower-priced novelty items like T-shirts are popular with students, while higher-priced merchandise are better targeted to alumni. Donating a few items to charity auctions and university fund-raisers is also a good way to gain visibility. If your business takes off, you can expand by contacting other universities in your area and offering to create similar items featuring their logos.

THE GOING RATE: Prices vary from $18 to $20 for T-shirts up to $380 for a gold pendant and chain. Janet and Sherry's biggest sellers in their jewelry line are $30 sterling silver earrings and a $65 silver pendant and chain. Men have also been buying their $75 money clips, $25 silver lapel pins and tie tacks, and $60 gold lapel pins and tie tacks.

HOST GARAGE SALES

It used to be that garage sales were a way to get rid of accumulated junk that you—and usually nobody else—wanted anymore. And to be sure, if junk gives you joy you can still find plenty of those types of sales, in addition to the occasional church or civic group rummage sale. But in recent years many sales have upped the quality and quantity of their offerings, and going "garage sailing" has become a sort of recreational activity. Plenty of people would like to get in on the action, but can't for a variety of reasons including lack of space, time, or energy.

If your home has good access to a major highway or well-traveled street, you can make money by hosting garage or tag sales. You'll need good organizational skills, patience, and eyes in the back of your head, but it's worth it—you can make several hundred dollars in a weekend without ever leaving your own property, plus get a lot of socializing in, too.

Basically, there are two main ways to host a garage sale. You can lease out space to other vendors, who then man their own table and collect their own money. The vendors pay you a flat fee. Or, you can take in other people's items, handle the selling yourself, and tag each piece with a code that you note on a sales slip. Then, at the end of the day tally each contributor's total, take a 10 percent commission for yourself, and give the rest of the money to the contributor.

The first strategy works best if you don't have a lot of friends or family to help you man tables and cash boxes. The second strategy works best if you have access to free (or nearly free) help to run your sale.

Some costs are associated with running a sale. You'll need cash boxes, signs for at least four intersections, balloons to mark the mailbox, tables, price and "sold" stickers, and name tags. You should advertise your sale on local bulletin boards and the classifieds section of your local paper.

There are estate sale experts who will, for a percentage of the profits, price, tag, advertise, and sell a home's goods. If you have upscale antiques or collectibles, such a service may make sense for you, but for the general garage sale all you need are your own skills and energy.

TOP TIP: Many first-timers will have no idea of pricing. Suggest 25 percent of the original price unless the item is a collectible (such as Barbies or Depression glass), in high demand (such as children's toys), or extraordinary (designer clothing).

GETTING STARTED: How do you find contributors for your sale? Through local bulletin boards and weekly neighborhood papers, plus outreach to neighborhoods with apartment buildings or town homes where frustrated garage sale wanna-bes are living. Decide beforehand whether you have the manpower and correct vehicle (such as a van or truck) to offer loading and unloading services, and charge $15 extra for them if you do.

THE BOTTOM LINE: Charge 15 percent of your clients total sales or a flat fee of $30 per table.

APPENDICES

◆

ORGANIZATIONS AND ASSOCIATIONS

SECTION 1: ARTS AND CRAFTS

American Craft Council
72 Spring Street
New York, NY 10012
212-274-0630
(Publishes *American Craft* magazine and *Craft Horizons*)

American Home Sewing and Craft Association
1375 Broadway
New York, NY 10018
212-302-2150

Association of Crafts & Creative Industries
PO Box 2188
Zanesville, OH 43702-2188
614-452-4541

Embroiderer's Guild of America
335 West Broadway
Louisville, KY 40202
502-589-6956

Professional Photographers of American Association
57 Forsyth Street NW, Ste. 1600
Atlanta, GA 30303
404-522-8600
(Publishes *Professional Photography* magazine)

Society for Calligraphy
PO Box 64174
Los Angeles, CA 90064
310-306-2326

Society of Scribes
PO Box 933
New York, NY 10150
212-475-1653

Window Coverings Association of America
825 S. Waukegan Road, Ste. A8-111
Lake Forest, IL 60045
847-480-7955

SECTION 2: BUSINESS SERVICES

American Accounting Association
5717 Bessie Drive
Sarasota, FL 34233
813-921-7747
(Publishes *Accounting Horizons*)

American Association for Medical Transciption
PO Box 576187
Modesto, CA 95357
800-982-2182; 209-551-0883
(Publishes the *Journal of the AAMT*)

American Institute of Professional Bookkeepers
6001 Montrose Road
Rockville, MD 20852
800-622-0121
(Publishes the *Journal of Accounting, Taxation, and Finance for Business*)

American Library Association
50 East Huron Street
Chicago, IL 60611
312-944-6780
(Publishes *American Libraries* and *Booklist*)

American Society of Indexers
PO Box 48267
Seattle, WA 98148
206-241-9196
(Publishes the book *Starting an Indexing Business*)

Association of Independent Information Professionals
245 5th Avenue, Suite 2103
New York, NY 10016
212-779-1855

The Authors Guild
330 West 42nd Street
New York, NY 10036
212-563-5904

Editorial Freelancers Association
71 W. 23rd Street, Suite 1504
New York, NY 10010
212-929-5400

The Foundation Center
79 5th Avenue
New York, NY 10003
212-620-4230

The Graphic Artists Guild
11 W. 20th Street, 8th Floor
New York, NY 10011
212-463-7730
(Publishes *Graphic Artists' Guild Handbook*)

Independent Computer Consultants Association
933 Gardenview Office Parkway
St. Louis, MO 63141
314-997-4633
(Publishes *The Indepedent*)

International Association of Business Communicators
1 Hallidie Plaza, Suite 600
San Francisco, CA 94102
415-433-3400
(Publishes *Communication World*)

International Association for Exposition Management
PO Box 802425
Dallas, TX 75380
214-458-8002

Meeting Professionals International
1950 Stemmons Fwy, Ste. 5018
Dallas, TX 75207
214-712-7700
(Publishes *The Meeting Manager*)

National Association of Claims Assistance Professionals
5329 S. Main Street, Suite 102
Downers Grove, IL 60515
800-660-0665
(Publishes the *Claims Advisor*)

National Association of Desktop Publishers
462 Old Boston Street
Topsfield, MA 01983
508-887-7900
(Publishes the *NADP Journal*)

National Federation of Abstracting and Information Services
1518 Walnut Street
Philadelphia, PA 19102
215-893-1561
(Publishes *Guide to Careers in Abstracting and Indexing*)

National Society of Public Accountants
1010 N. Fairfax Street
Alexandria, VA 22314
703-549-6400
(Publishes *National Public Accountant*)

Society for Technical Communication
901 N. Stuart Street, Ste. 904
Arlington, VA 22203
703-522-4114
(Publishes *Technical Communication* journal)

SECTION 3: PERSONAL SERVICES

American Association of Individual Investors
625 N. Michigan Avenue, Suite 1900
Chicago, IL 60611
312-280-0170
(Publishes *AAII Journal*)

American College of Sports Medicine
PO Box 1440
Indianapolis, IN 46206
317-637-9200

American Council on Exercise
5820 Oberlin Drive, Suite 102
San Diego, CA 92121
800-825-3636 or 619-535-8227

American Massage Therapy Association
820 Davis Street, Ste. 100
Evanston, IL 60201
847-864-0123
(Publishes *Massage Therapy Journal*)

Association of Bridal Consultants
200 Chestnutland Road
New Milford, CT 06776
203-355-0464

Association of Image Consultants International
1000 Connecticut Avenue NW, Suite 9
Washington, DC 20036
301-371-9021; 800-383-8831
(Publishes *Fashion News and Views* magazine)

Association of Professional Genealogists
3421 M Street NW, Suite 236
Washington, DC 20007
703-920-2385

The Board for Certification of Geneologists
PO Box 5816
Falmouth, VA 22403

International Lactation Consultants Association
201 Brown Avenue
Evanston, IL 60202
847-260-8874

La Leche League International
1400 N. Meacham Road
Schaumburg, IL 60173
800-LA-LECHE; 847-519-7730
(Publishes *New Beginnings* magazine)

National Association of Investors Corporation
711 W. 13 Mile Road
Madison Heights, MI 48071
810-583-6242
(Publishes the *Investor's Manual* and *Better Investing*)

National Association of Professional Organizers
1033 La Posada Drive, Suite 200
Austin, TX 78752
512-454-8626; 512-206-0151
(Information and referral hotline)

National Geneological Society
4527 17th Street N.
Arlington, VA 22207
703-525-0050
(Publishes *NGS Quarterly*)

SECTION 4: EDUCATIONAL AND
ENTERTAINMENT SERVICES

American Homebrewers Association
PO Box 1679
Boulder, CO 80306
303-447-0816
(Publishes *Zmurgy* magazine)

Child Care Information Exchange
Box 2890
Redmond, WA 98073
206-883-9394

Children's Bureau
U.S. Department of Education
Washington, DC 20201
202-708-5366
(Information on sound day-care practice; request their
publication *What Is Good Day Care?*)

The Foundation for Music-Based Learning
PO Box 4274
Greensboro, NC 27404
910-272-5303
(Publishes *Early Childhood Connections*)

Music Teachers National Association
441 Vine Street, Ste. 505
Cincinnati, OH 45202
513-421-1420
(Publishes *American Music Teacher Journal*)

National Association for the Education of Young Children
1509 16th Street NW
Washington, DC 20036
800-424-2460; 202-232-8777
(Publishes *Young Children* journal)

National Guild of Piano Teachers
PO Box 1807
Austin, TX 78767
512-478-5775
(Publishes *Piano Guild Notes* journal)

The Puppeteers of America
5 Cricklewood Path
Pasadena, CA 91107
818-797-5748
(Publishes *The Puppetry Journal* and the *Playboard* newsletter)

SECTION 5: HOUSE AND GARDEN

American Beekeeping Federation
PO Box 1038
Jessup, GA 31545
912-427-8447

American Boarding Kennels Association
4575 Galley Road
Colorado Springs, CO 80915
719-591-1113
(Publishes *Pet Services Journal*)

American Dog Breeders Association
PO Box 1771
Salt Lake City, UT 84110
801-298-7513

American Dog Trainers Network
161 W. 4th Street
New York, NY 10014
212-727-7257

American Honey Producers Association
PO Box 584
Cheshire, CT 06410
203-250-7271

American Kennel Club
51 Madison Avenue
New York, NY 10010
212-696-8200

American Society of Interior Designers
608 Massachusetts Avenue NE
Washington, DC 20002
202-546-3480

Association of Pet Dog Trainers
P.O. Box 3734
Salinas, CA 93912-3734
408-663-9257 or 800-PET-DOGS
(Publishes the *APDT Newsletter*)

National Association of Dog Obedience Instructors
PO Box 432
Landing, NJ 07850

National Association of Professional Pet Sitters
1200 G Street NW, Suite 760
Washington, DC 20015
202-393-3317
(Publishes *NAPS Network*)

Pet Sitters International
418 E. King Street
King, NC 27021
910-983-9222
(Publishes *Professional Pet Sitter*)

SECTION 6: BUYING AND SELLING

American Marketing Association
250 S. Wacker Drive, Ste. 200
Chicago, IL 60606
312-648-0536

Direct Marketing Association
1120 Avenue of the Americas
New York, NY 10036
212-768-7277

GENERAL ASSOCIATIONS FOR HOME BUSINESS OWNERS

Association of Enterprising Mothers
914 S. Santa Fe Avenue, Ste. 297
Vista, CA 92084
800-223-9260 or 619-598-9260

Chamber of Commerce of the U.S.
Small Business Center
1615 H Street, NW
Washington, DC 20062
202-659-6000
(Publishes *Nation's Business*)

Home-based Working Moms
P.O. Box 500164
Austin, TX 78750
512-918-0670

The Home Business Network
RR 1
St. George, Ontario, N0E 1N0
Canada
(Publishes the book *Bringing It Home: A Home Business Start-Up Guide for You [and your family]*)

The Microloan Demonstration Project
Office of Finance, Small Business Administration
409 Third St. SW, 8th Floor,
Washington, DC 20416
800-8-ASK-SBA
(Provides loans of up to $25,000 for small business owners to cover start-up costs, working capital or purchase of supplies and equipment. Contact your local SBA to inquire, since the program is not available in every region.)

Mothers Home Business Network
PO Box 423
East Meadow, NY 11554
516-997-7394
(Publishes *Homeworking Mothers*)

National Association for the Cottage Industry
Box 14850
Chicago, IL 60614
312-472-8116
(Publishes *The Small Office/Home Office* journal)

National Association of Home Based Businesses
Box 30220
Baltimore, MD 21270
410-363-3698
(Publishes *Home Based Business Newspaper*)

National Association of Women Business Owners
1413 K Street NW, Ste. 637
Washington, DC 20005
301-608-2590

National Association for the Self-Employed
2316 Gravel Road, PO Box 612067
Ft. Worth, TX 75261
817-589-2475; 1-800-232-NASE (toll-free advice line for members)

National Chamber of Commerce for Women
Home-Based Business Committee
10 Waterside Plaza, Ste. 6H
New York, NY 10010
212-685-3454
(Publishes *Sample Business Operator Profile*)

Service Corps of Retired Executives Association (SCORE)
409 3rd Street SW, Ste. 5900
Washington, DC 20024
202-205-6762
(More than ten thousand business executives offer free
counseling to start-ups and small businesses.)

U.S. Small Business Administration
1111 Eighteenth Street, NW
Washington, DC 20036
800-827-5722
(Information and programs that assist small businesses; request
name of your local office and their publication *Handbook for
Small Business*.)

BIBLIOGRAPHY

SPECIALIZED BUSINESS BOOKS

SECTION 1: ARTS AND CRAFTS

The Art and Craft of Paper
by Faith Shannon
(Chronicle Books, 1994)

The Art and Craft of Papermaking
by Sophie Dawson
(Running Press, 1992)

Artist's Market
(Writer's Digest, published annually)

Beginning Jewelry: A Notebook for Design and Technique, 2nd
Edition
by Roger Armstrong
(Star Publishing, 1992)

The Book of Jewelry
by Jo Moody
(Simon & Shuster, 1994)

The Business of Sewing: How to Start, Maintain, and Achieve Success
by Barbara Wright-Sykes
(Collins Publications, 1992)

Careers for Crafty People and Other Dexterous Types
by Mark Rowh
(VGM Career Books, 1994)

Craft Supply Sourcebook: A Comprehensive Shop-by-Mail Guide,
3rd Edition
Edited by Margaret Boyd
(Betterway Books, 1994)

Creative Cash: How to Sell Your Crafts, Needlework, Designs & Know-How, 5th Edition
by Barbara Brabec
(B. Brabec Products, 1993)

Decorative Style Most Original
by Kevin McCloud
(Simon & Schuster, 1990)

How to Be a Weekend Entrepreneur: Making Money at Craft Fairs, Trade Shows and Swap Meets
by Susan Ratliff
(Marketing Methods Press, 1991)

How to Become a Professional Calligrapher
by Stuart David
(Taplinger, 1985)

How to Open and Operate a Home-Based Carpentry Business
by Charlie Self
(Globe Pequot Press, 1995)

How to Open and Operate a Home-Based Crafts Business
by Kenn Oberrecht
(Globe Pequot Press, 1994)

How to Open and Operate a Home-Based Photography Business
by Kenn Oberrecht
(Globe Pequot Press, 1993)

How to Start Making Money with your Crafts
by Kathryn Caputo
(Betterway Books, 1995)

How You Can Make $25,000 a Year with Your Camera
by Larry Cribb
(Writer's Digest Books, 1991)

Making Your Own Paper
by Marianne Saddington
(Garden Way Publishing, 1992)

Paint Magic
by Jocasta Innes
(Pantheon Books, 1987)

Photographer's Guide to Marketing and Self-Promotion, 2nd
Edition
by Maria Piscopo
(Allworth Press, 1995)

Photographer's Market
Edited by Michael Willinas
(Writer's Digest Books, published annually)

SECTION 2: BUSINESS SERVICES

Basic Business Library: Core Resources, 3rd Edition
by Bernard Schlessinger
(Oryx Press, 1994)

Bookkeeping on Your Home-Based PC
by Linda Stern
(Windcrest/McGraw-Hill, 1993)

Current Medical Terminology, 5th Edition
by Vera Pyle
(Health Professionals Institute, 1994)

Desktop Publishing Success: How to Start and Run a Desktop Publishing Business
by Felix Kramer and Maggie Lovaas
(Irwin Professional Publishing, 1991)

Encyclopaedia of Business Info Sources, 10th Edition
by James B. Woy
(Gale Research, Inc., 1994)

Finding Facts Fast
by Alden Todd
(Ten Speed Press, 1992)

The Graphic Artists Guild Handbook, 6th Edition
(Graphic Artists Guild, 1987)

Health Service Businesses on Your Home-Based PC
by Rick Benzel
(TAB Books, 1993)

How to Be a Successful Computer Consultant
by Alan R. Simon
(McGraw-Hill, 1993)

How to Make Money Writing Corporate Communications
by Mary C. Collins
(Berkley Publishing, 1995)

How to Open and Operate a Home-Based Secretarial Services Business
by Jan Melnik
(Globe Pequot Press, 1994)

How to Start and Run a Writing and Editing Business
by Herman R. Holtz
(Wiley, 1992)

HTML Publishing on the Internet
by Brent Heslop and Larry Budnick
(Ventana Communications, 1995)

The Independent Medical Transcriptionist
by Donna Avila-Weil and Mary Glaccum
(Rayve Productions, 1994)

Index and Abstract Directory, 3rd Edition
by J. Leanne Wofford
(EBSCO Publishing, 1996)

Indexing Books
by Nancy C. Mulvany
(University of Chicago Press, 1994)

Indexing Concepts and Methods
by Harold Borko and Charles L. Bernier
(Academic Press, 1978)

Indexing from A to Z
by Hans H. Wellisch
(H.W. Wilson Company, 1991)

The Information Broker's Handbook
by Sue Rugge and Alfred Glossbrenner
(TAB Books, 1992)

Information for Sale, 2nd Edition
by John H. Everett and Elizabeth P. Crowe
(McGraw-Hill, 1994)

Literary Market Place
(R. R. Bowker, revised annually)

Making Money with Your Computer at Home
by Paul and Sarah Edwards
(Jeremy P. Tarcher/Perigee, 1993)

The RBS Book
by Robb Cosgrove
(QT Inc., 376 S. Mendenhall Rd., Memphis, TN 38117)

Starting Your Small Graphic Design Studio
by Michael Fleishman
(North Light Books, 1993)

Stedman's Medical Word Books
(Williams & Wilkins, several volumes in the series)

Stedman's Medical Dictionary, 26th Edition
(Williams & Wilkins, 1995)

Teach Yourself Web Publishing with HTML in 14 Days
by Laura Lemay
(Sam's Publishing, 1995)

*The Tech Writing Game: A Comprehensive Career Guide for
Aspiring Technical Writers*
by Janet Van Wicklen
(Facts on File, 1992)

*The Upstart Guide to Owning and Managing a Desktop Publishing
Service*
by Dan Ramsey
(Upstart Publishing Co., 1995)

Word Processing Profits at Home, 3rd Edition
by Peggy Glenn
(Aames-Allen, 1994)

Writer's Market
(Writer's Digest Books, published annually)

SECTION 3: PERSONAL SERVICES

The Breastfeeding Answer Book
by Nancy Mohrbacher and Julie Stock
(La Leche League, 1991)

*Cite Your Sources: A Manual for Documenting Family Histories and
Geneological Records*
Edited by Richard S. Lackey
(University Press of Mississippi, 1985)

The Investment Club Book: Best Tips from Investment Clubs
by John F. Wasik
(Warner Books, 1995)

Massage: A Career at Your Fingertips, 2nd Edition
by Martin Ashley
(Enterprise Publications, 1995)

National Auto Research Black Book
(P.O. Box 758, Gainesville, GA 30503-0758, several editions
annually)

The Personal Trainer Manual: The Resource for Fitness Instructors
Edited by Mitchell Sudy
(American Council on Exercise, 1992)

The Safe & Sound Child: Keeping Your Child Safe Inside and Outside the Home
by Larry and Leslie Stone
(Good Year Books, 1996)

The Source: A Guidebook of American Geneology
by Arlene H. Eakle and Johni Cerny
(Ancestry Publishing Co., 1984)

SECTION 4: EDUCATION AND ENTERTAINMENT SERVICES

The Chicago Manual of Style: The Essential Guide for Authors, Editors, and Publishers, 14th Edition
by University of Chicago Editorial Staff
(University of Chicago Press, 1993)

The Complete Handbook of Homebrewing
by Dave Miller
(Garden Way Publishing, 1988)

The Craft and Business of Songwriting
by John Braheny
(Writer's Digest, 1995)

Guide to the Pianist's Repertoire, 2nd Edition
by Maurice Hinson
(Indiana University Press, 1994)

How to Teach Piano Successfully, 3rd Edition
by James W. Bastien
(Kjos, 1988)

Making Money Making Music
by James Dearing
(Writer's Digest, 1990)

The New Complete Joy of Home Brewing
by Charlie Papazian
(Avon Books, 1991)

Nursery School and Day Care Center Management Guide, 2nd
Edition
by Claire Cherry et al.
(Fearon Teaching Aids, 1987)

Songwriter's Market
(Writer's Digest, published annually)

Start Your Own At-Home Child Care Business
by Patricia Gallagher
(Young Sparrow Press, 1994)

SECTION 5: HOUSE AND GARDEN

*Backyard Cash Crops: The Source Book for Growing and Marketing
Specialty Plants*
by Craig Wallin
(Homestead Design, 1994)

Beekeeping: A Practical Guide
by Richard E. Barney
(Garden Way Publishing, 1993)

A Book of Bees: And How to Keep Them
by Sue Hubbell
(Random House, 1988)

Creating an Accessory Apartment
by Patricia H. Hare and Jolene N. Ostler
(McGraw-Hill, 1987)

The Directory of Unique Museums
Edited by Bill Truesdell
(Oryx Press, 1985)

Filmed on Location: A Guide to Leasing Your Property as a Film Location
by James Leonis
(Premiere Publishing Co., 1994)

From Kitchen to Market: Selling Your Gourmet Food Specialty
by Stephen F. Hall
(Upstart Publishing Co., 1992)

How to Open and Operate a Home-Based Catering Business
by Denise Vivaldo
(Globe Pequot Press, 1993)

How to Run a Housesitting Business
by Jane Poston
(order from her at 17008 E. Ninth Street, Tucson, AZ 85719; 602-884-8530)

Making Potpourri, Colognes and Soaps
by David Webb
(TAB Books, 1988)

Marketing Basics for Designers: A Sourcebook of Strategies & Ideas
by Jane D. Martin and Nancy Knoohuizen
(Wiley, 1995)

Pet Sitting for Profit: A Complete Manual for Success
by Patti J. Moran
(Howell Books, 1992)

Potpourri, Incense and Other Fragrant Concoctions
by Anne Tucker Fettner
(Workman, 1977)

Profits From Your Backyard Herb Garden
by Lee Sturdivant
(San Juan Naturals, 1995)

Sit and Grow Rich: Petsitting and Housesitting for Profit
by Patricia A. Doyle
(Upstart Publishing Co., 1993)

Small Space/Big Bucks: Converting Home Space into Profits
by Jack P. Jones
(TAB Books, 1993)

Squeeze Your Home for Cash: 101 Great Money-Making Ideas for Homeowners
by Ruth Rejnis
(Real Estate Education Co., 1995)

SECTION 6: BUYING AND SELLING

Do-It-Yourself Marketing Research, 3rd Edition
by George Breen and Albert B. Blankenship
(McGraw-Hill, 1992)

Guerilla Marketing: Secrets for Making Big Profits from Your Small Business
by Jay Conrad Levinson
(Houghton Mifflin, 1993)

Guerilla Marketing Online
by Jay Conrad Levinson
(Houghton Mifflin, 1995)

Guerilla P.R.: How You Can Wage an Effective Publicity Campaign . . . Without Going Broke
by Michael Levine
(HarperBusiness 1993)

Home-Based Mail Order: A Success Guide for Entrepreneurs
by William J. Bond
(McGraw-Hill, 1990)

How to Find Your Treasure in a Gift Basket
by Ron Perkins
(R. Perkins, 1991)

Making Money on the Internet
by Alfred Glossbrenner
(TAB Books, 1995)

*Marketing on a Shoestring: Low-Cost Tips for Marketing Your
Products or Services,* 2nd Edition
by Jeffrey P. Davidson
(John Wiley & Sons, 1994)

*Measuring Markets: A Guide to the Use of Federal and State
Statistical data*
(U.S. GPO, 1979)

Tradeshow 200
(information on the 200 largest tradeshows)
Cahners Publishing Co.
12233 West Olympic
Los Angeles, CA 90064
310-826-5696

GENERAL SMALL BUSINESS
BOOKS

The Best Home Businesses for the 90's
by Paul and Sarah Edwards
(Putnam's Sons, 1994)

Complete Work-at-Home Companion
by Herman Holtz
(Prima Publishing, 1990)

Growing a Business
by Paul Hawken
(Simon & Shuster, 1988)

The Home-Based Entrepreneur: The Complete Guide to Working at Home, 2nd Edition
by Linda Pinson and Jerry Jinnett
(Upstart Publishing, 1993)

Home Business to Big Business: How to Launch Your Home Business and Make It a Success
by Mel Cook
(Macmillan, 1992)

Home Business Made Easy: How to Select & Start a Home Business That Fits Your Interests, Lifestyle & Pocketbook
by David Hanania
(PSI Successful Business Library, The Oasis Press, 1992)

Homemade Money, 5th Edition
by Barbara Brabec
(Betterway Publications, 1994)

How to Run Your Own Home Business, 3rd Edition
by Coralee Smith Kern
(VGM Career Books, 1994)

How to Start a Business Without Quitting Your Job: The Moonlight Entrepreneur's Guide
by Philip Holland
(Ten Speed Press, 1992)

101 Best Home-Based Businesses for Women
by Priscilla Y. Huff
(Prima Publishing, 1995)

Publication #910 (Guide to Free Tax Services)
Publication #334 (Tax Guide for Small Business)
Publication #583 (Record Keeping for Small Business)
Publication #587 (Business Use of Your Home)
(Internal Revenue Service, Washington, DC 20403;
800-829-3676)

Running a One-Person Business
by Claude Whitmyer
(Ten Speed Press, 1994)

Small Businesses That Grow and Grow and Grow!
by Patricia A. Woy
(Betterway Publications, 1989)

Small Time Operator
by Bernard Kamaroff
(Bell Springs Publishing, 1995)

The Ten Best Opportunities for Starting a Home Business Today
by The New Careers Center, Inc. with Reed Glenn
(Live Oak Publications, 1993)

The Work-at-Home Sourcebook
by Lynie Arden
(Live Oak Publications, 1994)

Working from Home
Paul and Sarah Edwards
(Putnam, 1994)

Your Home Business Can Make Dollars and Sense
by Jo Frohbieter-Mueller
(Chilton Book Company, 1990)

Note: Many of the business books listed in this section are available from your library, local bookstores, or can be ordered through the Whole Work Catalog from the New Careers Center, Inc. 1515 23rd Street, PO Box 339-CT, Boulder, CO 80306; 303-447-1087.

MAGAZINES

SECTION 1: ARTS AND CRAFTS

American Craft Magazine (American Craft Council, 72 Spring Street, NY, NY 10012)

Calligraphy Review (2421 Wilcox Drive, Norman, OK 73069)

Computer Quilter's Newsletter (4072 E. 22nd Street, #329, Tucson, AZ 85711)

Craft and Needlework Age (225 Gordons Corner Plaza, Box 420, Manalapan, NJ 07726)

Crafts 'n Things (Clapper Publishing Co., Inc., 2400 Devon, Ste 375, Des Plaines, IL 60018)

Crafting Traditions (5400 S. 60th Street, Greendale, WI 53129)

Doll Reader (6405 Flank Drive, Box 8200, Harrisburg, PA 17105)

Draperies and Window Coverings (450 Skokie Blvd., Suite 507, Northbrook, IL 60062)

Family Handyman (7900 International Drive, Suite 950, Minneapolis, MN 55425)

Fine Woodworking (63 S. Main Street, Box 5506, Newtown, CT 06470)

Giftware News (Box 5398, Deptford, NJ 08096)

Jewelry Crafts (4880 Market Street, Ventura, CA 93003)

Lapidary Journal (60 Chestnut Avenue, Suite 201, Devon, PA 19333)

Quilter's Newsletter Magazine (Box 4101, Golden, CO 80401)

Quilting Today (2 Public Avenue, Montrose, PA 18801)

Professional Photography (The Professional Photographers of America Association, 57 Forsyth Street NW, Ste. 1600, Atlanta, GA 30303)

Rodale's Craft and Needlework Age (33 E. Minor Street, Emmaus, PA 18049)

Studio Photography (445 Board Hollow Road, Suite 21, Melville, NY 11747)

Window Fashions (4225 White Bear Pkwy, Ste. 400, St. Paul, MN 55110)

Woodwork Magazine (42 Digital Drive, Novato, CA 94949)

SECTION 2: BUSINESS SERVICES

Boardwatch (5970 South Vivian Street, Littleton, CO 80127)

The Claims' Advisor (The National Association of Claims Assistance Professionals, 5329 S. Main Street, Ste. 102, Downers Grove, IL 60515)

The Chronicle of Philanthropy (1255 23rd Street NW, Suite 700, Washington, DC 20037)

Database (462 Danbury Road, Wilton, CT 06897)

Home Office Computing (555 Broadway, New York, NY 10012)

Information Today (143 Old Marlton Pike, Medford, NJ 08055)

The Independent (Independent Computer Consultants Association, 933 Gardenview Office Parkway, St. Louis, MO 63141)

Internet World (20 Ketchum Street, Westport, CT 06880)

Journal of the AAMT (American Association for Medical Transcription, PO Box 576187, Modesto, CA 95357)

Journal of Accounting, Taxation and Finance for Business (The American Institute of Professional Bookkeepers, 6001 Montrose Rd, Rockville, MD 20852)

Macworld Magazine (501 Second Street, San Francisco, CA 94107)

The Net (150 North Hill Drive, Brisbane, CA 94005)
Online (462 Danbury Road, Wilton, CT 06897)
PC Computing (50 Beale Street, 13th Floor, San Francisco, CA 94105)
PC Magazine (One Park Avenue, New York, NY 10016)
Publish Magazine (501 Second Street, Suite 310, San Francisco, CA 94107)

SECTION 3: PERSONAL SERVICES

Ancestry (Box 476, Salt Lake City, UT 84110)
Barron's (200 Liberty Street, New York, NY 10281)
Business Week (1221 Avenue of the Americas, 39th Floor, New York, NY 10020)
Forbes (60 Fifth Avenue, New York, NY 10011)
Fashion News and Views (The Association of Image Consultants International, 1000 Connecticut Avenue NW, Suite 9, Washington, DC 20036)
Geneological Helper (Box 368, Logan, UT 84323)
Heritage Quest (Box 329, Bountiful, UT 84011)
Massage Therapy Journal (The American Massage Therapy Association, 820 Davis Street, Ste. 100, Evanston, IL 60201)
Money (1271 Avenue of the Americas, New York, NY 10020)
Morningstar (225 W. Wacker Drive, Suite 400, Chicago, IL 60606)
New Beginnings (La Leche League International, 1400 N. Meacham Road, Schaumburg, IL 60173)
Wall Street Journal (200 Liberty Street, New York, NY 10281)

SECTION 4: EDUCATIONAL AND ENTERTAINMENT SERVICES

American Music Teacher (Music Teachers National Association, 441 Vine Street, Ste. 505, Cincinnati, OH 45202)

Clavier (200 Northfield Road, Northfield, IL 60093)

Early Childhood Connections (The Foundation for Music-Based Learning, Box 4274, Greensboro, NC 27404)

Keyboard (411 Borel Avenue, Suite 100, San Mateo, CA 94402)

Piano Guild Notes (National Guild of Piano Teachers, PO Box 1807, Austin, TX 78767)

Playboard and Puppetry Journal (The Puppeteers of America, #5 Cricklewood Path, Pasadena, CA 91107)

Young Children (The National Association for the Education of Young Children, 1509 16th Street NW, Washington, DC 20036)

Zmurgy (American Homebrewers Association, PO Box 1679, Boulder CO 80306)

SECTION 5: HOUSE AND GARDEN

American Bee Journal (Dadant, 51 S. 2nd Street, Hamilton, IL 62341)

Bakery Production and Marketing (1350 E. Touhy Avenue, Box 5080, Des Plaines, IL 60018)

Bee Culture (Box 706, Medina, OH 44258)

Cat Fancy (Box 6040, Mission Viejo, CA 92690)

Cooking for Profit: The Business of Food Preparation (PO Box 267, Fond du Lac, WI 54936)

Country Living (224 W. 57th Street, New York, NY 10019)

Dog World (29 N. Wacker Drive, Chicago, IL 60606)

Fine Gardening (63 S. Main Street, Box 5506, Newton, CT 06470)

Garden Design (100 Sixth Avenue, 7th Floor, New York, NY 10013)

House Beautiful (1700 Broadway, New York, NY 10019)

Metropolitan Home (1633 Broadway, 41st Floor, New York, NY 10019)

Organic Gardening (33 E. Minor Street, Emmaus, PA 18098)

Professional Pet Sitter (Pet Sitters International, 418 E. King
    Street, King, NC 27021)
Victoria (224 W. 57th Street, 4th Floor, New York, NY 10019)

SECTION 6: BUYING AND SELLING

Gift Basket Review (1205 W. Forsyth Street, Jacksonville, FL
    32204)
Incentive (355 Park Avenue S., 5th Floor, New York, NY 10010)

GENERAL SMALL BUSINESS PUBLICATIONS

Business Startups (2392 Morse Avenue, Irvine, CA 92714)
Entrepreneur Magazine (2392 Morse Avenue, Irvine, CA 92714)
Homeworking Mothers (Mothers Home Business Network, PO
    Box 423, East Meadow, NY 11554)
Inc. (38 Commercial Wharf, Boston, MA 02110)
Income Opportunities (1500 Broadway, Suite 600, New York, NY
    10036)
Opportunity Magazine (18 E. 41st Street, New York, NY 10017)
Small Business Opportunities (1115 Broadway, 8th Floor, New
    York, NY 10010)
The Small Office/Home Office (National Association for the Cot-
    tage Industry, Box 14850, Chicago, IL 60614)
Success (230 Park Avenue, 7th Floor, New York, NY 10169)